The Hatpin Menace

SELECTED OTHER WORKS BY KERRY SEGRAVE
AND FROM MCFARLAND

Chewing Gum in America, 1850–1920 (2015)

Wiretapping and Electronic Surveillance in America, 1862–1920 (2014)

Beware the Masher: Sexual Harassment in American Public Places, 1880–1930 (2014)

Policewomen: A History, 2d ed. (2014)

Extras of Early Hollywood: A History of the Crowd, 1913–1945 (2013)

Parking Cars in America, 1910–1945: A History (2012)

Begging in America, 1850–1940: The Needy, the Frauds, the Charities and the Law (2011)

Vision Aids in America: A Social History of Eyewear and Sight Correction Since 1900 (2011)

Lynchings of Women in the United States: The Recorded Cases, 1851–1946 (2010)

America Brushes Up: The Use and Marketing of Toothpaste and Toothbrushes in the Twentieth Century (2010)

Film Actors Organize: Union Formation Efforts in America, 1912–1937 (2009)

Parricide in the United States, 1840–1899 (2009)

Actors Organize: A History of Union Formation Efforts in America, 1880–1919 (2008)

Obesity in America, 1850–1939: A History of Social Attitudes and Treatment (2008)

Women and Capital Punishment in America, 1840–1899: Death Sentences and Executions in the United States and Canada (2008)

Women Swindlers in America, 1860–1920 (2007)

Ticket Scalping: An American History, 1850–2005 (2007)

America on Foot: Walking and Pedestrianism in the 20th Century (2006)

Suntanning in 20th Century America (2005)

Endorsements in Advertising: A Social History (2005)

Women and Smoking in America, 1880 to 1950 (2005)

Foreign Films in America: A History (2004)

Lie Detectors: A Social History (2004)

Product Placement in Hollywood Films: A History (2004)

Piracy in the Motion Picture Industry (2003)

Jukeboxes: An American Social History (2002)

Vending Machines: An American Social History (2002)

Age Discrimination by Employers (2001)

Shoplifting: A Social History (2001)

The Hatpin Menace
*American Women Armed
and Fashionable, 1887–1920*

KERRY SEGRAVE

McFarland & Company, Inc., Publishers
Jefferson, North Carolina

LIBRARY OF CONGRESS CATALOGUING-IN-PUBLICATION DATA

Names: Segrave, Kerry, 1944– author.
Title: The hatpin menace : American women armed and fashionable, 1887–1920 / Kerry Segrave.
Description: Jefferson, North Carolina : McFarland & Company, Inc., Publishers, 2016. | Includes bibliographical references and index.
Identifiers: LCCN 2015049028 | ISBN 9781476662152 (softcover : acid free paper) ∞
Subjects: LCSH: Women—United States—Social life and customs—19th century. | Women—United States—Social life and customs—20th century. | Hatpins.
Classification: LCC HQ1419 .S44 2016 | DDC 305.4097309/034—dc23
LC record available at http://lccn.loc.gov/2015049028

BRITISH LIBRARY CATALOGUING DATA ARE AVAILABLE

ISBN (print) 978-1-4766-6215-2
ISBN (ebook) 978-1-4766-2217-0

© 2016 Kerry Segrave. All rights reserved

No part of this book may be reproduced or transmitted in any form or by any means, electronic or mechanical, including photocopying or recording, or by any information storage and retrieval system, without permission in writing from the publisher.

On the cover: Victorian hat styles for the summer of 1900 advertisement, May 1900 issue of *The Delineator* magazine (The Old Design Shop); *inset* March 1910 editorial cartoon (Library of Congress)

Printed in the United States of America

McFarland & Company, Inc., Publishers
  Box 611, Jefferson, North Carolina 28640
    www.mcfarlandpub.com

Table of Contents

Preface	1
Introduction	2
1. Big Hats	5
2. Hatpin Fashion	36
3. The Hatpin as an Offensive Weapon	46
4. The Hatpin as a Defensive Weapon	73
5. Group Use of the Hatpin	95
6. Accidental Use of the Hatpin	102
7. The Hatpin Abroad	109
8. Agitation, Hysteria, Crusades and Legislation Against the Hatpin	116
Chapter Notes	181
Bibliography	192
Index	205

Preface

This book looks at the controversy in America that began in the mid- to late 1880s and swirled around the country until around 1920, with the peak of intensity and hysteria surrounding the fashion accessory occurring a decade earlier.

The story began with a lowly hat fastener that nobody paid much attention to until the arrival of big hair fashion for women, coupled with a sudden and continuing big hat fashion craze that hit America. Along with that came the birth and flowering of the modern advertising industry. It all led to a growth in the physical size of the hatpin, and that was when it all got really scary for men. Suddenly, men had to think about passing laws regulating women's fashions. Even when this was accomplished, the police were said to be too bashful to approach women in the streets and to enforce those laws. Men were genuinely trepidatious about taking public transit, as all those protruding hatpins threatened and endangered them. Some men went so far as to argue that a woman with a hatpin was more dangerous than a man with a gun.

It was perhaps the only time in American history that virtually all American women went out and about armed with a deadly (though legal) weapon. And the hatpin was an effective weapon indeed. It was used in a variety of ways, both offensively and defensively. This was the time of the first feminist movement, and women were becoming more vocal about their inalienable rights. Arguably, women needed a weapon during this time as they were regularly assailed, assaulted, and harassed on the streets and in public places. As the patriarchy grew fearful over the issue of armed women, they set out determinedly to disarm them.

Research for this book was done using online databases with the Library of Congress's "Chronicling America" being the most useful. Also highly useful was newspaperarchive.com.

Introduction

Before there were wars over hatpins there were skirmishes over big hats. Chapter 1 looks at the problems society had to deal with when big hats became all the rage and kept getting bigger and bigger. Anybody sitting behind such a woman could see very little except the hat. Removing a hat in public was not something that women usually did, and it was even more difficult when big hats were affixed to the big hair on a woman's head with big hatpins. It was also the fashion for many women to wear hair pieces—rats, puffs, falls, and so forth, which made big hair even bigger.

Chapter 2 looks at hatpin fashion as the newly emerging advertising industry was determined to sell more merchandise to more people and to turn desires into necessities. The hatpin changed from a somewhat smallish, nondescript item into a much longer and much more elaborate item, a fashion necessity, and (in some cases) expensive jewelry.

Chapter 3 looks at how women used the hatpin as an offensive weapon. This was the "dark" side of the hatpin. For example, women being arrested by the police often drew hatpins from their heads and launched attacks on those officers. On occasion they were used on fellow citizens as women fought with other women, using hatpins, or engaged in other felonious behavior.

Chapter 4 looks at the use of the hatpin as a defensive weapon. Examples include women forced to fight off mashers (as sexual harassers were called in this period) and highwaymen intent on stealing their money. Women were almost always praised for using their hatpins in this manner. This was the "good" side of the hatpin.

Group use of the hatpin is the subject of Chapter 5, which outlines how women used hatpins in concert, ranging from several women on a transit vehicle suddenly operating as a unit to subdue a harasser, to striking women using hatpins in confrontations with scabs, to suffragettes using their hat fasteners in large mob actions against the police. Chapter 6 looks at the accidental use of the hatpin. This ranged from a handful of bizarre deaths in which the wearer was tragically, and fatally, impaled on her own hat fastener, to playful encounters between friends that often had equally tragic results.

How foreign nations dealt with the hatpin question is outlined in Chapter 7. Many European countries found themselves confronting the same problems and solutions with respect to the hatpin as did America.

The last Chapter, 8, looks at the agitation, hysteria, crusades, legislation, and legislative attempts made throughout America as a frantic patriarchy sought to deal with the hatpin. It was largely fear, hyperbole, rhetoric, and overreaction that drove the patriarchy as it tried to respond to this new breed of independent, aggressive females.

1

Big Hats

The period covered by this book was one of great social change in America. As wealth and literacy spread and as people moved to cities more and more public amenities arrived, from places of amusement to places for education. Advertising as we know it today took hold in the nation and the people came under the sway of fashion and false "needs" as never before. It drove the market for hats and hatpins (and everything else under the sun) as never before. During this period the feminist movement was very strong and societal changes affected women to a greater extent than men. The focus of women's lives moved from hearth and home to include that of the world outside. Women demanded more freedom of movement and they went out and about by themselves or in groups. Never before had women demanded, and taken, and enjoyed such uncontrolled (by men) and non-chaperoned movement. It led to a backlash from men as women out alone were subjected to waves of sexual harassment, attempted and completed assaults, and so forth. They also came under fire for their hatpins. At the start of this period the hatpin was simply a virtually unnoticed item that was part of a woman's wardrobe and used to secure hats to their heads. But as its use as weaponized fashion became more and more obvious and more and more commented on, the attacks on the item intensified.

During this time men and women wore hats all the time when outdoors. When they went indoors into public places such as theaters, cinemas, restaurants, and so on, men always took their hats off; women almost always kept them on. And that was where some of the trouble started. Social convention dictated that women keep their hats on, but other factors were also involved. Men's hats fit their heads and thus no fasteners were needed. The hat remained secure, except perhaps in a high wind. Nor did a man need to look in a mirror to see if his hat was on correctly: since it fit the head he could tell from its feel on his head if it was sitting correctly, and a slight movement would fix it if it was off. On the other hand, women's hats fit the hair. Most women in this era wore long hair, but not hanging down, loose. It was balled up along the sides and back and top of the head. As well, many women added false bits of hair—falls, puffs, rats—to their own to create even bigger hair. On top of that went hats that grew in size over this period (as fashion dictated) and had to be secured to the head with hatpins, usually several, and these grew in size over time. Taking off or putting on such a hat in a public place, such as a theater or restaurant, required a fair amount of time and effort, and access to a mirror. Taking it off could mess up the hair arrangement, with its elaborate layering and false pieces, requiring repair work. Even when a theater had a "women's room," females were loath to line up and wait their turn. In short, women in this period did not like to continually take off and put on their hats.

Prior to the late 1880s little or no attention was paid to hatpins, but then it all began to change. It was bad enough that women were going out alone, or just with other females, but they were all going about with what was increasingly seen not as an item of wardrobe, an item of fashion, but as a weapon. That did not sit well in the council chambers of patriarchy. Before the hatpins wars, though, were the big-hat skirmishes.

Just before Christmas in 1891 an editorial in a Texas newspaper decried the big hat by writing: "At last a deathblow is about to strike the fashion of wearing large hats to theaters. Men have pleaded and protested, and there is even reason to believe that some of them have sworn." He continued: "The newspapers have attacked the hats and their wearers and have expended eloquence and wit upon them. A wicked Boston paper even started the assertion that none but servant girls wore large hats to theaters. All in vain." It was reported that an Iowa man had set in motion a precedent. He went to a theater and paid his money for a ticket. However, he saw nothing but the backs of two "capacious hats whose brims met and shut out the stage." He went to the box office and demanded a refund but none was given. So he sued the establishment's management "for obtaining money under false pretenses." Concluded the editor, "This is virtually the last of the high hat…. Opera house managers will have to choose between proscribing high hats or paying for damage suits." His enthusiasm was, of course, premature.[1]

One year later, the editor of a St. Paul, Minnesota newspaper remarked, "The long-suffering individual who has been accustomed to disburse his wealth at the box office window for the privilege of viewing the horticultural and ornithological exhibit on the headgear of the woman in front of him is growing more and more discontented with his lot." He went on to mention a plan then being implemented in Boston in which theater managers were printing prominently on their playbills the following: "Will you aid the management in its work of hat reform? Wear a small bonnet. Remove your large hat during the performance. The theater is well heated and protected from draughts." This Minnesota editor thought the idea was good but the specific Boston wording amounted to a "pathetic appeal." He recommended the following wording be adopted by managers of St. Paul theaters: "Ladies will not, and others are requested not to, wear large hats during the performance."[2]

When a Washington, D.C., newspaper editor lashed out at big hats in October 1894, his article featured an editorial cartoon depicting a hapless man stuck behind a big hat in church, at a lecture, at a concert, at the theater, and unable to see anywhere. Among the subheads for the piece were the following: "The public looking for an early deliverance from its [big hats] tyranny," and "No longer to be considered good form to wear obstructive headgear—pertinent suggestions." He wondered if the total abolition of feminine headgear at theaters and other places of amusement was on the menu or might just work as well for women to adopt a theater bonnet. He also worried that

> WILL YOU AID THE MANAGEMENT IN ITS WORK OF HAT REFORM? WEAR A SMALL BONNET, REMOVE YOUR LARGE HAT DURING THE PERFORMANCE. THE THEATER IS WELL HEATED AND PROTECTED FROM DRAUGHTS.

This is in the right line, but it is weak and apologetic. Moreover, its jocose allusion to draughts doesn't go well with the general seriousness of the subject. Of course, no woman wears a hat to keep off draughts, and any ironical allusion to this feature of the case simply tends to throw ridicule on the whole affair. A more concise and emphatic appeal, and one which we recommend to the favorable consideration of the managers of Twin City theaters, is the following:

> LADIES WILL NOT, AND OTHERS ARE REQUESTED NOT TO, WEAR LARGE HATS DURING THE PERFORMANCE.

When a newspaper editor commented that the wording on a theater playbill requesting women to remove their big hats was not tough enough, he suggested the above wording be used instead.

fashion for the coming winter was for hats to be higher and wider "if not now, then when, in the name of suffering humanity and equally grieved hu-woman-ity, can the tall hat grievance be made a burning question and forever and always settled—by burning up the hat. In other words, the doom of the tall hat has been spoken. It has been written hundreds of times, but now it has to go." He further fumed: "It shall no longer be said of woman ... that she will also deliberately pile such architectural effects in millinery on top of her head that the pleasure of every hapless person behind her at the play is turned into a sort of blind and hopeless misery. This ought to be the very strongest kind of argument, but everyone knows it is not, for it is weak from over use." According to the editor there was a crusade that fall to convert those women away from wearing such hats. He admitted some had been weaned off the habit but no specifics were presented. This newspaper had no particular theater bonnet in mind, leaving it to the ladies who were said to be the best judges of that issue. Reportedly, opinions had been solicited among the most fashionable and most frequent theatergoers and all were unanimous that the big hat was a nuisance and an unnecessary evil and had to go. One suggestion was to have a theater employee stationed at the door to take big hats from women, give them a check so that they could collect them after the show. One thing that was unacceptable to this editor were the time delays for reforms to be implemented; these, he believed, should happen immediately.[3]

On January 30, 1895, in Springfield, Illinois, Alexander J. Jones, one of Cook County's representatives in the Illinois Legislature introduced into the House a bill on the issue of hats. He stated that he was opposed to the wearing of large hats in theaters and was going to regulate the practice. The bill he introduced made it a misdemeanor for any person to occupy a seat in any place of amusement to obstruct the vision of any other patron of said place of amusement by wearing any hat, bonnet or other unsightly head covering after having been notified to remove same. It required the authorities of such places of amusement to secure the observance of the order, and to remove any person who violated the provisions of the act. People who persisted in wearing their hats after receiving due notification were to be fined $25, as were the managers of theaters who neglected to enforce the law. No more was heard of this bill.[4]

The Minnesota newspaper editor returned with a piece in February 1895 to announce that the "pest" had returned: "It is here. It is full grown." A reporter from that paper had made a recent visit to the metropolitan venue in that city and estimated the size of a hat directly in front of him at 18 inches across and 15 inches high (including the feathers); "and it was

The horrors of the big theater hat and how it blocked the vision of men, as seen by an editorial cartoonist in 1894.

only one of many." Admitted in the piece was the fact that many ladies "of good taste and refined habits" who were there displayed the habit of wearing small hats or of removing their head covering altogether while in the venue "but there were enough large hats present to interfere seriously with the vision of many ticket-holders." The editor thought there was no excuse for the behavior of those women who wore large hats. Quoting from a magazine, he declared himself in agreement with the idea that "the size of the hat a woman wears on her head in the theater is in inverse proportion to her breeding."[5]

Other legislative efforts were underway in Ohio in the spring of 1896.

On March 24 of that year, the Ohio House defeated Fosdick's hat bill after it had been amended to place the responsibility for non-compliance with the proposal upon the theatrical managers and exempting the hat-wearing women from punishment. The vote was 47 in favor and 45 opposed, but, as it lacked a constitutional majority, the bill failed. Reportedly there were "numerous humorous amendments" to the bill proposed by House members who did not take the whole affair seriously. One of them required the Ohio governor to annually appoint a chief inspector of hats; he was to appoint deputies in all cities in the state. It was also observed that on the day the vote of Fosdick's bill was held a number of supporters of the bill were absent and it was said that an effort would be made to have the bill reconsidered at some time in the future. And it was reconsidered. It passed, becoming a law in April 1896.[6]

A commentator in Washington, D.C., reported that the Ohio bill (as originally proposed) made it a misdemeanor for any woman to wear a hat that caused an obstruction for those behind her in any place of public amusement. Then the amendment made it a misdemeanor for theatrical management to allow such behavior to take place in their venues. Somewhat smugly the Washington editor thought that Ohio may have need for such a law as the one formulated by Fosdick but "moral suasion" worked well in Washington "where the women are affluent as to common sense." He added that his newspaper, the *Star*, called the attention of Washington "womanhood to the selfishness and impropriety of high hats in theater audiences and there was immediate and gratifying response; charmingly small bonnets or no bonnets at all are the fashion." Such instances

A collection of hats taken from a fashion column in September 1895. While these hats are not particularly small, the era of the *really* big hat was still in the future.

of high hats in Washington theaters were now rare, he added, with only occasionally a woman from one of the rural districts wandering in "with a big flower-bed on her head."[7]

On the evening of January 19, 1897, Mr. Watson in the House of Delegates in Missouri introduced a bill aimed at women who wore high hats in theaters. A motion to kill the bill failed by a vote of eight to seven. Managers of venues who permitted high hats would be fined not less than $10 and not more than $25. Under the provisions of the measure it was made the duty of policemen, who witnessed violation of the bill, to arrest the offenders after the close of the show. The offender was to be released upon payment of $3 to the police officer, which sum was to be forfeited in case the offender failed to appear for trial. If the offender appeared for trial and was found guilty, a fine of not less than $3 and not more than $5 was to be assessed.[8]

The Kansas City, Missouri, City Council defeated an ordinance, in January 1897, for the suppression of the high hat in theaters. In doing so, declared the editor of a city newspaper, "It placed itself on record as opposing an intelligent public sentiment. Nobody seriously disputes that the prevailing style of headwear for ladies is a nuisance in a theater, and there is no good reason why proper steps should not be taken to abate it the same as any other nuisance." He believed that such an ordinance was not so much needed in Kansas City as in some other places "for most of the ladies of this city have voluntarily recognized the rights of theatergoers to have a fair view of the performance for which they have paid, and politely remove their hats before the curtain rises. But it is to be regretted that there are some who do not, and it is to these that the ordinance was intended to apply." According to this editor, the agitation against the high hat "is being taken up in nearly every city of importance in the country." He predicted "Kansas City will yet have an anti-hat ordinance, or a theater regulation that will make an ordinance unnecessary."[9]

At about the same time an ordinance against certain kinds of theater headgear was passed by the Chicago City Council but had not yet been acted upon by Mayor Swift. Mayor Waggener of Atchison, Kansas, had just vetoed a similar ordinance. Waggener invoked the U.S. Constitution in his veto by citing "equal protection of the laws" and arguing that the high-hat ordinance was an unjust discrimination against women. Also, Indianapolis, Indiana, had just had an anti-hat bill passed and the question of whether or not to veto the measure was then under consideration by Mayor Taggart.[10]

Still in January 1897, a bill to abolish the "big hat nuisance" in theaters came from a senate committee in the West Virginia Legislature with a recommendation against its passage. A state senator there explained to a reporter that, in his view, the West Virginia Legislature "is not a convention of French milliners to tell the women of West Virginia what they shall wear."[11]

Kansas State Senator Hanna introduced an anti-hat theater bill into his Legislature on February 9, 1897. It read: "It shall be unlawful for any person, male or female, to wear upon his or her head any hat, bonnet or anything excepting his or her natural head adornment at any theatre or public entertainment." The penalty for violation of the bill was a fine of from $5 to $10.[12]

By February 26, 1897, both branches of the Louisville, Kentucky City Council had passed an ordinance prohibiting women from wearing hats in theaters and public halls. Reportedly, Mayor Todd would sign that bill on the following day.[13]

During the first couple of months of 1897 the battle against big hats was intense. According to journalist S. C. Schenck the ordinance that had just been passed by the Chicago City Council was expected to abate a nuisance "which has existed longer than Chicago has." He mentioned that efforts had been made in many places, but the theater hat had always won. Among the many wins Schenck considered to be "empty victories" was the one represented by the Fosdick law in Ohio. When it became law it was thought the huge plumes and other huge features on the hats would be banished forever. They were not. The Ohio law prohibited the wearing of big hats, but it left to the reluctant theater managers the task of drawing the line. A few sporadic efforts to enforce the law were made, but managers of those venues did not like to offend patrons—so the law became "a dead letter." Sometimes the resulting measures had what Schenck saw as curious complications. In Indianapolis, for example, where such an attempt at banning was made, a woman who had been forced to remove her hat retaliated by refusing to allow a man who wanted to go out between the acts to pass her. She insisted that he was interfering with her comfort as much as her hat interfered with that of the man behind her. In St. Louis, a man who found himself sitting behind "a monstrous creation of the milliner's art" became so exasperated in his futile attempts to see what was happening onstage that he took revenge by putting on his tall silk hat and ignoring the protests of the woman behind him. He was arrested, fined, and "canonized as a martyr to men's rights." Besides the numerous attempts to legislate the theater hat out of existence there had been many crusades of an unofficial character, added the journalist, such as newspaper editorials against the nuisance: "But it has all been a waste of effort." Reportedly, a "well-known" woman said recently that women did not refuse to remove their hats because of a natural perversity or malice. "She does not wear a hat because it is necessary, but because it is part of her costume ... and to ask her to leave it in a cloakroom or hide in her lap something which she admires and which she thinks adds to her beauty when she has it on her head is preposterous and unreasonable. Chicago Alderman Plotke was the one who framed and introduced Chicago's hat law. He was committed to his crusade and declared he meant "to fight the theater hat in Chicago until it dies the death."[14]

At a meeting of the San Francisco Board of Supervisors on March 15, 1897, Supervisor Rottanzi introduced an ordinance that made it a misdemeanor, punishable by both fine and imprisonment, for a person to wear a high hat in a theater. Owners and managers of theaters were also prohibited from admitting women to their theaters whose hats were above the limit prescribed by law. That ordinance was referred to the Judiciary Committee, which was to report on it at the next meeting. Anyone found guilty of violating the measure faced a fine of not less than $3 and not more than $20, or imprisonment in the county jail for not more than one day, or by both fine and imprisonment. For owners and managers of venues, the fine was not less than $10 and not more than $25, or imprisonment of not less than two days nor more than ten days, or both fine and imprisonment.[15]

A story in a newspaper in July 1897 stated that the women of Indianapolis not only removed their hats in theaters and other places of public amusement but also did so in church. It happened this way: In the First Baptist Church of that city there was an organization called the Woman's Circle—with 125 members, many of them "prominent" society women. At a meeting Mrs. D. M. Parry suggested that it would be an excellent idea for the members of the circle to remove their hats in church and that all the women in the congregation would be sure to follow their good example. It was adopted by the group as a resolution and passed unanimously. On the following Sunday those ladies implemented their plan and it was said to have been "enthusiastically received" by other women in the congregation. Other churches in Indianapolis were said to be considering adopting the same idea. Parry told a reporter, "I do not think the church ought to be behind the times in any good thing and now when there is a movement to prevent hat wearing in theaters and other places of public amusement I think it is high time for the church to take action, too." She added, "I have always thought that the complaint of men that hats and bonnets, especially

Gray Felt Shepherdess

Velvet folds, trimmed entirely in royal blue silk, edged with the new fringe trimmings, rhinestone and gilt buckle—a tasty and artistic hat of simple, yet rich, effect. We will give you this hat if you can buy similar quality elsewhere for less than $7. Our wholesale and retail price.

$3.15

The Dewey.

Beautiful Silk Velvet Turban

This splendid hat is a reproduction of one of Mme. Pouyanne's latest models. Simple, magnificent. Made entirely of shirred silk velvet, with fancy breast on side to match—bandeau of taffeta silk ribbon and shirred silk velvet. A hat that would be cheap elsewhere at $15. Our wholesale and retail price.

$6.45

The Pouyanne.

All Black Felt Hat

With velvet folds—large tam crown of silk velvet—one of the new style bows in front—fancy black breast on the side—taffeta silk ribbon on bandeau. One of the up-to-date hats. Elsewhere similar hats are sold for $10. Our wholesale and retail price.

$4.10

The Beaumont.

Misses' Hat of French Felt

Three shades of taffeta silk—shirred rosettes—draped with taffeta silk—cut steel buckle, bandeau trimming of taffeta silk. Every woman will vote this the biggest bargain for the money ever heard of. Couldn't buy one elsewhere less than $8. Our wholesale and retail price.

$4.55

The Lulu.

Bright Finish Fur Felt

Large velvet bow, edged with ruffled chiffon—crystal buckle—Shepherdess shape, with bandeau trimming of chiffon—a beautiful and chic hat. Priced elsewhere, you couldn't get one like it for less than $12. Our wholesale and retail price.

$5.98

The Trixie.

Beautiful Poke Bonnet

This is the well known Directoire style, satin-covered, with velvet folds—two elegant ostrich plumes—rhinestone buckle—double velvet ties—a great hat in perfect style. Would cost you double elsewhere. Our wholesale and retail price this week.

$13.80

The Directoire.

when heightened by flowers and other trimmings, are a nuisance was not without some justice, and I am now convinced, after our experience of last Sunday, that we women are not only more comfortable ourselves without hats, but escape giving a cause of offense to others." Mrs. Arthur Jordan, president of the Woman's Circle, said that the Sunday they first implemented the idea was the first one for some time that she had been able to get more than a partial view of the face of the minister during his sermon and she declared she had never appreciated a sermon so much before.[16]

Complaints were made about hats worn at Morton's Opera House in Paducah, Kentucky, on the evening of January 21, 1898. It was reported that "the dress circle looked like an oasis of palm trees in the desert of Sahara, and the kicks heard from behind were loud and long." The journalist thought there was only one remedy for such behavior: "the enactment of a law making the perpetual and unnecessary nuisance a misdemeanor." As far as he was concerned, nothing else would work.[17]

An ad from a Kansas City, Missouri, millinery in 1898, touting the latest fashions in hats; they would only grow bigger in all possible directions.

As of February 1901 the city of San Francisco had an ordinance in place relative to not wearing hats in theaters. It read as follows: "No person shall wear any hat, bonnet or other head covering within any licensed theater in the city and county during the rendition of any programme on the stage or platform of such theater, but every hat, bonnet or other head covering shall be removed from the head of the person wearing the same during the time of performance in such theater or during the rendition of the performance on the stage or platform of such theater; provided, that the above inhibitions shall not be held to include skull caps, lace coverings or other small or closely fitting headdress which does not interfere with or obstruct the view of the stage or platform of such theater of persons in the rear of such wearers while in such theater."[18]

New Orleans also had an ordinance in place in 1901 that forbade the wearing of high hats in theaters. The first person to be arrested for violating that ordinance was an actress who was fined $15.[19]

In January 1902, Fourth Ward Representative Thomas Kinney introduced a measure into the St. Louis House of Delegates prohibiting the wearing of high hats in theaters. He did so, it was said, because "his vision came in contact with an immense Gainsborough hat in the Columbia Theater, thus inhibiting him from witnessing the performance." Under his measure the managers of theaters and other public amusement venues who permitted patrons to wear hats or bonnets would be subject to a fine while patrons who ignored the law and obstructed views would be asked to give the attending police officer $3 as evidence of good faith, and to ensure their appearance in court. At the performance in question Kinney said he asked the woman with the huge hat, "very politely" to remove her hat but she twisted around and said she would do no such thing. Under his measure, "No person shall wear any hat or bonnet within any licensed theater in the city of St. Louis during the time of performance or during the rendition of any programme on the stage or platform, but any such hat or bonnet, shall be removed from the head during the time of such programme or performance, provided, however, that the above inhibitions shall not be held to include skull caps, lace coverings or other small and closely fitting head dress which does not interfere with the view of the stage or persons in the rear of such wearers." This ordinance, of course, was almost exactly the same as the one then in place in San Francisco. Managers who permitted violations of the measure were to be fined not less than $10 and not more than $50. No person was to be arrested during the performance, but it was made the duty of every policeman who observed any infraction to place an offender under arrest at the end of the show and for that offender to pay the officer $3. If the offender did not appear in court later, that $3 deposit was declared forfeited. In the case of a trial the offender, if convicted, would be subject to a fine of not less than $3 and not more than $5 for each offense.[20]

Apparently the situation was changing and moral suasion was indeed having an effect, at least in some places. An article in the same Minnesota newspaper that had often editorialized with a passion against the nuisance commented in December 1903 that big hats remained the fashion and were

Some big hats featured in a July 1904 newspaper. Note the elaborate decoration on the tops of these hats; that was the coming thing.

the fashion the year round. "These hats can be worn to the theater with evening wraps, but must be taken off at once [in the theater]," noted the journalist. He also observed, "A week or two ago a woman sat through two acts of a play at the Metropolitan with her large hat on, and the sight was so unusual that everyone stared." The reporter thought it was just absent-mindedness on her part and that "nothing can more completely spoil one's pleasure at a play than to sit behind a large hat; but nothing can quicker ruin a woman's temper than to have to take off her hat. The woman who has a carriage and can go down to the theater without any hat is all right but the unfortunate woman who goes in the car [public transit] and has to take off her coat, furs, and hat after she gets there, considers the thing almost more trouble than it is worth." The same reporter also spoke to the difficulties involved in hat removal by noting, "In the first place, it is very difficult for a woman who has put on her hat before a mirror to take it off without a mirror and have her hair look decently. Then when she come to put on her hat again she is quite likely to get it on backwards or over one eye." The piece ended with the observation that "the custom of women taking off their hats has become universal, and this was done mainly because of complaints of masculine grumblers whose point was well taken."[21]

More big hats, from November 1905; these were touted to be used for "walking."

Wings and Breasts Used Largely on New Hats.

Still more big hats; these were featured in a newspaper in September 1906.

Famed columnist Cholly Knickerbocker weighed in on the subject of women and hats with a November 1907 column on the issue. That author's name was a house pseudonym of the Hearst newspaper chain, used by whatever male columnist happened to be writing the column at the time. But since the column was about women's issues, mostly, the author was listed as Mrs. Cholly Knickerbocker. Along with the article was an artist's collage of huge hats. Cholly wrote: "Women have certainly no sense of proportion or they would not so willingly adopt all the most outrageous fashions. Just now the hats are positive caricatures. Small women disappear bodily under them, stout women accentuate their size, tall women look like grenadiers of the British Guard, pretty women are swamped, plain ones look plainer—and yet they wear them, and yet the headgear rises and grows and swells in height and width and ponderosity and price." That quote was attributed to Lady Violet Greville of England. Cholly ended his piece by declaring that smaller hats were growing in popularity but he produced no evidence to support that idea.[22]

The *Los Angeles Herald* published an article in March 1908 that contained a collage of huge hats. The hats were drawings with blanks for the faces. A photographer for the paper went out on the street and took photos of women, some of which were then inserted into the blank spaces. The piece then told its readers that if a reader identified herself under one of

Mrs. Cholly Knickerbocker (pseudonym for a male columnist) discussed hats in 1907.

the drawn hats "and have enough nerve to admit it" she could get a free six-month subscription to the newspaper by coming down to the office and pointing herself out. The article went on to declare that Los Angeles was the victim of the strange "Merry Widow Hat" disease. It was, of course, a satirical article and went on to declare the disease sufferer had "a mania for strange and outrageous headgear, and insists on wearing great disks in the place of hats and piling thereon a mixture of all the flowers that ever grew in garden and in field." Reportedly, the disease was milder in Los Angeles than it was in New York City, where the disks measured 36 inches and 40 inches from brim to brim, while in Los Angeles the extreme limit was 28 inches, while the majority of hats shown in local shops had a diameter of 20 inches to 21 inches. That style was all the rage and demanded by all, according to hat shop reports, and that style was to be adopted by all women, from children on up to old age. At store counters where umbrellas and parasols were sold, clerks reported that sales had fallen off by nearly two-thirds in that spring because women were buying hats big enough to serve as protection against both showers and sun. Blame for this particular style was given to Franz Lehar and his operetta, *The Merry Widow*, which had its debut in 1905. A United Kingdom run in 1907 had set off a craze for the large hats worn by the title character in that piece. For a brief time, "Merry Widow" became a sort of generic name for huge hats. In Los Angeles those hats were on sale with the cheaper ones running from $5 to $15 and expensive ones, "creations" running from $30 to $45 and $50 "trimmed." The reporter on this piece saw one in a store that was trimmed with a "whole flock of blackbirds," while another one contained "a tower of violets and roses that makes one dizzy to contemplate."[23]

Not long after the Merry Widow story in the *Los Angeles Herald* an editorial cartoon appeared in an Arizona newspaper and in other papers. Apparently it originated in an Indianapolis publication. It spoofed the fashion for gigantic hats and all the novel uses to which they could be put.[24]

In October 1904 the superintendent of a large, new, uptown apartment building in New York City, told a reporter that the most frequent objection to his apartments was their lack of closet and wardrobe space. "The increasing size of women's hats and the demand Fashion makes on her followers is putting us in a bad way," the superintendent supposedly said. "One woman told me there was a time when she could easily put her clothes in an ordinary wardrobe and be well dressed. To-day it is altogether different, for no woman is well dressed unless her garments match from her head to her heels."[25]

In Springfield, Illinois, a measure was introduced on April 23, 1909, into the Illinois House of Representatives in the name of George C. Hilton of Chicago, by Mr. Cermak in Hilton's absence and, if passed, the measure would provide a fine of from $100 to $200 for anyone who made, sold, or wore a hat larger than the maximum dimensions laid down in the bill. As contained in the bill the specifications were: diameter—no more than 18 inches; crown, not more than one cubic foot in diameter; weight, not more than five ounces. With respect to the trimmings on the hat, the use of stuffed birds, skins of lizards, snakes, fur, or anything else liable to decay and to become the roosting place for microbes and germs was forbidden; feathers—no plume, aigrette [egret crest] or feather was allowed to project more than six inches beyond the crown. Also in the bill was a clause that

These were faces of real women snapped on the street, unknowingly, by a photographer for a Los Angeles paper in 1908. Those faces were inserted under drawn big hats. A woman who recognized herself was entitled to a free subscription to the paper if she presented herself to the paper's office.

This editorial cartoon appeared in publications around the county in the spring of 1908, spoofing the rage for big hats.

forbade the use of hatpins that projected more than six inches beyond the crown. The bill make it a misdemeanor to manufacture or sell such a hat that did not comply with the measure or to wear such a headpiece in walking or driving upon the public thoroughfares, or in any house, hotel, place of amusement or other public place or in any public vehicle. Retail outlets were also forbidden to exhibit hats of a banned size "but the exhibition of

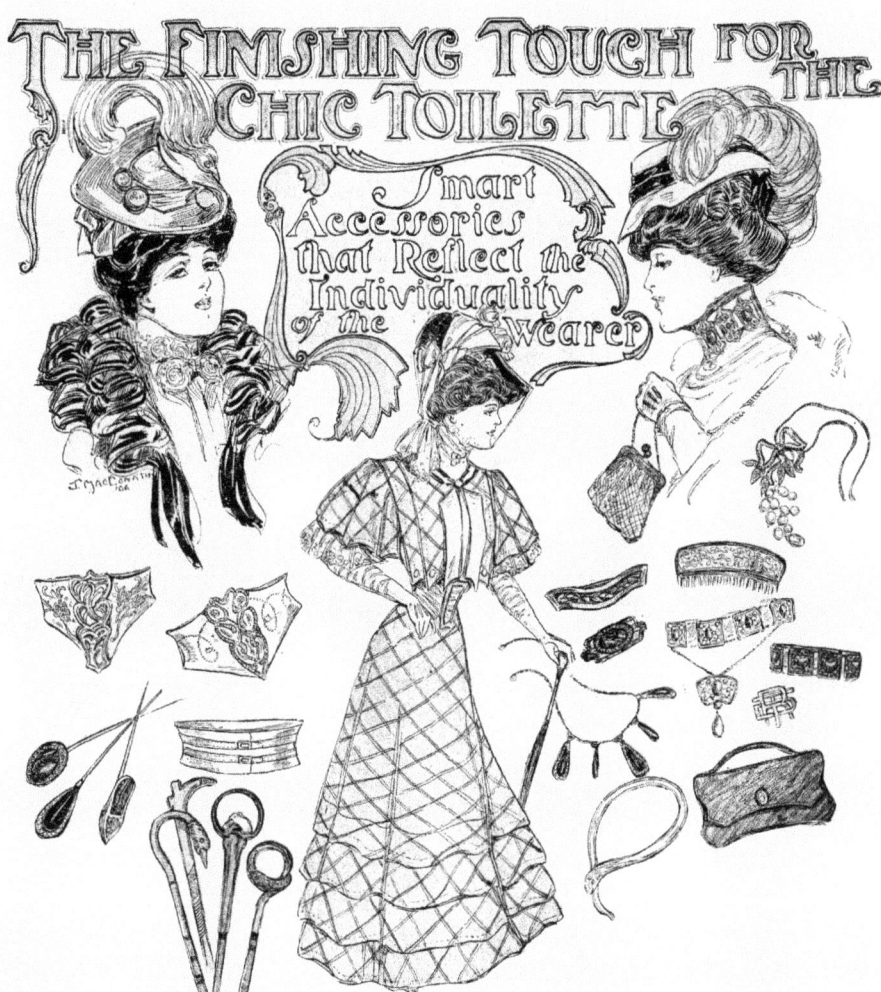

The power of advertising can be seen in this October 1906 ad, illustrating just how many fashion-oriented items the well-dressed woman needed, beyond the big hat. Note: near the lower left side a few hatpins are pictured.

ancient and freakish types and models of hats and headgear for purposes of education or amusement is permitted."[26]

On the following day the "real reason" for the Hilton hat bill was said to have come to light. The informant was Mrs. Hilton herself; she did not agree entirely with her husband's views. "I was down at Springfield while the suffragist people were there," she said. "Many of them wore such big hats that it was impossible for the members of the legislature to get around.

Top: The fashionable woman of 1906 needed a special hat for every occasion. Even for skating, where the hat was, obviously, big. Also, it did apparently nothing at all to keep a woman's ears warm in the cold weather. *Bottom:* More big hats, from May 1907; notice that these feature small gardens on the top.

I think that those big hats did more damage to the cause of women suffrage than anything else that happened there. The poor legislators were always bumping their faces against big straw hats, or scratching themselves with feathers or long hatpins." Legislators, when interviewed by the reporter, acknowledged that the information from Mrs. Hilton was correct. The position of the opposition to the hat bill was stated by Mrs. Oliver W. Stewart, president of the Illinois Woman's Suffrage Association. She declared, "If the Illinois legislators would use some of their energy in considering woman suffrage or some of the other important issues before them instead of thinking up such ridiculous measures as this hat bill, they would be of greater service to their state."[27]

One day later a scathing editorial about the proposal was published in an Illinois newspaper. The editor declared the bill "would be funny, were it not for its serious side. The subject offers much food for the jokesmiths, though when the taxpayer considers how little has come from the present session of the legislature the humor of this freak bill is a bit sour." He continued: "The legislator who proposed it needs a hot towel laid on his head. This antidote for brainstorms can be obtained at any barber shop and is usually applied for the asking without charge." In conclusion, the editor thundered: "It is unfortunate that a man must make himself ridiculous as a substitute for being distinguished. And to think of the people of Illinois actually raising the salaries of legislators recently and paying for having the lawmaking body turned into a farce comedy.[28]

A couple of weeks later it was reported that Hilton's hat bill had "sailed along" to third reading and was expected to be called up in the following week for debate. Hilton was said, by his friends, to be assembling a collection of hats of all shapes and sizes to be introduced as exhibit A in support of his bill during that debate. Said a reporter: "Although the bill was regarded as more or less of a bit of humor when it was

This editorial cartoon appeared in May 1909 and spoofed the Illinois lawmakers as they considered a bill to regulate women's hats. It also took shots at those hats, and at hatpins.

Stunning summer hats, as featured in a May 1908 ad. They just kept growing and growing.

first sprung, many of the members are declaring they are for it, and it will not be surprising if the bill is passed by the house."[29]

On May 10, 1909, Mrs. Hilton was heard from again in the media. It was an article that focused on the idea that while Mr. Hilton waged war on "freak" hats, Mrs. Hilton was "wearing a freak hat everywhere." Moreover, she could see nothing objectionable in a big hat and long hatpins. When she went shopping or to the matinee she wore one, a "sort of hybrid Mary Garden-Merry Widow thing, and she pins it fast upon her head with 20-inch hat pins that her husband is just now so busy legislating against." She told the journalist, "I wasn't consulted. Mr. Hilton started this crusade of his without my knowledge or consent." By this time an emergency clause had been tacked on to the bill giving it effect as soon as it was passed. Mrs. Hilton added, "George will be defeated for reelection if this bill passes."[30]

George Hilton continued to defend his measure. A day after his wife spoke out, George grumbled, "There is a real necessity for this measure. A person cannot walk through a store or a streetcar now without incurring danger of having his eyes put out. Those 20-inch hat pins must go." Late in May the bill was defeated in the Illinois Lower House.³¹

A few days later another editorial on the subject appeared. This one was brief, and observed: "A resolution was recently introduced in the Illinois legislature to limit the size of women's hats. Must be lots of bachelors in that sedate body to thus tempt the wrath of the women scorned."³²

Late in January 1910 a report observed that a dignified inquiry "into a comical situation" would be made the following day by the Interstate Commerce Commission. It had been found that for three years express companies had been trying to reduce the size of women's hats. The hats not only took up a lot of space but had to be handled as carefully as glass. Express companies appeared to have increased the rates on hats and other millinery articles, but milliners and the wearers had paid the extra freight charges rather than abandon the fashions. Finally, though, milliners appeared to the Commerce Commission on the ground that rates were not only excessive but unjust. It was claimed by the milliners that rates of various articles that went to make up hats had nearly doubled since 1906 and that big hats had still further boosted the rates. The formal complaint to the Interstate Commerce Commission was made in the name of the Milliners' Jobbers' Association, composed of 65 wholesale jobbers located west of Columbus, Ohio.³³

That hearing was held in Chicago on January 28, 1910, before Commissioner James S. Harlan. According to the journalist, "It is evident that the express

FREAK HAT LEGISLATION MAY COST HIM HIS JOB

MRS. GEO. C. HILTON AND HER 18-INCH HAT, FASTENED WITH 20-INCH PINS.

This illustration shows Mrs. George Hilton and her "freak" hat.

This sketch shows women, all wearing big hats, in a restaurant in October 1908. It illustrated the fact that women rarely took their hats off indoors in public places. Too much work was involved.

companies had thrown off for all time the tyranny of the 'big lid.' Through their representatives they declared they would rather go out of business than stand it any longer." During the previous two years the express firms had been putting up the rates on hats until they were then nearly twice what they had been in 1906 and the hat makers were before the commission to find out why. C. W. Stockton, the president of one of the express companies, did most of the talking for all the express firms. "When we first began making rates on women's hats the hats were small, neat, compact affairs that looked like a pat of butter and were fastened to the wearer's head with a little string," he said. "We charged by the pound at that time. Since then the hats have been growing steadily in width, length, height, and the fourth dimension, but they haven't grown an ounce in weight. Why, five years ago, you could get from 500 to 3,000 women's hats into any ordinary express car. Now you have to take the double doors off to get one in."[34]

Legislative efforts to deal with big hats were almost finished, but not

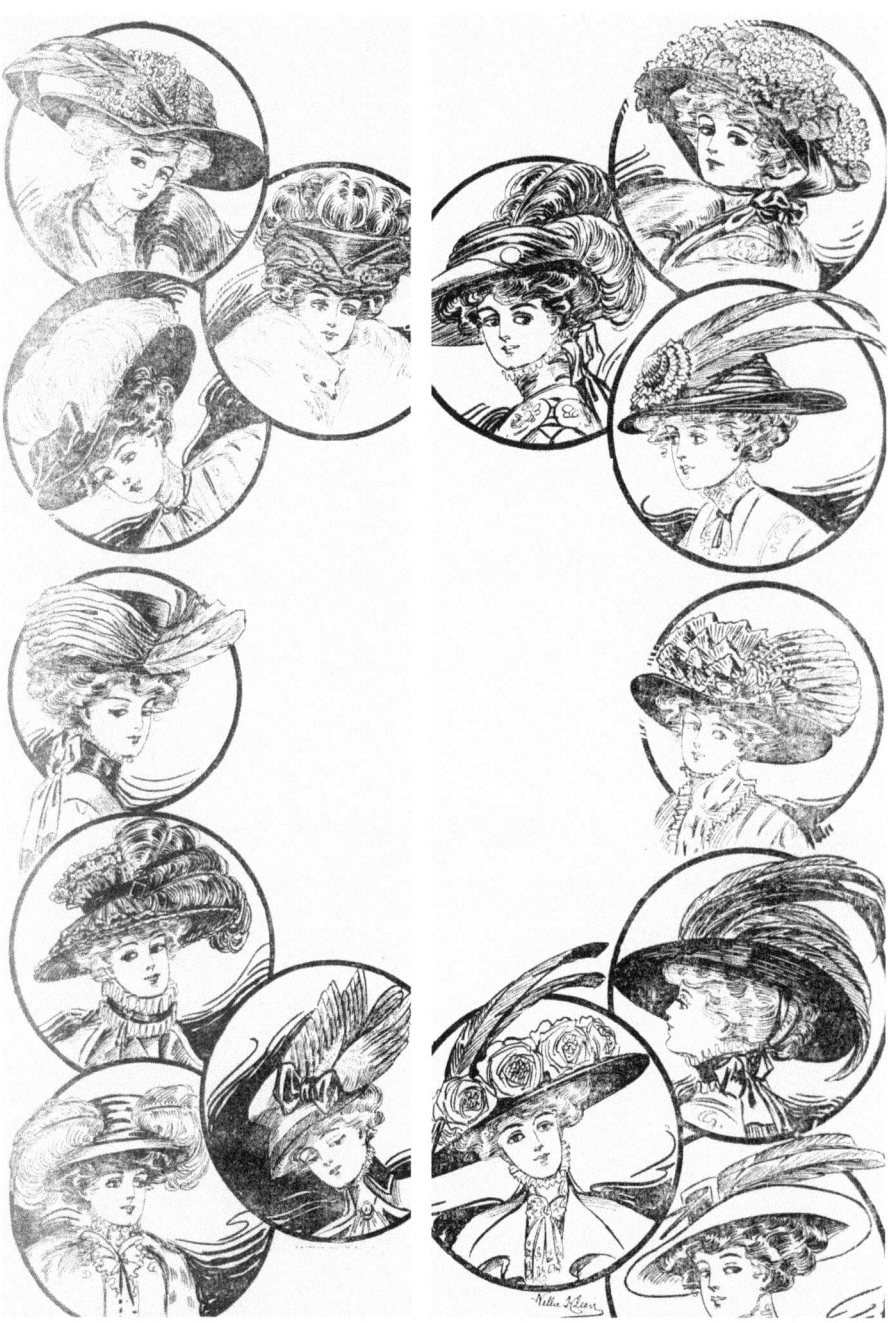

A baker's dozen plus one of the latest big hats that appeared in a newspaper at the start of 1909.

quite. At Annapolis, Maryland, a state legislator introduced a bill to limit the size of women's hats to ten inches in diameter. Walter Wittig was the father of the bill. When a female reporter went to interview him he admitted that not even his wife knew of his intent. Although he was an antisuffragist he still had virtually no support for his bill. A newspaper editor called it another freak bill and concluded, "But the gayety of nations is being well cared for by the men who are sent to State legislatures and to Congress. Some are unconscious humorists but, nevertheless, will live longer as humorists than as solons."[35]

An article published in April 1910 with respect to Chicago noted that as to the wearing of hats in public places, it is "not enough that women are

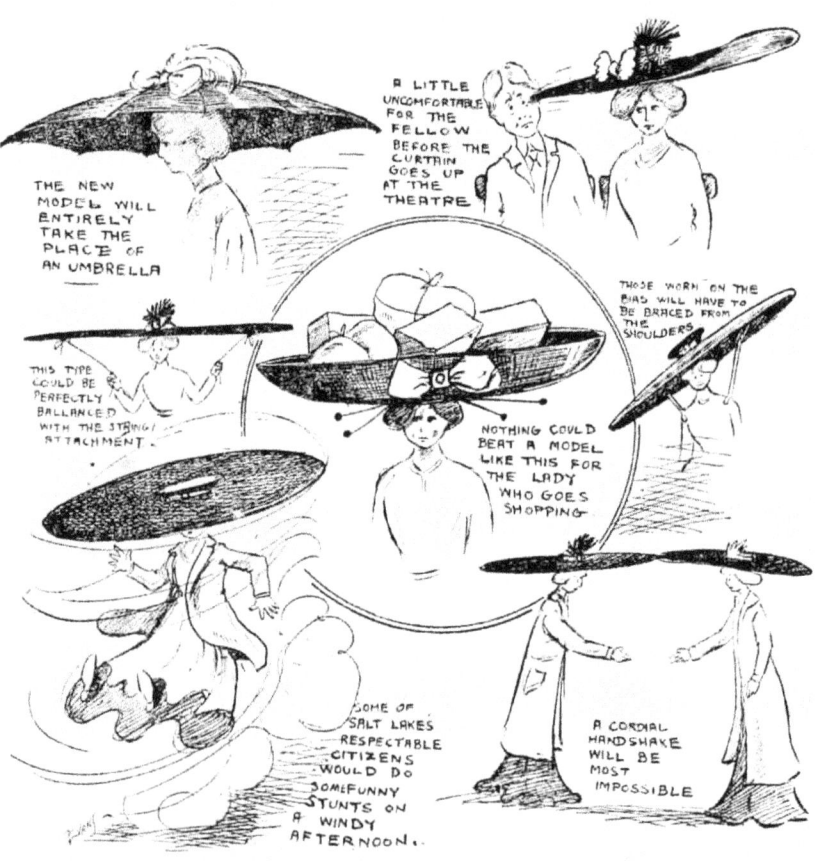

An editorial cartoon from March 1910 that came up with some novel uses for the big hats.

required by law to remove them in the theatres, but there are churches in which the rule is enforced. Signs politely request that large hats be removed during the sermon in order that the congregation may see as well as hear." Said one "fashionably dressed" woman regarding the church rule: "It really spoiled my pleasure in my new hat. For my part, I would rather be inconvenienced a little in having to peer around to see the minister than be obliged to take off my hat."[36]

An April 1910 article stated that when the Merry Widow hat lost popularity a year or so earlier there was hope that smaller hats would emerge. But it was not to be: big hats were still the dominant fashion. That caused an newspaper editor to muse, "Mere man dares not express an opinion, but he can and does hope that rationalism will prevail among the designers, and that the beauties of the small hat will be pointed out to the purchasers."[37]

A story about big hats that was partly spoof and, presumably, partly true, appeared in the California press in May 1910. In a skyscraper, in Alameda, California, a fire of "mysterious origin broke out in the hat of a woman on a local electric car this afternoon. Before the blazing structure of straw, willow plumes, flowers and chiffon could be disconnected from the coiffure of the hysterical wearer by conductor J. J. Farrar, who organized himself into a volunteer fire department, the elaborate and costly creation of the milliners had burned to the rim. There was no insurance." Farrar had some difficulty in locating the hatpins, but he persisted, removed them, and threw the burning hat from the car. While the woman involved thanked the transit employee she refused to give her name. She had boarded the streetcar and been on it for only a few minutes when a small boy sitting near her yelled, "Fire, fire; lady, your bonnet is on fire."[38]

Hat etiquette often found its way into print. In New York City in October 1909, tightly packed multitudes of spectators crowded together on the sidewalks to watch the great land parade. It was the 300th anniversary of Henry Hudson's discovery of the Hudson River and the 100th anniversary of Robert Fulton's first successful commercial application of the paddle steamer. At that open-air parade were many women who took off their hats, as "they do in obedience to custom in a theatre," wrote a journalist. At that outdoor event they did so because people behind them asked them; sometimes, the hat interfered with the wearer's view. For example, one woman with a big hat said she could only look straight ahead and could not turn her head to the left or right because the hat would bang and scratch those nearby. A woman who was wedging her elbows sideways to make a little more room for herself asked a policeman to take her hat off for her, so she would not lose her place, which would happen if she lowered her elbows. That police officer then "fumbled among the feathers and bows on her hat and found the hat pins one after another and pulled them out and put them in one of her hands and then he lifted off her hat and put that in the other."[39]

In the summer of 1910 a newspaper reporter in London had investigated "why the gigantic matinee hat still continues to be worn in spite of all protests, and has found the reasons to be many and weighty." For one thing, the women who had paid a high price for their hats did not want it to be flung about in a public dressing room. For another, "She cannot go to a matinee without a hat. She lunches in her hat, her hair must be dressed to suit the hat, and she is probably going out to tea in the hat after the matinee is over." Furthermore, "She has no time to wait her turn in the tiny dressing room to find her hat, or for her turn at the mirror to restore [her] coiffure, which is disarranged by the removal of the hat." Many women, it was stated, had ceased to attend matinees because they did not care to remove their hats. The article went on to state that if, as stated by prominent American women, the church attempted to adopt the custom of theater patrons by having women remove their hats, the "churches will be practically empty, especially at morning services, when a woman's coiffure is arranged for the day. If women attended church in the evenings dressed as they do for the theater there might be an excuse for removing the hat, but not otherwise."[40]

Mrs. Francis Earl Brown, a member of Los Angeles high society, posed in 1910 for a wedding portrait. If the trend toward bigger and bigger hats continued, the time would soon arrive when the hat was larger than the wearer.

At around the same time another article (taken from a millinery trade journal) remarked that both the press and the pulpit were still hanging on to the "fruitless effort" to diminish the size of women's hats. Male correspondents, it was argued, were trying to get women "not to follow style, but to follow man's idea of what the women of the country ought to wear." However, it was argued, those combined efforts would have no effect on women because fashion ruled supreme: "Her votaries are legion, and will follow her diction, whether it be large hats or small hats, switches, coronets, puffs, 'rats,' or curls … women will have their own way in this matter, let pulpit and press scold as it will." One clergyman was described as being foolish enough to state for publication that "big hats were a hindrance to the salvation of souls." Let him bar his pews to the fashions of the day in women's wear "and he will have very few souls to his credit." According to the author of this article, the only sensible remark made by a clergyman on the subject was attributed to a New York man who said women could wear hats as large as they desired in his church: "If necessary, a woman may have a whole pew to herself." In conclusion, the journalist declared: "Exercise a little patience, friends, the styles will shortly change, when small hats and big sleeves will return to bother us."[41]

Even representatives of women's clubs spoke out against the big hat, at least on rare occasions. As of November 1910, the Ebell Club of Oakland, California, had gone on record as no longer allowing women to wear hats at club meetings. And the Ebell Club of San Francisco was said to be not far behind. More and more clubwomen were reportedly going on record

WAR STILL WAGED BETWEEN HATS LARGE AND SMALL

This article, published at the end of 1914, declared there was a war on between large and small hats. Large hats still held sway, but they were in for a rapid decline within a few years.

against the tall hat as a feature of club meetings. Mrs. D. E. F. Easton, president of the Cap and Bells Club (also said to be working towards a ban on the hats) said, on November 27, that at recent club meetings she had requested members of the club to remove their hats and that as of the first of the coming year she would recommend to the board of directors that all members be required, formally, to remove their hats during all programs given by the club. On the December events calendar sent out to members was the notice: "Please remove the hat while the program is being rendered." Mrs. Henry Eickhoff, chairperson of the music committee of the California Club, said her club had no rule for removal of hats during meetings but felt there should be. "The structures that ladies are adorned with are not suitable things to wear at a meeting—beautiful as they might be," she said diplomatically. Mrs. John Martinon, of the Laurel Hall Club and the Channing Club, was friendly to the big hats, not finding them objectionable. Mrs. Huntley of the Ebell Club of Oakland was outspoken in her opposition to big hats: "When it is considered that the hats worn by women today are larger than they have ever been, and to my mind, altogether too large, it is no more than fair that the members should be requested to remove their hats. One can not sit behind one of these immense hats and see the stage. People for six and even eight rows back have to crane their necks to get a look at the speaker." She insisted her club would enforce the hat rule. "The trouble is in the hats," she reasoned. "They are too large as worn at the present time."[42]

But the era of gigantic hats was coming to a close. An article in late 1914 discussed fashion in hats with one of its subheads reading, "War still waged between hats large and small."[43]

Less than a year later an article argued that "small hats of head size

Tailored Chapeaux of Velour And Felt Will Do Away With Hatpins

Small Hats of Head Size Fit Tightly and Eliminate the Troublesome Hatpin From the Equation.

This 1915 illustration showed the small hat that was beginning to make headway in the fashion scene. It had the added advantage of not needing any hatpins to attach it to the head.

fit tightly and eliminate the troublesome hatpin from the equation."⁴⁴

In the fall of 1917, Broadway and film actress Irene Bordoni had a bylined article in which she described her favorite hat—a small, close-fitting one. She said she liked it "because it is very light and fits smugly, needing no hatpins and always looking well."⁴⁵

This 1917 article featured actress Irene Bordoni endorsing the idea of the small hat. Also noted in the piece was that hatpins were not needed. The big hat was then on its way out.

2

Hatpin Fashion

Hatpins moved from being an almost unnoticed item of a wardrobe to a necessary item of fashion, which was regularly hyped and touted by the expanding and exploding advertising industry. The size and style of hatpins were altered regularly as women were urged to buy more and more of them. Through the 1880s hatpins were about five inches in length, perhaps varying by an inch in either direction. The head of the pin was usually a simple white or black ball. And that was about it. And then advertising took hold.

According to an 1893 news report, the spoon craze had then died out: "But a new one is springing up in its place, as silly a fad as ever tempted the soul of woman to extravagance. It is the collection of hat pins. Many of these pins would serve for daggers 'tis true; but the usefulness of the dagger is, after all, circumscribed." While this account looked like a news story it was just as likely a plant by the ad industry to create a craze for collecting hatpins.[1]

By late in 1895 it was reported that hatpins were growing in elaborateness and expensiveness with each passing day. Rhinestones, silver, steel, gilt, gold, and even jewels were being employed and the "most useful and inexpensive black headed hat pin is no longer possible." There were only two changes that could possibly be made in hatpins. One was to alter the head and make it more elaborate by, for example, adding jewels. And that was done. The other possible change was to alter the length of the item. Since making pins shorter than the four or five inches (then a standard pin size) was not feasible; the only option seemed to be to make the pins longer. And that was done.[2]

By the summer of 1905 jewelers were said to be turning out more hatpins than ever, although, noted a reporter, "There has been a rumor of a crusade against hatpins." One reason for that increased demand for pins was said to be that according "to Fashion's decree, it is no longer correct to secure one's headgear with odd pins, but it must be fastened in place by four pins of the same design." The reporter went on to add that "most women—although they may not admit it—realize that the hatpin in the process of adjustment is one of the very best means of attracting attention to a well-shaped head and beautifully coiffured hair—to say nothing of the hat."[3]

A 1906 newspaper article was mostly about the hatpin as a fashion accessory. Its subtitle was: "New uses for a woman's weapon." The journalist began his story by observing, "Just a few years ago the hat pin was an inconspicuous little thing with a black or white head, which was used solely for the practical purpose of fastening on a hat." He went on to declare, "Here and there handsome hat pins appeared and were looked upon as articles of needless extravagance. The decorative hat pin of today is considered an absolute necessity and women possess an abundance of them sufficient to meet every need of the modern hat." According to this journalist, the hatpin had three purposes: it held the hat in place; it adorned it with "sparks of light and color in jeweled heads"; and it gave individual shape to the hat. It was mostly a nonsense article filled with advertising hype and little else.[4]

An editorial cartoon that appeared in June 1906 newspapers showed the huge arm of American

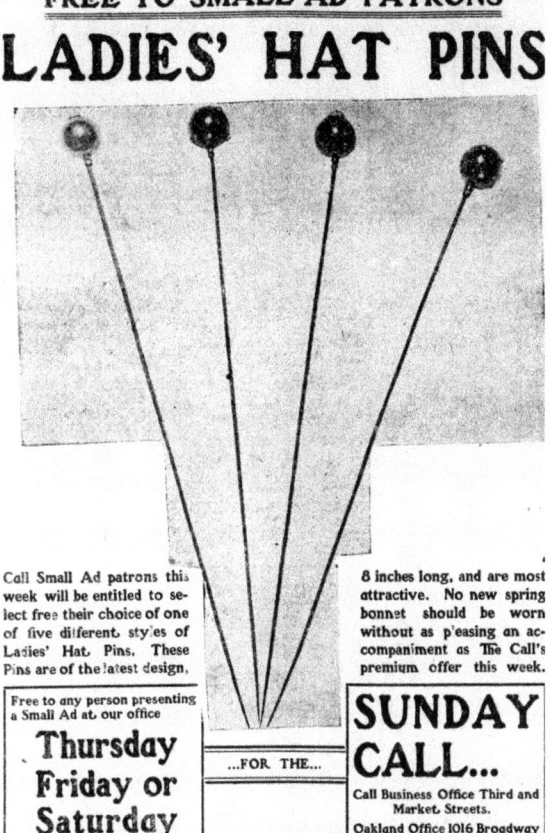

A San Francisco newspaper of 1905 offered free hatpins—eight inches long—to people who placed a classified ad in their paper.

womanhood using a hatpin to secure Senator Reed Smoot to the wall of the United States Senate building, pinning him through his clothing. There had been a controversy regarding the seating of Smoot, who had been elected to the senate by the Utah legislature in 1903. The premise of the controversy surrounding Smoot's seating was reported to be over the Church of Jesus Christ of Latter-Day Saints's practice of polygamy. Smoot subscribed to that religion; he was an apostle, a high church position. That issue came to a conclusion in 1907 when the U.S. Senate voted to exclude him, but the vote fell short of the two-thirds majority needed to expel a member, and thus Smoot retained his seat. It was an issue that galvanized many women at the time. None of this, of course, had anything to do with hatpins or hats, but the fact the editorial cartoonist chose to depict women's wrath with a hatpin was testament to the growing prominence of what was once an innocuous item in a wardrobe, and to its uses as a weapon.[5]

Still, in 1906, another fashion article appeared touting the pin as a hot fashion item. It told the story about a woman in a hat store who liked a

A 1906 editorial cartoon about a political scandal involving a United States senator was one that was closely followed by women. The scandal had nothing to do with hatpins, but the cartoonist chose to present women's power and strength by using one. That was a testament to the increasing prominence of the pin, the growing controversy surrounding the fashion item, and its potential use as a weapon.

hat but thought there was no good place on it for her pins. The milliner in the shop suggested ways to perhaps move something on the hat to make a space for her pins. However, the prospective buyer declined; she thought the suggestions did not work. She would look elsewhere to find a hat to suit and fit her pins, not the other way around. Jewelers were reported to be receiving innumerable orders to set old stones such as family heirlooms, and so on, into hatpins.[6]

Later still in 1906 a reporter declared, "One might as well give up all ideas of being in the fashion if she keeps on her new feathery hat with the same pins that fasten her toque or sailor." Pins were then designed, the reader was informed, to "accompany every separate bonnet; indeed, many of the new imported creations of the milliners' brains have the pins already in position to jab through one's tresses." That is, those hats could be bought in the store with the pins already attached to it, rather than the customer having to select pins.[7]

At the end of 1907 a female customer voiced her dissatisfaction about the size of hatpins: "How in the world do they [pin makers] suppose we can make these mammoth hats stay on our heads

This 1908 ad for hatpins that were available at a jewelry store emphasized the elaborate nature of the new pins as the advertising industry took over all aspects of American life.

if we only have these tiny things to fasten them with?" She held up one hatpin that was about seven inches long and said, "It's no use using three or four pins if they won't reach clear across your hat."[8]

By early 1909 a reporter remarked that the variety in hatpins was "a condition for wonderment and a cause for comment. From four to seven are used in one hat, and the fashion demands that they be alike." While a great deal of money could be spent on a hatpin, most were still relatively inexpensive; according to this piece, one dollar would buy "four exceedingly good ones." Lower quality pins were cheaper still.[9]

Just one week later another journalist observed that the hatpin "is no longer treated merely as a necessity but as a most pronounced ornament. Often six or eight huge pins are worn at once, and as much care is spent in choosing them as on all the rest of the costume."[10]

A fashion article in the spring of 1909 concentrated on the increasing size of the pins. It included an illustration of a vase-like holder for hatpins. For decades women had been storing their pins at home in an ordinary pin cushion. But the hatpins were growing so long that the dressing table pin cushion could no longer accommodate the extra length. A reporter stated, "Not since some inventive mind thought of the long pin for holding a woman's hat securely on her head has this weapon of utility and defense assumed such imposing proportions as to head and such prominence as it has of late. The new style of millinery demands hatpins of gigantic size, and in large numbers." That led to a new need for a place to put them when they were not in

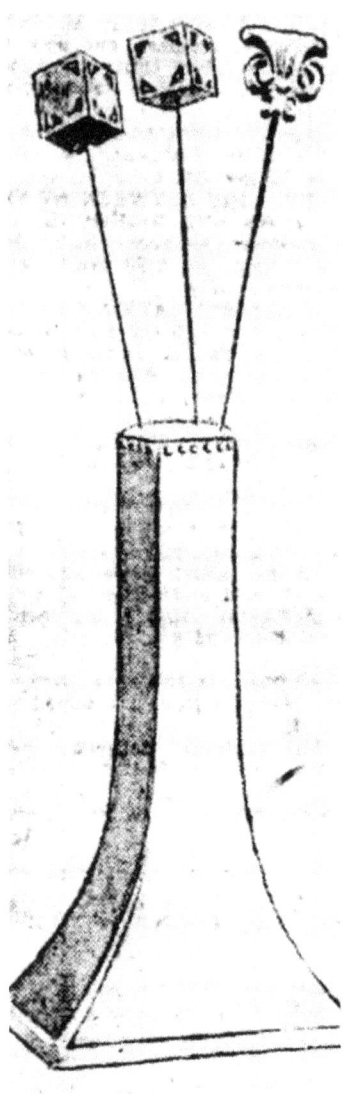

Traditionally, women had stored their hatpins on their dressing tables by sticking them into the ordinary and ubiquitous pin cushion, but, by 1909, the pins were getting so long that there was a supposed need for a special receptacle for them, a tall vase.

use because those new and longer hatpins "are much too long to find a safe anchorage in an average pin cushion.... The new holders are much longer than any that have ever been made before."[11]

Rhinestone hatpins were hyped in early 1910, along with other fancy designs. "Now that hatpins play such an important part in the accessories of the correctly dressed girl and woman they are much more carefully chosen and matched up than formerly," the story read. "Four, at the least, are required to hold the modern hat securely on the head, and in many cases five and six are worn."[12]

Several million hatpins with eyes like needles were imported into the United States every year, it was reported in 1910. That was all a tariff dodge that saved manufacturers many thousands of dollars. There was no tariff on imported needles; there was, however, a tariff on imported hatpins. Therefore, the steel shanks for hatpins were made with eyes (and thus were, theoretically, needles) and came into America duty-free. Once in America, those eye holes were filled with solder and heads put on them after they had passed inspection. And thus, needles were transformed into hatpins.[13]

A fashion reporter observed in October 1910: "This is the greatest season for big hat pins in history. Hat pins large enough to hold powder puffs, mirrors, trinkets and small change are being shown by the

An ad that appeared in a San Francisco paper in the summer of 1910.

manufacturing jewelers." The story continued: "So huge are the new designs that many of the ornamental heads have hinged lids. When the lid is lifted the powder puff and receptacle for knickknacks is disclosed. The inside surface of the lid is a tiny mirror." Guards were also made in order to cover the point of the pin. They were also said to be ornamental, and matched the head. Those guards could also be used interchangeably for many pins. Those hatpin heads and guards were often stylized animals such as roosters, pheasants, owls, and so forth. In some designs the rooster from comb to claws was three inches long (and that was just the head of the hatpin).[14]

So extreme was the above story that it produced a spoof in another paper just a few days later: "Carelessly opening the top of her hatpin, Clarice took out a piece of soap, a towel and a pitcher of water. Having washed her hands Clarice carefully drew from the hatpin a new hat, which she put on with every evidence of satisfaction. With the aid of a hand mirror and a powder puff from the same receptacle her toilet was completed, and when Clarice had replaced the various articles and snapped shut the lid of the hatpin she resumed her strap [hanging] in the West Farms express [transit vehicle]."[15]

By 1911 the war against hatpins was well underway and was very intense in the 1910–11 period. The issue of hatpins began to be treated somewhat differently by fashion journalists. An ad appearing in the summer of 1911 featuring a new style of small hat that was hyped for motoring, golfing and theater

A NEW CAP FOR MOTORING, OCEAN TRAVEL, GOLFING AND THEATRE WEAR IS CREATING A FURORE

As the war on the hatpin reached its zenith, ads such as this became commonplace. It touted a smaller style of hat and noted in the text that no hatpins were needed.

wear. The ad emphasized: "No hatpins needed."[16]

During that same summer, Julia Bottomley wrote a piece about the Panama hat, which was not especially small. The background drawing to the illustration showed the Panama hat of old, along with a gigantic creation on top of it. "The owner of a panama hat should not use hatpins to fasten it on with," she advised. "Hat fasteners should be sewed to the head band and thrust into the hair to secure the hat to the head. It is almost a crime to thrust pins through the beautiful, painstaking weave of which the hat is made. The evidence of carelessness shows a lack of appreciation. When one sees a fine panama punctured with holes it is a mark of inelegance in the wearer."[17]

A few weeks later a fashion reporter named Ethel Lloyd Patterson declared, "Take off your puffs and rats and things; if you have any hair of your own, bind it closely to your head well down over the ears." She explained that the new hats for fall and winter "are all very small and won't need any hatpins because "they will be worn pulled well down over the ears and without any hatpins to hold them in place."[18]

A 1911 article on the Panama hat suggests that hatpins were not needed for this type of hat and that to use them to fasten it reflects a lack of sophistication on the part of the wearer. While the Panama hats featured were not especially small, note the older style in the lower right of the illustration. It is gigantic in size and also featured a mountainous creation on the top.

However, the hype for hatpins had not completely died out. Toward the end of 1911 an ad from a jewelry store touted hatpins as a fashion item. The Tulsa jeweler who placed the advertisement insisted the hatpin was a piece of jewelry and the discerning customer could spend as much or as little as she cared to "invest."[19]

A fashion article that appeared in March 1912 argued that, as fashion dictated, women would "discard the enormous, wicked looking hat pins so prominent last season." The new ones were "of only moderate length, without any dangerous protruding point."[20]

A different way of dealing with the hatpin was reported from London, England, late in 1912. It was said that small machines would be in use in West End shops there "which will bring emancipation to long suffering man from the menace of the protruding hatpin." In the future, hatpins would be "cut to measure." Whenever a woman bought a new hat, whatever its size, she would be supplied with hatpins to fit, made while she waited. "In the past hatpins were made only in one or two sizes, six or nine inches

Left: At the end of 1911 a Tulsa jeweler placed an ad in the papers for hatpins. Here, they are openly touted as pieces of jewelry and that the discerning woman could spend as much as she liked, or as much as she cared to "invest." *Right:* Another ad, this one from 1913, touting hatpins as a fashion statement. Women were encouraged to come to the store and see, and of course buy, some of the new fashionable hatpins. Would any woman want to go around wearing last year's hatpins?

long," the female reporter declared. But all that would change now. A shopper bought a hat, and the saleswoman, with the aid of her guillotine-like machine, clipped the hatpin to the exact size, protruding only a fraction of an inch.[21]

Over the years various remedies had been suggested for the dangerous point of the hatpin, as a guard to protect people from the point. One of the more common ideas was for something like a cork to be stuck on the end of the point. However, nothing ever caught on; no suggestion even managed to pass the fashion test. A new device was introduced at the beginning of 1915. It was designed to hold hats on without the use of hatpins and was designed by Ora Cue, described as a famous millinery lecturer and designer. Her device consisted of a lining around the inside of the crown of the hat that was adjustable with a cord drawn through it—used to tighten the device. As with all such devices and ideas generated to affix a hat to a woman's head without hatpins, it went nowhere.[22]

Many devices came and went that were designed to affix the hat to the head without using hatpins. This 1915 ad featured one such idea: a lining inside the hat somehow held it in place. None of these devices ever made any headway anywhere, not even for a short time. Only when short hair became fashionable for women, and the small hats came into fashion, did the hatpin finally disappear.

3

The Hatpin as an Offensive Weapon

From the mid–1880s onward, the use of the hatpin as a weapon was chronicled. Sometimes the fashion item was used as a defensive weapon; that is, a use for which the woman wielding the item was lauded, or at least not condemned, and not subjected to any punishment. Sometimes the fashion item was used as an offensive weapon; that is, it was put to a use for which the woman involved was indeed subject to punishment. On rare occasions the victim of the hatpin–toting female was the woman herself.

On November 11, 1887, Mrs. McPherson, who lived at the Chelsea Hotel in New York City, fainted while shopping in Macy's department store. She fell backwards to the floor and her hat pin was forced into the base of her skull. It was not assumed that she was badly hurt until she was taken into a back room of the store, where someone noticed blood trickling down the back of her neck. An examination discovered the pin had penetrated her brain, inflicting a mortal wound. She was reported to be then "dying" in a New York City hospital. She was described as a rich and handsome woman of 35 who had five young children. Doctors at the hospital were said to have described her case as hopeless. A newspaper account read: "Daggers and pins and feminine ornaments of that sort are relics of the barbarous times when women wore genuine weapons in their hair." McPherson may not have died; it was not uncommon for newspaper stories of this time period to report somebody as "mortally" or "fatally" wounded, only to have them survive. It was even more common for newspapers not to bother following up on stories. Such was the case here, as no more was reported of McPherson.[1]

An accident occurred in the afternoon on December 25, 1890, on

Eleventh Avenue in New York City. An unknown, elderly woman slipped and fell to the sidewalk. When she was picked up she was found to be as if dead; an examination disclosed the fact that a long hatpin had been driven into her brain when her head struck the sidewalk. When she fell a crowd gathered and she was carried into a nearby store. She was unconscious and an ambulance was summoned from Roosevelt Hospital but, before it arrived, the woman had died. No identification was found on the woman's person and she was estimated to be about 60 years old. A brief editorial on the accident declared: "Hatpins are a useful part of a woman's wearing apparel and they have not heretofore been accounted dangerous. But greater care in the use of them appears to be one lesson of this accident."[2]

Carrie Pelsgrove, 17, resided near New Castle, Kentucky. At the beginning of March 1895 she went ice skating with a group of her friends, on a pond near her home. During the afternoon a race was held and she was bumped by one of her friends. She fell to the ice, driving a hatpin into her brain. Pelsgrove died before she could be taken home.[3]

Mrs. Mary Jenks was walking along the street in Washington on the morning of September 10, 1896, when she was run down by a bicyclist. She was knocked over and fell on her head. A hatpin was broken off and punctured her scalp. When she was taken to the Emergency Hospital two inches of hatpin were removed from her head. Jenks was not otherwise hurt and apparently recovered.[4]

As the result of an accident early in December of 1901, Miss A. L. Rodgers of Oakland, California, was lying "dangerously ill." She was walking along a downtown street in Oakland on the afternoon of December 7 when a boy allowed an awning at one of the stores on the street to descend upon her head. The awning struck one of her hatpins at such an angle that it was forced into her head. She uttered a scream, but recovered in a moment and withdrew the pin with her own hands. She thought little more of the incident but later in the afternoon she fainted and was taken home by friends. A doctor was called and he discovered the pin had almost pierced the brain cavity. Rodgers was then under treatment and it was hoped that she would recover. Nothing more was reported on the accident.[5]

In the middle of October 1904, Emma Wynn was walking along a street in Chester, Pennsylvania, when a football kicked by a youth fell on her hat, driving a hatpin through her scalp to the length of one inch. She fell to the sidewalk unconscious and was taken to a hospital, where the flow of blood from a severed blood vessel was checked.[6]

Mrs. Nellie Beaver was riding a bicycle along a San Francisco street on May 1, 1908, and was run into by a streetcar; as a result her hatpin was driven with terrific force partly through her skull. She was then at the hospital with her recovery said to be "doubtful." A policeman had lifted the woman from under the car; she was unconscious. An attempt to remove her hat revealed the embedded hatpin. The victim, Mrs. Beaver, was 30 years old. Nothing more was heard of the incident.[7]

When Mrs. Peter MacDonald was thrown from a buggy in a runaway on a steep grade near Boone, Iowa, in July 1910, a hatpin penetrated four inches into her brain. As a result she, reportedly, lay near death in a local hospital. She had been found unconscious by the roadside by a farmer driving home from Boone. He put her in his wagon and drove to the hospital.[8]

Mrs. Laura Clas, wife of A. C. Clas, described as one of the best-known architects in the northwest and the designer of the new Milwaukee $20 million civic center, filed a lawsuit in September 1910 against the Soo railroad for $5,000 damages because of an injury she sustained from a hatpin while travelling in Minnesota. In her complaint, Laura said she had boarded a train at Brooks, Minnesota, and that it started to move so suddenly she was thrown to the floor of the car and was badly scratched and bruised. The main injuries were due to her hatpins, she declared.[9]

A "simple" hatpin was said to have been the cause of the death of its wearer in Paris, France, in September 1912. The young woman in question slipped and fell as she

Nellie Beaver was one of a number of females who were injured (or even killed) by their own hatpins. Beaver suffered head injuries when her hatpin was jammed into her skull in May 1908, after she was knocked off her bicycle by a streetcar.

was descending from a streetcar. The hatpin became dislodged and was driven right through the woman's scalp. Death was thought to have been instantaneous.[10]

One of the most regularly occurring uses of the hatpin as an offensive weapon came about when some miscreants used it on policemen, or tried to, or on other officials of the justice system. Sadie Dietz (alias Jennie Harris) of New York City was held in custody on January 5, 1893, on a charge of robbing waiter Simon Green in a café. The woman started cursing when taken to the prison as Matron Lynch led her to the top balcony, where she could not disturb other prisoners. This further enraged Dietz, who turned on Lynch and stabbed her over the left eye with a steel hatpin that was five inches long. It broke inside Lynch's face, but was later extracted. Dietz then faced the added charge of felonious assault. No more was reported on this case.[11]

When Lottie Sherwood, 22, was arrested for being intoxicated on the streets of New York City in January 1893, she attempted to stab an Officer Hughes with her hatpin when she was taken out of her cell to be transported to court. At Jefferson Market court she was held for examination on a charge of disorderly conduct.[12]

Frances Waters, a New York City woman, was arraigned on December 30, 1893, in Jefferson Market court for streetwalking. The arresting officer was named Hall. After she had been sentenced to jail for three months, she made an attack on him. As she was being led away she broke free from the escorting court officer's grasp and ran towards Hall, whom she clawed and pounded. He threw her aside and then she came at him again, this time with a long hatpin in her hand. Four court officers managed to subdue her and removed her from the court and escorted her to prison.[13]

On the evening of June 22, 1895, the police patrol wagon in Kansas City, Missouri, was ordered out to pick up a drunken woman. On the way back to the police station the detainee became abusive and was ordered to keep quiet by an Officer Lillis. Without saying a word she drew a long steel hatpin from her hat and tried to stab Lillis. It required the efforts of two policemen to subdue her. At the station she gave her name as Cora Stoner.[14]

During July 1895 in New York City Jennie Brown, a 28-year-old homeless woman was arrested by an Officer Schulen for being drunk and disorderly. During the incident Brown tried to stick Schulen with a hatpin. When she failed in that effort she tried to bite him.[15]

New York City Policeman Florence J. Driscoll found a drunken female on the street on the evening of December 3, 1896. When she refused to move on after he had ordered her to do so, Driscoll arrested her. On the way to the station she suddenly turned on him, drew her eight-inch-long hatpin from her hat and thrust it at the officer's left eye. The point of the pin hit the bone just at the corner of the eye and bent nearly double; fortunately, his eye was unharmed. When they reached the station, the woman gave her name as Nellie Lang, aged 38. However, the desk sergeant recognized her as Mollie Lawler, whom he had arrested 20 years earlier when he was a patrol officer. Back then, she had been arrested for stabbing a sailor, who nearly died of his wound. Mollie, then 18, was sent to the state prison by Recorder Hackett for ten years. Nothing more was reported on Lawler's current arrest.[16]

The Lang incident prompted an editorial response that was published in a New York City newspaper the following day. The editor remarked that the hatpin stabbing was only one of several such episodes that had occurred within the past few weeks. Not long ago, he said, Policeman Essig arrested Mary McGovern or "Hat Pin Mary," as she was termed in the Tenderloin area of the city because of her propensity to use that "women's weapon," and took her to the station. On arrival there she pulled a long hatpin from her hat and made a jab at Essig's eyes. He dodged and only received a scratch. Not long before that, Mary jabbed Officer Thompson in the arm when he arrested her. Yet another policeman, Officer Mulcahey, was said to carry a scar on his neck from "Hat Pin Liz," a Tenderloin resident who came by her sobriquet in the same manner as Mary McGovern did.[17]

Early in 1897, Bridget Harris of New York City wandered into Youman's coal office and said she wanted a quarter. When she was ignored, she repeated her request. Finally, someone in the office told her to leave. She declined. Then somebody summoned a policeman. An Officer Fletcher came and, along with company employee Michael Finley, tackled the woman. She squirmed away and drew out a long hatpin. Fletcher and Finley felt they needed assistance and so reinforcements were called for. Three other policemen responded, at which point she surrendered. A few days later in court she received a sentence of six months on Rikers Island. It was written in the report that Bridget Harris was known as "the man-eater" because she carved them up with knives or hatpins. She had already served two terms of six months each on Rikers Island, and three New York State prison terms of one, two, and three years, respectively.[18]

Aggie Sylvia was another New York City Tenderloin-area denizen. She made regular appearances in court for offenses such as drunkenness and disorderly conduct. In February 1897, an Officer Lanzenbeck, who had arrested her, was leading her out of court when she drew a hatpin and tired to jab him in the eye. Said a reporter, "The education of every Tenderloin policeman includes a lesson on this very point." On this occasion Lanzenbeck avoided the hatpin thrust. Aggie was promptly re-arraigned and another charge was added to her record.[19]

New York City policeman Billings had been, reportedly, stabbed so many times by irate women that he had long since ceased to regard that sort of attack as felonious assault. In his latest episode, wherein he was stabbed in both hands, he preferred to bring the single charge of "drunk and disorderly" against the woman in question. At his station his fellow officers knew him as "Hatpin Billings." On a Saturday night in the spring of 1898 he came across Mary Mulroney, drunk and disorderly on the street. With some difficulty, he took her to the station where the 35-year-old woman drew a long pin from her hand and lunged at him. He leapt back and took a stab to one hand and was stabbed in the other before subduing her. When she was brought into Jefferson Market Court, the magistrate said to Billings, "You must prefer a charge of felonious assault against the woman. There has been too much of this thing, and it must be stopped. This is a good time to begin." Billings agreed, and Mulroney was held over for trial, in lieu of $1,000 bail. No more was reported on the case.[20]

In Detroit in December 1898, Bertha Hurse tried to kill a guard in the county jail with her hatpins. When the guard arrived at her cell to collect her and take her to court for her appearance she made a lunge at him with two big hatpins and tried to stick them in his eyes. He managed to avoid the attack and got her to court on time, where she was fined $5 by Justice Whelan for stealing 25 cents from a little girl.[21]

On the morning of January 26, 1900, Lizzie Davenport was arraigned in Harlem police court in New York City before Magistrate Pool on a charge of disorderly conduct. The 20-year-old was committed to the workhouse for six months. Policeman Petry led her from court, during which time she created a fuss. Davenport assaulted the officer with her umbrella and then drew a long hatpin from her hat and stabbed him twice in the shoulder.[22]

Deputy Sheriff Wall of St. Paul, Minnesota, went to serve papers in a legal action against Laura Brown Johnson in March 1900. The bone of contention was 30 volumes of the *World's Best Literature*, which the company (Harper's Weekly Club Publishing) sold on the installment plan. Johnson had not been keeping up the payments on the set of books. When Wall reached her home, Johnson ordered him off the premises. Wall went ahead and entered her home and proceeded to take the books. Johnson then stabbed him with a long hatpin, after which she grabbed some of the books and ripped out some pages. Wall finally took possession of what remained of the books and left.[23]

Mary Riley entered a police station at 10 p.m. on August 20, 1900, and told Desk Sergeant Timothy Cullinane that she had come to post bail for a woman who had been arrested. Cullinane asked if she was a householder; when Riley said no, Cullinane told her she could not sign the bail bond. She then snatched a long hatpin from her head and made a thrust at the officer. Falling short of her target, she rushed around the desk and again tried to stab the officer, missing him yet again. He subdued her with the help of other officers, at which point Mary Riley was herself locked up on a charge of disorderly conduct.[24]

Detective Glennon of the New York Police Department saw two women on Fortieth Street on the night of August 31, 1900, and ordered them to move on. He said this admonishment angered the women, who then attacked him viciously. One used a hatpin and tried to stick it in his eyes. He was stabbed twice in the face. Other policemen aided him in arresting the pair. They gave their names as Olive Haskell, 17, and 22-year-old Belle Brown.[25]

While some female prisoners were being moved around in the Raymond Street jail in Brooklyn, New York, on December 27, 1900, Nellie Jones, serving a 15-day term for public intoxication, made a rush for Matron Fannie Handy. The matron was knocked down after eight other prisoners joined the assault. Warden McGrath answered the alarm and was immediately beset by a number of these women, who used hatpins to gouge his face and hands, leaving him with blood streaming from his face. Several more deputies arrived on the scene and quelled the disturbance.[26]

In Seattle early in the morning of March 24, 1901, Annie Curtis, described as "a fallen woman," made a vicious attack upon a jailer by the name of Corbett at police headquarters. She had been arrested several hours earlier on a charge of assaulting one Edward Parsons in a box in a concert hall when he refused to buy her a bottle of wine. Around 2 a.m. Corbett went to her cell where she was making a disturbance. As Corbett opened the cell door she lunged at him and plunged a hatpin into his chin. Other officers arrived to subdue her. One of them extracted the pin from Corbett's chin. That led to Curtis, whose police record described him as "unsavory," being charged with assault.[27]

On April 4, 1901, Annie Curtis was fined $75 by Justice Cann on a charge of assault and battery. Her lawyer asked for clemency, claiming she was distraught over being separated from her children. Justice Cann found her guilty of simple assault and battery, instead of "murderous assault," as stated in the original charge. Apparently, the clemency plea worked. Corbett was unsatisfied with the ruling and so informed the court.[28]

Kate Joyce, 27, of New York City, was arrested in July 1901 on the charge of drunkenness and creating a disturbance. When she appeared in West Side Court the shrieking woman launched an attack on Policeman Kerr with a hatpin. Other officers joined Kerr in subduing the woman; however, Kerr would not press charges against Joyce.[29]

Police officers Pierce and Hartford arrested James Hammell and his wife, Irene, and their friend Mrs. Mary Ryan, all of whom were fighting on the street, before a large crowd. When the police placed all three under arrest, they joined forces against the policemen. The two women attacked with hatpins, fingernails, and feet. The crowd then turned on the policemen, which necessitated reinforcements being called out before order was restored and the three prisoners were taken away to the lockup.[30]

Detective McNally, a 22-year veteran of the Jersey City Police Department, was reported, at the end of March 1904, to be dying at his home from blood poisoning. He had arrested a female shoplifter one week earlier and while he was taking her into custody she stabbed him in the right leg with a hatpin. McNally treated the wound with home remedies but blood poisoning had set in. Several doctors were working to save his life, but the medical opinion was that he only "had a small chance of recovery." There were no other published reports on his condition.[31]

Florence Busco was held on March 31, 1904, for stabbing New York City policeman Cornelius Willense with a hatpin. While he was taking her name at the desk at the station house she pulled out a hatpin and stabbed Willense in the eye. The pin pricked the eyelid but did not enter the eye proper. She had first been arrested for disorderly conduct.[32]

A woman assaulted Mr. Thilo F. Barnum on the street in New York City on October 23, 1904. She was drawn to his $1,500 diamond scarf pin and tried to rob him of it. She slapped him in the face and tried to grab the pin. While the pair scuffled, two police officers arrived on the scene, alerted by the commotion. The would-be robber, Alice Moulton, then pulled out a long hatpin and began lunging at everyone within reach. Patrolman Debbs rushed her, only to be stabbed in the leg with the hatpin. She was then arrested, taken to the station, and charged with attempted highway robbery.[33]

Mrs. J. Gunderland resisted arrest, on a charge of disorderly conduct, on an early November 1904 evening in St. Paul Minnesota. She had succeeded in jabbing Patrolman Burke in the neck and arms with a hatpin. Earlier that night she went to the saloon, where her husband worked as a bartender, and began to quarrel with him. She finally became so loud that he called an officer; a struggle ensued. Mrs. Gunderland was charged with disorderly conduct.[34]

Eighteen-year-old Christina Pendergast of New York City was held on charges of disorderly conduct and malicious mischief, on March 7, 1905. When she was refused a drink in a saloon she kicked in one of the bar's windows. Officer Kelleher arrived on the scene and arrested her. While he turned his back to her to call for a wagon to come and collect her, Christina drew a hatpin from her hat and stabbed him half a dozen times in the face.[35]

Anna Raetta Neumann, sentenced to five years in jail for shoplifting in Minneapolis, made a desperate attempt to break free of the police officers who were transporting her to the prison in Stillwater, Minnesota. Near the prison door she used a hatpin and held her escorts at bay for a few moments, finally being overpowered by the officers and taken inside the prison.[36]

Minnie Kelly, familiarly known about the Jefferson Market Court in New York City as "Hatpin Minnie," ended a six-month stay at Riker's Island prison on September 25, 1906. She then celebrated so thoroughly that she was in court once again on September 26, charged with intoxication. Magistrate Cornell sentenced her to another six months on the Island. As she was being led away she broke loose from the officer escorting her and attempted to stab Sergeant Carey of the Court Squad with her hatpin. He dodged it. She was then led out, screaming obscenities all the way. Two years earlier she attempted to stab Magistrate Wahle with a hatpin after he had imposed a six-month sentence on her.[37]

According to an October 1906 report, the first command the presiding officer gave when his men on the Spokane, Washington, police force arrested a woman was: "Search the hens for hatpins." Whenever and wherever the police arrested a woman the first thought they had was: "Has she a hatpin on her person?" The article argued that the average Spokane officer "fears not keen cutting dirks or sixshooters as feminine toys, but he is in mortal dread of the treacherous hatpin. Often rusty and always long, one prick to the hilt in the vitals means the end of any bluecoat who receives the full length of a hatpin from an enraged woman." Within the past three years in various cities, read the report, several deaths had been directly attributable to hatpin stabbings. (Of course no details were provided; it was merely a reworking of the earlier NYPD article. Even though this article was supposedly about Spokane and included alleged quotes from Spokane officers, no names were given.) "Until it becomes unlawful for a woman to carry a hatpin, men will be in danger. As lawmakers accept the

'Garden of Eden' theory that man was made first and the laws are made mostly for him, they are casting about for some remedy to protect the male from the insidious weapon. Meantime the police of Spokane and other cities always bear in mind the injunction: 'Search the hens for hatpins.'"[38]

An angry woman with a hatpin and a badly scared special police officer armed with a revolver caused a commotion on a city street in Salt Lake City on the night of June 29, 1908. Mrs. Emma Steer, a name well known to the police, and Special Officer C. C. Riley were the participants. Steer stabbed Riley several times with a long hatpin and Riley drew his revolver and fired one shot into the air. Officer Bert Seager heard the commotion and put an end to the disturbance, although no one was arrested. Nothing was reported as to the cause of the commotion except that Steer declared after the row that she attacked Riley with her hatpin because he insulted her.[39]

Policeman Harry Bands of Duquesne, Pennsylvania, was reported to be in serious condition at his home as a result of being stabbed with a hatpin while taking a prisoner to the workhouse. That stabbing occurred in a streetcar on a Monday night in July 1909. When the officer told his prisoner they would transfer to a less crowded vehicle, she declined to leave the car. It was alleged that she drew a hatpin from her hat and stabbed the officer in the stomach. Despite his injury, Officer Bands compelled the woman to board another car, which ultimately took the miscreant to a workhouse. Returning home later that night, Officer Bands became ill. A doctor was summoned and the officer was diagnosed as being in serious condition. No more was reported on this incident.[40]

In 1909, an unnamed police matron in New York City was quoted as saying, "You have always got to keep your wits about you when searching a woman. They could get you in a minute with a hatpin or some weapon. We take any hatpins the first thing [during an arrest]. Many a policeman has been wounded and nearly lost his eyesight from a hatpin stab, and a matron was stabbed so badly that she had to undergo a serious surgical operation. We search the bow on a hat, linings, hems and every particle of clothing to the fingertips of gloves. We take every rat, comb and hairpin out of the hair and search it."[41]

Officer Timm of the Omaha Police Department had to do battle with one Frances Cantell, who tried to stab him with a hatpin while he was placing her under arrest sometime in August 1909. She made three or four jabs at him but he averted all of them and finally disarmed and subdued her. Apparently he stopped her only because she was a white woman "parading" down the street with George Williams, a black man, a display the officer deemed "disgraceful."[42]

On the night of August 31, 1909, in Portland, Oregon, a Jennie Smith attacked a city jailer by the name of Burke as she was being released from a cell. Jennie had been jailed for being an "undesirable citizeness"; while incarcerated she loudly predicted dire things would happen when women earned equal rights. A male friend came and bailed her out. As she was making her exit she lunged at Burke with a hatpin. He disarmed her and then told her the amount of bail just paid was not enough to cover this additional breach of peace. Jennie was led back to her cell.[43]

While making his rounds on the morning of November 5, 1909, Officer Bernard met J. Hallenburg, a sailor, who complained that one May Brown had robbed him of $11; the officer then located the woman and questioned her about the allegation. In reply, she pulled out a hatpin and sprang at the policeman, stabbing him some 20 times about the face and neck. She was finally overcome by Bernard and arrested. He was taken to the hospital.[44]

Commenting on the attack on Bernard, police captain Claude G. Bannick stated, "It's a dangerous weapon when a woman starts something." Seattle city attorney Ralph Pierce remarked, "It's far worse than most concealed weapons." He mentioned the focus was then on the new 13-inch-long hatpins that had surfaced a few days earlier. According to the reporter, "The new hatpin is a most innocent appearing weapon for both offensive and defensive purposes when hidden in a hat. But when firmly grasped in the middle it is a dangerous weapon and will pierce anything but cast steel.... The new hatpin is nearly as firm as the ordinary stiletto and it is sufficiently thin to leave no tell-tale mark." Bannick and Pierce were of one opinion when it came to this newly discovered pin: "It should be banished."[45]

Detective Walter Hogan, of the Spokane, Washington, police force, narrowly escaped serious injury (and possibly death) when Mabel Webber, whom he had seized as a robbery suspect, made a furious attack on him with a hatpin. A lunge at the detective's heart was averted but not before the pin had penetrated to a depth of half an inch on his left side, just above the heart.[46]

Stabbed in the abdomen by a steel hatpin while attempting to arrest a woman who was creating a disturbance in Globe, Arizona, on June 14, 1910, Deputy Marshall C. W. Morris sustained serious injuries that, reportedly, could lead to the lawman's death. When he tried to arrest the woman in a restaurant after a disturbance, she hit him over the head with a bottle and thrust a hatpin into his abdomen. It broke off during the struggle. Only later did Morris realize he had been stabbed. He went for medical help and had a four-inch section of hatpin removed from his stomach. Morris was listed in critical condition, with the threat that peritonitis could result from the injury caused by what a reporter termed "the strange weapon."[47]

Fed up with litigation, Mrs. Rose Lander shrieked at the man she was suing that she was tired of his fooling around and then stabbed him with a long hatpin. Although the pin penetrated Samuel Levy's coat it went no deeper when it was deflected by a notebook he had in an inside breast pocket. He got nothing more than a scratch. All this activity took place in a courthouse in New York City, in January 1913. After the first stab, Levy fled down the hall with Lander in pursuit. His cries for help drew a crowd and the now-frightened Lander dropped her hatpin and fled out the door of the building. Levy admitted to a reporter that he owed the woman money and would not pay it back. As a result she had sued him, but the litigation had dragged on and on.[48]

Ethel Franklin was arrested on the night of April 12, 1913, in Salt Lake City by Patrolman C. C. Carsensen on a charge of vagrancy. At that point she promptly charged her captor with "a wicked hatpin." The point caught on a button of his coat and thus did the officer no harm.[49]

With respect to the use of the hatpin as an offensive weapon, women found many, many other circumstances and situations in which to wield them. In Boston, Massachusetts, on May 8, 1888, Forest Johnson, a liquor dealer, died from the effects of the hatpin–related injuries inflicted upon him by Margaret A. Young. On the night of April 16, the young woman entered Johnson's saloon and called for a whiskey. Johnson considered her to be intoxicated already and refused to serve her. An altercation ensued: Johnson ordered her to leave the saloon, whereupon she drew her steel hatpin and made an assault on the barman. He put up his hands to protect his face and was stabbed in the fleshy part of his hand. The woman made her escape after the assault. Johnson removed the entire pin from his hand (or so he thought) and then went to a nearby physician to have the wound treated. The physician advised the barman to apply poultices to the wound, which he did for two days. At the end of that time the pain was unbearable and he submitted to an operation at City Hospital, during which approximately an inch and a half pin was removed from his hand. Blood poisoning, however, set in, resulting in his death. His assailant was arrested and remanded for trial. Nothing more was published on Margaret Young.[50]

A meeting of the State Board of Correction and Charities was held on October 21, 1891, at Rochester Asylum in Minnesota. As a result of that meeting a female attendant at the institute was discharged for have pricked a patient with a hatpin. No other details were provided.[51]

While services were held on the afternoon of April 20, 1894, in Stephen Merritt's Mission in New York City, a poorly dressed woman broke up the meeting by jumping from her seat into the aisle and shouting. She was recognized by doorman James Pollard as the same woman who had disrupted a service earlier that day, causing her to be ordered out. Pollard tried to eject her again but she pulled out a long hatpin and jabbed him in the leg. A minor panic ensued, during which people made a dash for the exit. Pollard went for the assailant again. This time he avoided several more thrusts and finally grabbed the hatpin from her. All the noise attracted a policeman, whereupon Pollard told him to arrest the drunken woman. At the station house she gave her name as Mary Grady, age 38. She was locked up on a charge of disorderly conduct.[52]

Mrs. Kitty McCord was arrested on October 21, 1895, at her home in New York City on a charge of having stabbed her husband with a hatpin at a dance in Fernando's Hall on the previous Saturday evening. McCord was said to be seriously wounded and staying at his mother's house; his chances of survival were listed as about 50 percent. Nevertheless, he refused to talk to the police about the case. "I won't say that she didn't and I won't say that she did" was his constant answer to the obvious question. Friends of the couple said that Tom provoked the attack and the only decent thing for him to do would be not to prosecute his wife. Five years earlier the presumed assailant was Kitty Hagan, then 18 years old; Tom McCord was then 20. After the two were wed, things went from bad to worse, and six months earlier Tom had deserted his wife and three children. He was out of work and went home to live with his mother. Kitty had her husband arrested for non-support a week earlier and when he appeared in Yorkville Police Court he promised to pay as much as he could. However, he sent no money to his wife and children, and he was reportedly drinking heavily. Kitty learned that her husband was going to Fernando's on that fateful day and went there to see him. They met on the dance floor, where an altercation broke out. As the crowd around the arguing couple eased away, Tom went back to dancing (though not with his wife) before suddenly falling to the floor. A doctor saw him and took him to his mother's house, where he had been living since deserting his wife. Tom had a wound in his chest that could have been made by a hatpin. Police were called to the dancehall to investigate the reported stabbing, but Tom would not cooperate with them. Said Tom: "I was dancing in Fernando Hall with Annie Belter when there was a little fuss and I felt a sharp pain in my chest as if I had been pricked. A little while after that I had trouble with my breathing, and that's all I have got to say. I don't know who stabbed me and that's straight." It was reported that the police were satisfied that Kitty stabbed her husband with a hatpin but they had no witness who would testify to that. Kitty was said to have an excellent reputation and had done her best to support her children.[53]

A few days later an editorial on the McCord case pointed out the fact that hatpins seemed to have an alarming effect on all men except those in the newspaper business: "They made fun of woman's ability to nail her hat to her head by pushing a rod of steel into the vacuum where a man keeps his brains. But every day sober folk hated to have to sit in the cars beside a woman who had two to four inches of sharpened steel sticking out beyond her head." After a while, the editor continued, the general public got used to it and men discovered hatpins made good pipe cleaners. "But now the hat pin is leaping to the front rank of murderous weapons. Within a month there have been two or three serious affrays in which women have stabled folks with these fine stilettos. The last case, in which a woman pierced her husband's heart with her hat pin, is the worst case of all." Concluded the editor: "If the vice spreads, we shall have to consider every woman armed when she has her hat on and, alas, she is privileged to wear her hat even at her prayers."[54]

Mr. Fowler took a girl with him to a Baptist church service in Sherman, Texas, in December 1895. The couple happened to sit in front of Maggie Jones, Fowler's former sweetheart. In a fit of jealousy, Jones stabbed Fowler in the back with her hatpin. It penetrated some two inches into Fowler's body, curving around the spinal column. Fowler fainted. He was carried from the church and the pin was extracted by a doctor. The victim was said to be in critical condition; no more was reported on the event.[55]

Emma Moore, Birdie Saunders and Benjamin Foster went on an excursion down the river near Washington, D.C., on June 18, 1896. Birdie took offense at another couple, Blanche Riley and Grant Holmes. The women fought with Blanche, who, in the fracas, was stabbed by a hatpin. That pin was left in her stomach, with only one-eighth of an inch projecting. Birdie and Benjamin were arrested. The latter had two pen knives, the former was minus her hatpin. Blanche took the stand in court and swore Birdie had stuck her with the hatpin while Benjamin held her. The judge sentenced the accused couple to 364 days in jail.[56]

Mrs. Jessie Bowen and Mrs. Maggie Kierce made the rounds of the saloons in San Francisco on the evening of March 29, 1897. In one of those bars they met F. Nougier, a waiter. They drank together until all three were drunk. When the women rose to leave, Nougier protested and grappled with Bowen, who thrust a hatpin deep into his left breast, where it broke off. Nougier was taken to the hospital while both of the women were arrested. The next day they appeared in court before Judge Campbell, who dismissed the charge against Kierce; Bowen was convicted on a charge of battery and sentenced to six months in the county jail. In passing the sentence, Campbell said it was a serious crime and he regretted that the charge had been reduced to battery, as she should have been punished with a term in the penitentiary.[57]

A San Francisco bookkeeper by the name of Edward Donohue had an adventure on a Saturday night in July 1897. He went to the Receiving Hospital on the following Sunday morning, complaining that he had been stabbed on the left side of his chest with a hatpin. Donohue explained that he had met a young woman on the street who said she was a stenographer. He took her into a saloon, as she wanted a drink. After they had a few drinks she seemed to "get angry," and when he tried to pacify her she stabled him with a hatpin. At least that was *his* story. Following the stabbing, Donahue went home and slept, but in the morning he awoke with considerable chest pain. A doctor examined him and found the hatpin had punctured a lung and broken off; he extracted a piece about three inches long. Donohue said he did not know the woman and did not think he could recognize her. He was married, with three children. According to the account, that incident was the third such case at the Receiving Hospital within a few weeks. The first case involved a married woman who stabbed a chance acquaintance in a saloon. Judge Campbell sentenced her to six months (the Bowen case cited above). The second case was that of a young girl named Smith, who stabbed a waiter in a Baltimore restaurant in the early morning hours of July 5. The case was said to be pending.[58]

An editorial on the Donohue case noted that the bookkeeper was at home in critical condition, but that he was expected to recover. It also summarized the three recent, and similar, assaults in San Francisco. That editorial was titled, "A Woman's Weapon."[59]

A young woman startled shoppers in a Sixth Avenue dry goods store on the afternoon of September 20, 1897, in New York City, by trying to jab a hatpin into a nearby person. She was taken into custody by the store detective. A policeman was called and she was taken to the New York Hospital, where she said she was Lizzie Harnett, age 27. Physicians at the hospital revealed that the woman suffered from nervousness and insomnia.[60]

A different account stated that the hatpin wielder was one of the salesgirls in the millinery department at the Siegel-Cooper store; she was said to have thrown the customers into a panic when she suddenly "went crazy." Harnett immediately stopped showing goods to a customer, ran back and forth, took up a hatpin and began to chase several customers around the store. At the police station she claimed her husband had once placed her in an asylum. A doctor had declared her nervousness was "the result of overwork and too great [of] worry." Harnett was sedated and then locked up.[61]

Harnett's behavior prompted an editorial from a New York City newspaper. It observed that "she gave impetus to the growing distrust of that article of feminine wear ... and compared to the broad rim straw hat, which was popular several years ago, the hatpin is almost innocuous." He continued by remarking that the styles of women's headgear daily continued to make the hatpin more and more necessary. "The sailor [hat] nearly always needs it, and the big hats, which are indicating in the shop windows a continuance of their favor through another winter, need it more than any other kind," he concluded. "Possibly the only hat which does not require it is just the sort of hat which no woman nowadays will consent to wear so long as she is in style."[62]

Herbert Crow was a young businessman who was fatally stabbed by a young woman on October 11, 1897, in Hastings, Nebraska. She used a hatpin. The pin entered his side and broke off. Crow refused to give the name of the girl or the reason she stabbed him. It was reported, though, that he had been stuck by his girlfriend in a jealous rage over another woman. He was 18 years old, and alive, even though the account called him "fatally stabbed."[63]

Several days later he was reported as "recovering" from his wound, but still refused to identify the girl. A day later Crow was said to have developed chest pains and was taken to a doctor's office for an operation. The steel hatpin was located in his left lung and the four-inch-long item was removed. Crow's further fate went unreported in the press.[64]

A very brief editorial on the Crow case declared: "The use of hat pins may become subject to legal restrictions if its use as a weapon of offense and defense continues."[65]

May Murphy of San Francisco, an employee of Empire Laundry, got into a fight with a female friend in July 1898 over a young male co-worker. For a time the rivalry between the two women continued, apparently without physical violence. But then as Murphy was leaving work for the day she was confronted by her rival. In the ensuing fight, Murphy stabbed her rival with a hatpin. Fellow laundry workers separated the pair. They met again on the evening of July 22, however, and this time Murphy was stabbed with a knife. She refused to name her assailant.[66]

Murphy's encounters prompted a very brief editorial that dealt, somewhat indirectly, with gender and class issues. The complete editorial read: "Perhaps the use of a hatpin in a fight between laundry ladies is legitimate. It is when a man is stabbed by this weapon that the rules of civilized warfare are violated."[67]

On the night of September 22, 1898, in a rear room of Morris' saloon in Scranton, Pennsylvania, a woman used a hatpin on another woman. The offender was a young woman named Gussie Regall, better known as Lizzie Croft, who was arrested. She and the victim quarreled and Croft tried to stab her with a hatpin. She was held on a charge of assault, in lieu of $500 bail. A reporter wrote, "The woman's mania for using a hat pin as an offensive weapon has made its appearance in Scranton."[68]

Martin Bowers, foreman for a contractor, swore out a complaint in San Francisco on February 1, 1899, for the arrest of Mrs. Emma Ward of that city, on a charge of attempted murder. Bowers said that while he was at work a few days earlier at a Union Street wharf, Ward threw red pepper in his face and tried to stab him with a hatpin. She finished her assault by threatening to kill him within 24 hours. She accused Bowers of being the cause of her 13-year-old daughter Hazel being sent away a week earlier to the Girls' Training Institute.[69]

Ward's activities prompted a newspaper editor to write that when the "gentler sex" overstepped the bounds it was necessary to get them back. "Let it be done kindly, and rather by reasoning than resort to the police," he argued. He added that there was an "unwritten law which grants to women the privilege of using a hatpin as a weapon of offense and defense. Are her feelings outraged, she can pluck from her headgear this ready implement and jab it where it will do the most good. She has frequently done so, even at the risk that for the nonce her hat will not remain straight, and nobody ever heard of her being punished for it. The hatpin in the hands of indignant beauty is suggestive, corrective; a pointed rebuke." He went on to declare: "While not seeking to curtail the remedial hatpin in its work of protecting virtue and chasing vice howling into the distance, there are circumstances under which it may not be properly employed." Then he mentioned the Ward case as being one of those examples. That is, it was unfair to blind him with pepper and then attack him with a hatpin. He had no chance to run. "If she persists in her reckless course the first thing she knows those Sacramento legislators will abolish the hatpin and decree that its place be taken by a ribbon or a string. And then where will she get off at?"[70]

On the evening of October 4, 1899, 60-year-old Samuel Stoddart was attacked by two women who dragged him into a dark alley and robbed him of $150. He tried to resist them but the women used a large hatpin and a pocketknife as weapons. He made it to the nearest police station, where he showed his left leg, which had been pierced to the bone by the hatpin. Stoddart had managed to secure the hat of one of his assailants. At the station a police officer identified it as belonging to Eva Marshall or Gertrude Smith, both of whom were known to the police. They were picked up and brought to the station, where Stoddart identified them as his attackers.[71]

On March 23, 1900, Joseph Lial, a caterer in the city of Salinas, California, was stabbed in the leg by a hatpin wielded by a jealous woman. It was a small wound but it penetrated a vital spot, causing the man to nearly bleed to death. Lial and the female assailant got into a shouting match that escalated into a physical fight over another woman. In a rage, she drew the steel pin from her headgear and stabbed Lial. He refused to identify the woman, or to say anything about the incident.[72]

Robert Elwood was a traveling salesman for a St. Louis shoe house. Early in October 1901 he was in Salt Lake City, where he sustained an injured thumb as the result of a hatpin attack. Elwood had arrived in Salt Lake, registered at a hotel and went out on the town drinking. He finally ended up at a "resort," run by Lillie Evans. He had some trouble with a woman at that establishment and demanded some money be returned. He was referred to Evans, who brushed him off by saying she knew nothing of the matter. Elwood then tried to pull a ring off one of Evans's finger, but two of the female employees immediately came to her aid; one of them bit his thumb. He ran outside, creating a disturbance, kicking at the door of the resort and then throwing a boulder through it. A warrant was issued, and Elwood was taken into police custody. He was booked on a charge of destroying property. After he pled guilty to the charge and agreed to pay for repair of the door, the judge fined him $10 and Elwood went on his way.[73]

When she was confronted with her sister and her sister's husband, John Brooks, who were quarreling, Mrs. Loretta O'Brien of Brooklyn, New York, thought herself justified in using her hatpin. During this incident, which occurred on March 20, 1903, O'Brien jabbed Brooks in the face with her hatpin, which broke in half. It took physicians at the hospital an hour to remove the pieces lodged in the victim's face. The couple had started to quarrel during Loretta's visit. When she entered the fray with her hatpin, she said that both her sister and her husband turned on her, causing her to act in self-defense. The point of the pin entered Brooks's face just below the left eye, passed through the roof of his mouth and penetrated the tongue. She was arrested but, said the news account, "No serious outcome is anticipated," that is, unless blood poisoning set in.[74]

A later story revealed that 23-year-old Loretta was being held on a charge of having stabbed 32-year-old Brooks. When the pin broke off it left about four inches of steel in his flesh. According to this account, when the couple started to argue, Loretta took her sister's side, whereupon Brooks ordered her to get out of his house. As she was somewhat slow to leave, Brooks started to physically put her out. Loretta thought he was going to strike her and so she stabbed him with her hatpin. An ambulance was called and Brooks was transported to the hospital. Loretta was arrested. Nothing more was reported on this case.[75]

In the presence of a huge crowd of 50,000, the World's Fair in St. Louis was formally dedicated on April 30, 1903. In the crush of the crowd the most serious injury was said to have been sustained by a fireman who was jabbed in the face by a woman with a hatpin. He was trying to persuade her not to crowd into a specially reserved space, setting off her fury. She was not arrested, and the fireman was treated at the hospital. While that was taken place, President Theodore Roosevelt was giving a speech at the event.[76]

That caused a St. Louis newspaper editor to comment, "That universal instrument of peaceful arts, the hairpin, is fast losing popularity in favor of a weapon of war, the hatpin. The fireman whose face was so painfully pricked by an infuriated lady in Thursday's crowd may head a society for preaching a return to old implements. The hatpin finds mankind defenseless."[77]

Two women, using hatpins, reportedly fought a battle on a Third Avenue trolley car in New York City on the night of May 30, 1903. The confrontation did not cease until both women rolled off the car and onto the street. Jealousy over one of the ladies' husband was said to have caused the fight. Rose Fox and Bessie Olembeck were on the same car, separated by the crowd of passengers. When one moved to get off, the other recognized her. First they traded angry looks, and then angry words, and then they began to jab at each other with their hatpins. Fox was said to have drawn her hatpin first; Olembeck quickly followed suit.[78]

Effie Smith and Bertha Winston quarreled over the affections of a man called Thomas Kane one night late in June 1903, in Chicago. Smith pulled a hatpin from her headgear and stabbed Bertha in the chest. Winston reportedly died within ten minutes. It was the first hatpin murder in Chicago. No more was reported.[79]

Emma Leonard, 27, and Kate Cherry, 21, were reported to be the first highwaywomen to utilize the hatpin as a weapon with which to hold up a victim. They tried that tactic on Frank Pilong of New York City early on July 31, 1903, and got $112. Pilong, cashier for the Fort Lee Ferry Company, had just made his collections and was leaving the ferry house. The women followed him, jumped him, and threatened to stab his face with their brandished hatpins if he cried out. They searched him and took the $112. While one of the women searched him for money the other one stabbed him in the face a few times; then they let him go. The women ran off but Pilong gave chase, yelling for the police. Finally the two women ran into the arms of a policeman, who arrested them.[80]

A meeting in Boston addressed by Booker T. Washington in Zion Church on July 31, 1903, broke into a riot, requiring a score of policemen to intervene. Two arrests were made and order was restored but not until one of the women, the sister of an arrested man, made effective use of a hatpin, which she jabbed into the neck of a policeman with such force that he was obliged to release his grip on his prisoner. A reporter observed that Maud Trotter, who "did such brilliant work with the hatpin, was released." Some 2,000 people had attended the meeting with the riot initiated by those in the audience who were opposed to the methods of Booker T. Washington.[81]

A stockman from Saco Montana by the name of F. B. McArthur was stabbed in the stomach by a hatpin in Kalamazoo, Michigan, on August 22, 1903. His assailant was an unidentified woman on the streets of Kalamazoo. McArthur was walking along the sidewalk in the middle of the day in a large crowd when a small boy brushed a little feather duster in the woman's face. The woman, thinking it was McArthur, grabbed her hatpin and jabbed it into his stomach. According to the news account, "McArthur cannot live." No more was reported on the incident.[82]

Because she thought Maggie Brown was paying too much attention to her husband, Mrs. Laura Scott attacked her with a hatpin, inflicting injuries to her face and head. The trouble occurred on the main street of Peoria, Illinois, in May 1904. That assault in front of a large group of spectators was said to have caused a "sensation." Laura Scott was arrested.[83]

Bertha Seller was held in custody on May 1, 1906, in New York City after it was revealed she had robbed and beaten a "defenseless man" and then fought two policemen and a streetcar crew. The victim was 19-year-old James Smith. He said he was walking down a New York City street the previous evening when Steller jumped out and started to strangle him. She went through his pockets, took $2, threw him into an alley, and made for a streetcar. Smith followed her, got on the same car, confronted her, and demanded his money. At that point she attacked him with a hatpin and a pair of scissors. A car conductor intervened but she jabbed him with her hatpin a couple of times and he backed off. He called for the police, who eventually arrived and subdued her. She had bitten, by then, one of Smith's fingers to the bone and left him with more than 20 stabs and gashes on his face and neck. Nor more was reported on Steller.[84]

A young woman by the name of Fernell was the victim of a painful assault on a crowded streetcar in Portland, Oregon, in July 1906. She and her escort squeezed onto the already-crowded car. As passengers jostled back and forth into one another, Fernell bumped into a woman in front of her. The latter flew into a rage and drew a hatpin from her hat and plunged it deep into Fernell's thigh. Other passengers tried to seize the assailant, but she escaped by jumping from the car.[85]

Joseph M. Neil, described as a "well-to-do athlete" was found dead in a room in the Greenwich Hotel in Greenwich, Connecticut, in the middle of December 1906. Witnesses had seen him walk into the room a short time earlier, in the company of a woman. One day later, the woman, believed to be his wife of a few weeks, was arrested in New York City. An autopsy on Neil's body showed that death had been caused by a hatpin that had penetrated his brain.[86]

A few days later it was reported that authorities were still investigating the death, while the police continued holding actress Catherine Neil, the victim's widow. Officials then had a theory that the woman, under the influence of drugs, may have murdered her husband while in an "abnormal

In a sensational case that involved references to alcohol and other drugs, actress Catherine Neil was suspected of having murdered her husband with a hatpin.

condition of mind, believing herself another person." Those officials thought she was a "morphine fiend and possibly a modern Dr. Jekyll and Mr. Hyde." Mrs. Neil claimed her husband died from heart trouble after a major drinking spree. The title of this article was "Low Life Murder."[87]

Some ten days later it was announced that "Goldie" Neil would be tried for the murder of her husband. In this account, it was argued that she killed him by pushing either a hatpin or a nail file into his brain by inserting in behind the eyeball. She had admitted to the police that she had two husbands "but excuses this on the plea that she thought the first one, William H. Finley, a policeman, was dead." Goldie gave her age as 25.[88]

It was charged that Goldie, in a fit of anger, and after prolonged dissipation from her "reckless husband," placed a sharp instrument—either a hatpin or a nail file—into his brain. He was dying when his wife called for medical aid. According to the physician, Goldie contended that her husband fell on a knife while intoxicated. She took a night train to New York City immediately after her husband's death, promising to return. She did not return and an investigation was launched, which culminated in her arrest. Then she declared that her husband committed suicide. Goldie explained bruises on her face and arms by saying her husband had treated her cruelly. A few weeks earlier she obtained a divorce from her first husband, who was a member of the New York City Police Department. Immediately thereafter she married Neil, a former prize fighter and blacksmith. He paid the cost of the divorce proceedings. Neil was partial to drink and it was alleged that he forced his wife to drink with him "and that he dragged her down to his moral level."[89]

Mae Ward used a hatpin on the house detective of the Hotel Gotham in New York City in January 1907 in a fight that disturbed the upscale hostelry and ended up in Yorkville Court on January 16. Charles Fleming was the hotel detective who testified that Ward kept going in and out of the hotel, sitting in the lobby, laughing loudly, and making insulting remarks as guests passed her. When he asked her what she was doing, she wouldn't answer; when he asked her to leave, she refused to do so. He physically moved her outside, whereupon she drew out her hatpin and stabbed him in the nose. Then he called the police. In court Magistrate Breen said to Ward, "Just because you're a good-looking young woman, you mustn't think you can go into one of our best hotels and make a disgraceful scene. I wish there was a charge of assault against you. I want to make a lesson of your case and I'll fine you the limit for disorderly conduct—$10."[90]

Pansy Street appeared in court in Salt Lake City on July 15, 1908, before Judge Diehl, charged with battery upon Mrs. Margaret Misell. On or about April 25 there was a dispute in a city department store between Misell, her daughter, and Miss Pansy Streit, who became Mrs. Pansy Street. The two women quarreled over a couple of rings, resulting in Street striking Misell in the face, giving her a black eye. Pansy was arrested for battery but, as she was then under 18, the case was sent to juvenile court. It was sent back to Diehl's court when it became know that Miss Streit had married and her name had become Street. Marriage meant she was no longer a juvenile. In court it was revealed that Misell followed Street up and down the aisles of the store, after their row, and that Misell jabbed Street with a hatpin a dozen times. Diehl did not believe the hatpin story and fined Street $15.[91]

Bonita was described as the leading woman with the Wine, Women and Song acting company, which had gone out of business suddenly while on tour in Cincinnati. On the morning of April 21, 1909, she was arrested in her room at the Sinton Hotel after a fight with the hotel clerk; she was then locked up by the police, who charged her with disorderly conduct. Later, she failed to appear in court, having skipped to New York City on a train. A fine of $5 and court costs was paid by her attorney. Prior to her arrest, the fight had taken place in the hotel elevator between Bonita and night clerk William Hetlich and watchman Adam Matz. She was armed with a hatpin. Both men were reported to have been "severely stabbed" during the scuffle and a doctor had to be called to tend to their wounds. The trouble started after Bonita tried to order drinks from the bar after it had closed. When she was refused service, a fight broke out.[92]

The Paducah Light and Power Company in Kentucky swore out a warrant on July 19, 1909, against a woman named Hattie Hall, who had created a disturbance on a streetcar the prior evening. It seemed the conductor refused to accept a nickel with a hole in it; this enraged the woman, who then lunged at the conductor, attempting to stick him with a hatpin.[93]

Determined not to be trampled on by the heedless men who swarmed the stations and crowded the coaches of every train out of Coeur d'Alene, Idaho, an unidentified woman took action on her own. On August 3, 1909, on the last train out of that city for Spokane, Washington, a number of men climbed into the overcrowded train. "I've used this hatpin before when a man tried to take advantage of me and I'll do it again," announced one woman in the rear coach. Her threats were said to have been heeded, after a few taunting and insulting remarks from the men in question. Problems involving men on such coaches were reported to include smoking in the cars, "roughness," and "loud talk and vicious remarks."[94]

Eva Tanguay was arrested at her hotel room in Louisville on March 1,

1910, on a charge of assaulting Clarence Hess, a youthful stage employee at MacAuley's Theatre in that city, with a hatpin. She was then appearing in *The Follies of 1909*. Tanguay was a superstar of the era, both on the legitimate stage and in vaudeville. At the police station she gave a bond for her appearance in police court on the following day, in the sum of $200. Hess also filed a suit against Tanguay, asking for $2,000 for physical damages. After a three-hour trial in Louisville police court on March 2, the actress was fined $40 and court costs on the complaint of Hess. He alleged that Tanguay had jabbed him with a hatpin. Hess appeared in court with his physician, testifying that the stage hand had three punctures in his abdomen.[95]

A report from Chicago in March 1910 stated that Chicago's first "hatpin divorce was granted by Judge Dupuy when he freed August Johnson from his wife, Hilda, on the grounds of cruelty." When asked the nature of the cruel treatment, Johnson said, in court, that his spouse had a predilection for sticking hatpins into him.[96]

Mrs. Ethel Zwerling wielded her hatpin on July 1, 1910, for some time and by doing so kept at bay a gang of men employed by the Edison Electric Lighting Company. The men had been instructed to set a pole in front of her New York City house and the hole had been dug when she rushed out, brandishing her hatpin. Some of the men were badly jabbed in the arms. When the police arrived, they arrested the miscreant. While she was away at the station house being processed, other workmen raised the pole, but Ethel vowed it would not remain up because she would cut it down. Many of her neighbors had promised to assist her in her war against the company and they announced that they planned to uproot all the poles in the area.[97]

Armed with hatpins, three young women held at bay seven workmen of the New York Telephone Company, on November 23, 1910, in New York City. Those workmen had dug a four-foot hole in front of the residence where the women lived, and started to erect a pole. Those women were sisters Ida, Bessie, and Annie Levine. Although the workmen protested the interference, pleaded with, threatened, and cajoled the women, they had no success. Reportedly, the police were called but also without success, although no details were given. The story ended with the speculation that legal action could follow.[98]

Miss Nellie Brown did not hesitate to follow Harvey Zemp across the continent when she considered he had jilted her, and attempt to avenge the injury she charged he had inflicted upon her. Brown had been raised in the mountains of South Carolina, where, it was said, unwritten law found ready sanction. In a court in Redondo Beach, California, a preliminary examination took place and Brown was held for trial; it was with difficulty that court officers restrained Brown from attacking Zemp with a hatpin while he was giving evidence. She was then being held in jail: A few days earlier she had shot Zemp at Redondo Beach while he was riding his bicycle and then turned the gun on herself with the intention of committing suicide, but Zemp, gripping his wounded arm, ran to her and took the gun away. The pair had grown up together in the mountains of South Carolina; when Zemp left for California it was with the promise that he would send for Brown. At first he wrote frequently, but his letters grew colder and fewer. She wrote, demanding that he send for her but received no reply. Weeks passed: Brown became convinced another woman was involved. She journeyed alone to California to find him. At the end of December 1910, Brown was placed on probation for two years, and the case was over. She promised to immediately return to the South.[99]

In police court in Washington, D.C., Sadie Johnson pled not guilty to striking conductor Eustice Marshall with a hatpin and raising a disturbance on a streetcar early on January 11, 1911. However, she was found guilty and fined $50 for assault and $20 more for the way she had acted. As she did not have the money to settle the account, she was taken off to jail.[100]

Mrs. Louis Saville had a heated argument with Solomon Stevens over a small irrigation ditch which Stevens had built across a truck garden owned by Saville. It all took place in Ogden, Utah, in June 1911. The two began to scuffle, Stevens said, and then she attacked him with a hatpin. Saville claimed that Stevens knocked her down twice and slapped her repeatedly. She was 45; he was 50. She swore out a complaint, lament-

Nellie Brown followed her sweetheart across the country, convinced he had jilted her. After trying halfheartedly to murder him, she tried to stab him with a hatpin in court.

ing the fact she had no stouter hatpin or revolver with which to deal with Stevens. He was arrested on a charge of assault and battery.[101]

A violent quarrel ensued between members of a party of young women returning from a Long Island resort to New York City early on the morning of August 14, 1911. Alveda Carpenter, 19, was reported to have been stabbed in the heart with a hatpin and to have dropped dead in the street. One of her companions was arrested and charged with murder.[102]

Two women engaged in a hatpin duel for possession of a seat in the courthouse at the murder trial of J. B. Sneed, in Fort Worth, Texas, on February 24, 1912. Their fight interrupted the arguments in the trial for ten minutes. Finally, the combatants, Mary Lang and Georgia Heath, were separated by the sheriff and order was restored. Both women received hatpin jabs on their arms, but suffered no serious injury.[103]

An enraged woman who had just been indicted by the grand jury for sending obscene literature through the mails, threw the office of United States commissioner Anson S. Taylor into an uproar by brandishing two long, sharp hatpins at assistant attorneys S. McComas Hawken and Sydney Mudd, Jr., the men who had prosecuted the case against her. After a struggle with several court officials, she was subdued. The attack took place at the end of July in 1912. Josephine Simpson, 35, had just recently been released from prison after serving five years for the exact same crime. The literature in question was a threatening letter to a woman, containing numerous obscenities. When a deputy marshal was about to remove her from the courtroom she suddenly jumped up, drew the two hatpins from her headgear and rushed at the two lawyers. About six years earlier, Simpson was employed as a servant by Mrs. Moser, whom she was alleged to have robbed. She was sentenced to serve a term of six months in the workhouse. Almost immediately after her release from the workhouse she began mailing threatening letters to Moser, couched in "extremely obscene language." In the letters she threatened revenge for he imprisonment. Arrested, found guilty of sending obscene literature through the mails, Simpson was sentenced to five years. Released only a few months earlier in 1912 she soon afterward, it was alleged, wrote another threatening letter to Moser. This led to her being arrested again.[104]

Attacked by a maid who lunged at them with a hatpin, after she had just received a notice of dismissal, Mary and Lottie Pickford, famous sisters of the movie world, and their mother, Charlotte, were saved from probable injury when their screams brought a chauffeur to their rescue. The girl, Katherine Ripkine, was overpowered and carried bodily out of the Pickford bungalow.[105]

In December 1919 the results of an organized effort in New York City to protect stores from holiday shoplifting became apparent in the women's courts of Manhattan and Brooklyn on December 14. Suspected shoplifters, who had filled three patrol wagons were arraigned in Manhattan, and a dozen or more in Brooklyn. At least a dozen women store detectives brought 50 tearful suspects before Magistrate Jean Norris in Manhattan. All had been apprehended in the act. According to the news account: "Some arrests were made only after vigorous battles in which hatpins were used or umbrellas broken on the heads of the detectives. The umbrellas were used as receptacles for stolen articles."[106]

4

The Hatpin as a Defensive Weapon

While the hatpin had been used by women many times in an offensive way (a way that usually led to problems for the woman wielding the item), it was also used many times in a defensive way, to fend off would-be robbers and assaulters and mashers (as sexual harassers were known in that time period). On a train near Chicago in August 1891 two young women had berths, upper and lower six. Opposite them in lower five was an obese man. He was drunk and kept swaying and backing into the curtains of number six as he tried to get ready for bed. Suddenly he jumped about four feet in the air and yelled that he had been stabbed through the curtains. When the porter arrived to see what the commotion was about, the girl in lower six said, "If there are any more big beasts in this car who attempt to sit on me they'll get jabbed with something worse than a hatpin. You tell them so, porter." The fat man said nothing more but went to bed and did not arise in the morning until the woman had left the car.[1]

In October 1895 a woman left San Francisco to study art in New York City. It was while she was there that she had the idea of making a hatpin a weapon of defense. "Of course you know that a woman can't go about alone with any degree of comfort when she gets away from western chivalry," she told a reporter. She stayed with her brother in Newark and used suburban trains almost every day. "I had a bookful of unpleasant experiences before I learned the magic power of that simple little hat pin," she said. As an example, she told of a man who squeezed in beside her, causing her to yield part of her seat to him. Still he encroached more, until she got fed up and drew her hatpin. The man eased away and yielded her seat back to her as she brandished her makeshift weapon. Since then, she employed the same tactic and considered herself safe. The reporter then spoke to other women who told him of different uses for the hatpin, such as the picking of locks, as a can opener, and as a paper cutter, but "first place was given, without a dissenting voice, to the story of the hatpin as a modern and always available weapon of defense."[2]

An article published in May 1897 told of an unnamed woman who rode the Chicago elevated trains (el) all the time, and who had found a new use for the hatpin on the el "crowder." One particular man sat too close to one or more women on the car, assuming they would not protest his "impertinence." Now, when this unidentified woman was faced with Mr. Crowder, she took out her hatpin and gave him a jab. It worked: he always jumped up and got out at the next stop.[3]

Two men who tried to rob a streetcar in Chicago on the night of January 9, 1898, were foiled by a woman passenger named Sadie Williams. Besides her, there were three other passengers (one female, two male) and one transit employee (a grip man) on the car. None of those three males came to the aid of Conductor Warren, the man being robbed. Warren was having a desperate fight with the two robbers and, just when he was about to lose, Sadie joined in the fight. Grabbing her long hatpin she lunged at the nearest robber. He screamed, released the conductor and turned on Sadie, who attacked him again. He quit the fight at that point and fled the car. Sadie then struck the other robber in the cheek with her hatpin. When the half-dazed conductor came to his senses, there was only Sadie and one passenger left on the car. The other passengers and robbers had all fled. Sadie replaced her hat, asked the conductor if he was all right and then promptly fainted. She was revived and escorted home.[4]

The story of Sadie Williams generated at least two editorials on the subject. One from a West Coast newspaper remarked that the hatpin enjoyed a modest popularity for it intended purpose: "Then all at once, the sphere of the hatpin widened. If a man in a public place crowded more than the exigencies of the jam seemed to warrant a sharp prod awakened him to a sense of error and suggested sudden reform. The pin became a weapon of defense. Far be it for us to say that it ever was a weapon of offense. Let the men who have been punctured by it examine their own consciences and make plait if they can." The editor related the Williams story and went on to declare, "But just now the hatpin is at the zenith of its fame. It has vanquished a robber.... This was no ordinary occasion. The hatpin forever!"[5]

An editor from an Eastern newspaper remarked: "It is no longer proper to speak of women fully attired for the street or shopping campaign as 'defenseless.'" After discussing the Williams story he stated: "By this act

4. The Hatpin as a Defensive Weapon 75

the Chicago girl has given the hatpin a startling prominence as a weapon of war. The modern hat-fastener is often nearly as large and as formidable as the stiletto and razor that have been by law banished from use in good society by males." He thought the girl's quick use of the item demonstrated the hatpin to be handier than the hip pocket razor. In conclusion, the editor wrote: "With a modern hatpin carefully sheathed in her headgear, therefore, it is easy to see that a resolute, up-to-date woman is a person not to be trifled with."[6]

Some three weeks after the robbery attempt, the West Chicago Street Railway sent her an "extremely complimentary" letter, along with a $10 check. Williams explained that when she saw the two robbers struggling with the conductor, she was not afraid: "All I thought of was helping him. The only weapon I could think of was my hatpin, and as soon as I could I jerked it out of my hat and jabbed it into the robber nearest me." In this account Williams was called, without explanation, Barbara Stack. Only in this specific story was she identified as such; everywhere else she remained Sadie Williams.[7]

As Bertha Lynch and Ada Robinson were walking along Main Street in Derby, Connecticut, on May 2, 1900, they were approached by two men who barred their way and demanded money. The women screamed and tried to run away. One man made a grab for Lynch's leg. In desperation, she drew a long hatpin, brandishing it as she faced the would-be robbers. They drew back in fear. She lunged for the nearest one and the pair ran off.[8]

In St. Louis in June 1900, Mrs. G. B. Swafford and a woman friend defended themselves with their hatpins against a

Sadie Williams, of Chicago, stepped forward in January 1898 and used her hatpin to drive off two men who tried to rob a moving streetcar. She enjoyed a brief fame as a heroine, even if she was misidentified as Barbara Stack in this one account.

threatened attack by strike sympathizers. The two women got off a transit car on their way to visit a friend when they were assailed by a number of men, who called them *scabs*, among other epithets. When one of the men made a movement, as though to attack, both women drew their hatpins and brandished them. The man and the others backed off.[9]

Rose Suedmeyer, 20, was set upon by a highwayman at 7 p.m. on the night of January 30, 1901, within one block of her home in San Francisco. She stabbed her assailant with a hatpin and he fled.[10]

A fight on the part of Mrs. Emma Gardner of St. Louis, in which she used a hatpin as a weapon, resulted in the arrest of Bud Franklin, who was locked up on a charge of attempting to steal Gardner's overcoat. While she was in the front office of her laundry business, she saw someone in the back room trying to take the coat. Emma cornered him with a hatpin and forced him to drop it. She then marched him out into the street and turned him over to a passing policeman.[11]

On the night of March 17, 1901, in Denver, Colorado, a woman named Georgiana Thompson had just returned home and was in her apartment reading when she heard a scratching at the keyhole, trying to pick the lock. As her apartment building had recently been plagued by a spate of burglaries, she was on her guard. She went to the door, flung it open and confronted a man on his knees and holding a length of wire. As he tried to rise, he collided with Thompson, who promptly sat on him. For the next half hour she used her hatpin on him every time he got fractious. Mr. Pomeroy, the apartment manager, eventually heard her cries for help and, seeing she had things under control, left her there and went for a policeman. The would-be robber later gave his name as G. G. Hilton.[12]

In April 1901, four young women from South Williamsport, Pennsylvania, battled with two tramps on the river bridge and inflicted severe punishment on them with their hatpins. Ella Mishow, Mabel Shaffer, Rose Gilson, and Emma Gilson, who ranged in age from 17 to 20, were on their way to Williamsport, traveling by way of the Maynard Street Bridge. Halfway across the bridge they were accosted by two men who attempted to assault Mishow and one of the Gilsons (they were sisters). As the struggle ensued, one of the females shouted, "Use your hatpins." All four immediately armed themselves and stabbed the men a few times before they gave up and ran off.[13]

A newspaper editor in Salt Lake City summarized a then-recent story that had come to his attention, in May 1902. Mrs. Mary Brockington and her daughter Virginia were walking along a street in Milton, Delaware, when they were attacked by a man who tried to steal the older woman's purse. She clung tightly to it until her assailant finally knocked her down. Then Virginia came to the rescue. Drawing a hatpin from her headgear, she stabbed him repeatedly before he fled the scene, screaming; he was later arrested. The editor then went on to give the footpads of America "a little admonition: Beware of the woman with the hatpin. That is to say, beware of all women." He said that because he believed that, quite often, the "undoing of some gentleman of the road is chronicled."[14]

While Hattie Marquardt was on her way home in July 1902 in Norfolk, Nebraska, she was followed by two men. One of them passed Hattie and then turned around and stopped her while the other man grabbed her from behind, demanding her money. She successfully fought them off with a hatpin, breaking it off in the hand of one of the assailants.[15]

So prevalent was it becoming that a woman drove off a would-be robber with her hatpin that a comic strip of the era devoted one of its daily entries to the issue. In the strip, Sallie Slick and her aunt Amelia do exactly that to a would-be robber. (For unexplained reasons, the location of the action was set in Italy.)[16]

Anna Nelson's use of a hatpin as a weapon of defense proved valuable in resisting the attack of a highwayman on the night of September 7, 1902, in Minneapolis. She was on her way home from church when a man leapt out of the bushes, ordered her to stop, and demanded her money. When she would not surrender her purse, he knocked her down. In the ensuing struggle she used her hatpin on him. He ran off and Anna continued home, even though she was badly injured from the fight. Both of her eyes were swollen shut and her lips were badly cut.[17]

Justice Robertson in the First District Police Court in St. Louis on September 15, 1902, stated emphatically that it was a woman's legal right to use a hatpin as a weapon to protect herself from the attack of a man. That decision came as a result of the case of Dolly (perhaps Dollie) Tracy of St. Louis. She had been arrested on the complaint of fellow citizen Joseph Posten, who charged that Tracy had stabbed him with a hatpin. Tracy admitted having used the hatpin but declared in her defense that he attacked her. Justice Robertson, after further questioning, stated that the pair fought on a city street; that Posten used his fists on her and was about the repeat the attack "when she resorted to the woman's most favorite weapon—noiseless, hard to see and capable of making a painful wound—the hatpin." Upon reviewing the incident, Justice Robertson told Tracy, "I think you were justified in using the hat pin on him. If you had stabbed him a few times more I believe you would have done right. You are discharged, but I shall fine Posten $10. You never should have been brought into court."[18]

So popular was the story of a woman who drove off a highwayman with a hatpin that a comic strip from July 1902 featured that theme, although the action was set in Italy, for unexplained reasons.

The Tracy case caused a newspaper editor to write: "The old-fashioned notion that the only protection by a woman should be her scream has given way to something more practical. A scream is a good thing so far as it goes, but it may not go far enough. A hatpin generally does if handled properly. In extreme cases it should go clear up to the hilt. The male victim can do the screaming." He went on to add that while it could not be ranked as a deadly weapon "it is a wondrously effective one. It chases away footpads and it could be used with discretion in providing more room in the street cars." He concluded: "We look to see the hatpin cut a wide swath in the world, and so far it has with scarcely an exception been applied where its use was entirely justifiable."[19]

When Tracy and Posten appeared in court, the latter showed several "ugly scars" to the court to attest to the hatpin attack, but it left Justice Robertson unmoved. "I believe that a woman is justified in using her hatpin in self-defense," he stated. "A hatpin may be an ugly and even a dangerous weapon, but I hardly think that it would come under the legal nomenclature of 'deadly weapon.'" He then added, "I think a woman may carry or wear a hatpin of almost any size and length without coming in contact with the law forbidding the carrying of dangerous weapons. I do not think a hatpin could be termed a concealed weapon even if it was the size and shape of a small dagger."[20]

Armed with only hatpins, two women in Chicago, on November 11, 1902, saved a man being beset by three highwaymen. They put the assailants to flight and saved James Walsh. That attempted robbery took place in an alley at 8 a.m. The three men set upon Walsh, took his watch and were beating up the retired coal merchant when the two women came to his rescue.[21]

Mayme Andrews of East St. Louis used a hatpin on a would-be masher on a Saturday evening in that city in April 1903. Andrews has just finished her day's work in a department store and was walking home when a man who was unknown to her insisted on walking beside her. When he accosted her, she did not reply to him and began walking faster. But the man matched her pace and almost touched her arm. As a last resort, Andrews withdrew her hatpin and pricked him on the shoulder with it. The man, after being jabbed, suddenly ran off down the street.[22]

A newspaper editorial in April 1903 commented on a new society in Brooklyn that was designed to eliminate the masher. The editor thought the group would have its hands full because "there are all too many street mashers, but they are far too bold to confine their advances to the goo-goo habit [making eyes at someone]. They can quickly be discouraged if the ladies use hatpins and umbrellas firmly and judiciously." He went on to say that "a long bold stare is, of course, annoying to most women, but the man who won't take a good look at a pretty woman as she passes on the street doesn't know what his eyes are for." He concluded by observing, "A good looking woman is entitled to the homage of an admiring glance, and we'll bet she never gets angry when she receives one. The general run of the men who bestow the glances have no intention of flirting or being disrespectful. They do it because they can't help it, and they would be mighty poor excuses for men if they tried to help it."[23]

Miss Leoti Blaker of Kansas stabbed an elderly masher with a hatpin in a Fifth Avenue coach in May 1903, during a visit to New York City. She ran a hatpin into his arm with enough force to elicit a scream from the "elderly stickee." Blaker had been in the city for a few days. As she told a reporter, "If New York women will tolerate mashing, Kansas girls will not." She got on the coach and sat down next to an elderly-looking man. His attentions proved annoying and embarrassing to her and she kept edging away from him as best as she could. Finally, he put his arm in back of her. "I became so enraged that I didn't know what to do," she explained. "At last I reached up and took a hatpin from my hat. I slid it around so that I could give him a good dig, and ran that hatpin into him with all the force I possessed." According to Blaker, the man screamed when stabbed but said nothing else; he promptly got off the coach at the next corner. She also told the reporter that the hatpin as a weapon of defense was without equal and as a masher exterminator it had met with such unqualified success that she recommended it to all Gotham girls who were annoyed by the attentions of "evil-minded men." Blaker said that the first time she discovered the hatpin to be an excellent means of self-defense was when a tramp tried to grab her pocketbook while she was walking through some woods: "I had my hat in my hand and was pushing the hatpins back and forth when the tramp jumped out at me. I up and jabbed him in the face so that he ran away screaming." She added that she didn't propose to be annoyed while she was in New York City "so I will carry an extra hatpin in my shirt waist ready for action."[24]

Rosa Wilson was a showgirl at the Casino in New York City. At the end of May 1903 she announced that she had "begun a hatpin war on mashers." She had been riding in a Broadway streetcar when a man entered and stood before her as she hung onto a strap. He nudged her several times with his knee (blaming the motion of the car), leered at her, and so forth. Rose reached toward her hat and drew out a nine-inch pin. The masher did not notice that activity. Once again he nudged her with his knee, promoting her to stab him in the leg a few times. He yelled and quickly fled the car. Wilson admitted to the reporter that she had used her hatpin "vigorously" and said she meant to treat all other streetcar mashers in exactly the same fashion.[25]

When Lulu Rayner was arraigned in police court in Washington, D.C., on September 7, 1903, on a charge of assault and battery upon George Dent, she pled guilty. Dent said she stuck him on the arm with a hatpin; Rayner countered that she did so because he tried to hug her. Judge Scott, however, discharged her and let her go home, saying a woman had a right to stick a man for taking such liberties.[26]

On the evening of September 6, 1903, in Chicago, 19-year-old Emily Myers defender herself from the attacks of a highwayman. She put the would-be robber to flight by jabbing him in the wrist with her trusty hatpin. Myers had gotten off a streetcar and started walking to her home. Suddenly, a man with a red handkerchief over his face appeared next to her and demanded her purse. He tried to seize it, but she held on. She then drew out her hatpin with the other hand and began jabbing him. He tried to grab her hand, but was stabbed in the wrist. With a cry of pain, he let go of her and ran off.[27]

MISS LEOTI BLAKER, OF KANSAS, STABBING ELDERLY MASHER WITH A HATPIN IN FIFTH AVENUE COACH

This 1903 sketch depicts Leoti Blaker, of Kansas City, newly arrived in New York City. She faced what many women found themselves subjected to on crowded transit vehicles—the masher. Blaker jabbed her hatpin into the "elderly stickee."

At Lockport, New York, on a night in September 1903, Nellie Eckhardt, a young woman from Buffalo, went to the rescue of her escort, William Neuse, when he was attacked by a gang of ruffians. She used her fists, an umbrella, and a long hatpin so proficiently that the assailants fled.[28]

In November 1903, Edward L. Green, a black man, was under special guard in the Bronxville jail in New York City as the authorities feared he might be lynched. Green was charged with having attacked a young woman employed as private secretary by former New York State senator Isaac Mills. She was on her way home when Green grabbed her and was in the process of strangling her when she drew a hatpin and stabbed him. Her screams drew rescuers and a posse was formed that later that night found Green.[29]

By the vigorous use of her hatpin, Clara Hansen saved herself from injury at the hands of a man who attacked her on the night of January 11,

1904, while she was walking home in Salt Lake City. He seized her from behind, threw her to the ground and started to choke her. Clara gave him several jabs with her hatpin and he finally ran off. Her screams drew help, but the assailant had already escaped into the night.[30]

So common had the use of a hatpin as a weapon of defense become that an illustrated instructional piece on the topic was published in the *New York Tribune* on February 7, 1904. The piece began with a rhetorical question: "What shall we do in case we are attacked by some thief or ruffian?" The male readers would generally answer, "Carry a revolver." According to the piece, however,

> few women possess the nerve necessary to use a pistol with effect when attacked. Then there is the objection to a revolver in the possession of a woman that she would be averse to suspecting the motive of every man she met, and would probably fail to draw the revolver until too late, for fear of making a foolish mistake. What, then, can be provided for her that will be formidable to a foe, yet absolutely safe, so far as she is concerned, and every ready at hand, whether wanted for use or not? [The obvious answer is the hatpin; specifically one designed] primarily for use as a weapon of defense. It is in reality a stiletto, masquerading as an innocent hatpin. It is made of fine steel that will bend but will not break, as sharp as a needle, and hardened at the end so that it can be used with deadly effect as a dagger, and with a handle that enables a woman to grasp it for use as a weapon and hold it so that it cannot easily be pulled from her hand.[...] There are times in every woman's life when a suspicious-looking character arrives on the scene and a voice whispers to the woman, "Beware of him." While most women would shrink from pulling out a revolver, it is an innocent act to put the hand to the hat and draw out one of her stiletto-like hatpins. With this in her hand the nervous woman is ready for the stranger, whatever his intentions. If he is an honest man he will probably take no notice of the woman's actions. If he is a thief, it is more than probable that he will mark the act and let the woman pass unmolested.[31]

The instructional article cited above was reprinted in several other newspapers in America over the following month or so. A paper in Kansas printed the full text, including an addendum:

> It is an axiom with the members of the police force that the woman with the hatpin is more to be feared than an armed and desperate burglar. The reason is that the burglar's hand could not travel hipward [to a gun?] without a bullet or a club disabling his arm. The woman with the hatpin, however, has to be watched with lynx eyes, and even then is likely to have the weapon concealed up her sleeve for use when opportunity comes.

When the Kansas paper reprinted the New York piece it did not name any source, even though it reprinted the story verbatim. The extra bit added at the end changed the tone of the article from the good, necessary, defensive use of the hatpin to one of an improper use of the item.[32]

Jennie McCarmont of St. Louis was assaulted on the night of July 10, 1904, while she was walking along a street in that city. The assailant was a man, she said, who attempted to rob her. She pulled out a hatpin and stabbed him with it several times in the body and on the face before the police arrived. They had heard her screaming. The assailant ran off, but the police officers caught and arrested him. Jennie identified him as her attacker. He was not named in the news story.[33]

Mrs. W. D. Whalen of Omaha had a dangerous encounter as she walked home one day in November 1904. Two men jumped out from a hiding place and demanded she hand over her valuables. She yelled out and pulled out a hatpin, despite the fact that one of the men was aiming a revolver at her. Those two men suddenly gave up and ran off into the night.[34]

That same month in Omaha it was reported that a man had been terrifying women in the leading residential area of the city for about two weeks. He had been nicknamed "Jack the Hugger" by the media. Helen Pickett was walking along the street one night when "Jack," as it was believed, seized her by the waist. At that point Pickett drew her hatpin and used it on the masher. Jack ran off, howling with pain.[35]

Mrs. William Willisten of Marinette, Wisconsin, saved herself from robbery by three men on Main Street in February 1905. One of the men grabbed her purse but, as he did so, she seized a pin from her hat and jabbed it deep into his arm. The man gave a yell and all three of the men disappeared down an alley.[36]

Lillian Lundquist returned home from the theater on the evening of July 23, 1905, in Oakland, California. She got off the streetcar near her home and stared walking to her destination. A man stepped up to follow her for a bit and then accosted her. She screamed and tried to free herself from his grip, but he was too strong. Then she drew a hatpin from the back of her hat and drove it into the man's side. With a cry of pain, the man released her and ran down the street.[37]

On August 14, 1905, Nettie Sayman of South Chicago jabbed a highwayman into flight after he had knocked her fiancé into unconsciousness. When he made a lunge for her purse she drew her hatpin and thrust it into the assailant's arm. A brief struggle followed during which he received several more stabs before he gave up and fled, crying in pain.[38]

Carrie Bullocks, a mill girl, was passing a secluded spot surrounded by woods in West Millville, New Jersey, while returning home from her place of employment. Just then a man jumped out, grabbed her, put a hand over her mouth, and threw her to the ground. She managed to fight him off with a hatpin; he fled into the woods. Carrie's father headed an armed posse of 30 citizens who searched for the assailant for many hours. However, he was not found.[39]

Two young women successfully defended themselves against the attack of a lone footpad who stopped them on a St. Louis street on December 29, 1905. Lizzie Finnegan and Lulu Moss got off a streetcar and started to walk home. Suddenly a man jumped out and tried to grab Moss's purse. Both women drew hatpins and jabbed him. He quickly gave up and fled the scene.[40]

Elizabeth Kirshman of Atlantic City, New Jersey, was attacked by a man near the beach in the cottage section of the city in the first month of 1906. When he seized her she fought him off by drawing a hatpin and stabbing him in the face. He fled. A crowd had assembled, drawn by her cries, and they chased the man and cornered him under the boardwalk. He was dragged out and "handled roughly" by the crowd before the police could intervene. He was arrested and jailed, but not named in the account.[41]

A 17-year-old woman by the name of Annie Hubble was accosted early on the morning of January 25, 1906, as she was on her way to work at the Lincoln mills in Chester, Pennsylvania. The man threw an arm around her and "addressed her with endearing terms," said the account. Taking a long hatpin from her headgear she plunged it into the chest of her assailant who, fled, howling with pain.[42]

Mary Harrington, yet another milliner, was pursued as she traversed a Cleveland street in March 1906. He followed her when she left a restaurant, matching her steps before finally speaking to her. She pulled a long pin from her hat and jabbed the fellow in the arm. The masher shrieked and scrambled away.[43]

It was reported in May 1906 that hatpins as weapons for women to fight off pocketbook snatchers and highwaymen was advocated by Captain Boardman, chief of detectives on the Washington, D. C., police department. That advice to the women of Washington was given by Boardman in order that they might defend themselves from the "negro highwaymen" who had held up and robbed eight white women, in separate incidents, within the past 18 days. The police were said to be opposed to women carrying revolvers for fear that some of them might get excited and start shooting "with disastrous results to innocent parties." Boardman believed the hatpin was "as deadly a weapon as a woman should be entrusted with" and pointed to two or three cases in St. Louis and Chicago where highwaymen were fought off by women with hatpins.[44]

4. The Hatpin as a Defensive Weapon 85

Shortly thereafter, Boardman's comments drew a response from the New York Police Department. According to the account, a New York detective told a reporter for a Washington, D. C., newspaper: "New York policemen are amazed at the suggestion made by a Washington detective that the women of this city arm themselves with hatpins as a means of defense against possible assault." He added that the reason for the surprise "is that the woman with a hatpin is feared by the police of New York more than the Italian or Spaniard with his dagger or stiletto, the darkey with his razor or the American tough with his revolver." He added, "Most of the women of the street are provided with these hatpins, and use them with terrible effect on the slightest provocation. As policemen are their most frequent targets they have naturally become very leery of them. The great danger from these long steel pins is that they are easily concealed and you are not apt to discover their presence until it is too late." This unidentified New York detective continued by saying, "Of course it would be all right if women used these deadly weapons alone on brutes who attack them with evil intent, but our experience in New York has been that they are mainly used as weapons of women of bad repute to assist in robberies or to resist arrest by the police. Several policemen have already been killed in that way [no details provided and, in any case, it was not true] and most of us are always guarding against the possibilities of the same fate." His conclusion: "Hatpins may be a good weapon for the women of Washington but in New York we would like to have a law prohibiting their use entirely."[45]

Mr. and Mrs. Morris Benach returned to their New York City apartment one afternoon in late May 1906, only to find a burglar in their home. The two men began to scuffle; the burglar seemed about to prevail and was soon on top of Benach, who was then on the floor. It was then that Mrs. Benach joined in. She drove a hatpin deep into his flesh, causing him to scream. About that time a policeman arrived. He arrested and removed the burglar, who gave his name as Joseph Miller, but was known to police as Felix Gross.[46]

Beatrice Grandy appeared in court on July 3, 1906. She was charged with maliciously stabbing George T. Derby in the back with a hatpin, puncturing his lung; for several days the boy's life hung in the balance. Beatrice testified that she and her sister met several young men on a street in Norfolk, Virginia, one of whom was Derby. She said he attempted to push her off the sidewalk and that she stabbed him in self-defense. Several prominent residents of the neighborhood testified to the good character of Grandy. The jury hearing her case acquitted Beatrice after having deliberated for just three minutes.[47]

Florence Young, one of the members of the Buster Brown acting company then playing in Los Angeles at the Grand Theater, succeeded in driving off a robber who attacked her and tried to get her purse, in early January 1907. For several evenings before the attack Young had noticed a man who had been following her while she was on her way home from the theater. On January 6, the same young man jumped out at her and grabbed her purse. She held on, screamed, and made several jabs at her assailant with a hatpin. He gave a cry of pain, let go of Florence, and ran off. She reported the matter to the police, who unsuccessfully searched for him.[48]

On a crowded Chicago street in December 1906, May Gates, cashier of the A. G. Morse Confectionery Company, was transporting $5,000 from the bank to her employer's office to meet the firm's payroll. She had returned from the bank by streetcar and was almost at the firm's door when five masked and armed men attacked her and dragged her into an alley, trying to wrench her handbag from her grip. She held then at bay for a time with a hatpin, drawing a crowd in the process. At that point, some of the robbers drew their revolvers just as the police arrived. Some 20 to 30 shots were fired as the robbers tried to flee on a streetcar with two of them captured; the other three escaped. One policeman and one bystander were slightly wounded by errant bullets.[49]

Eighteen-year-old Maggie Kennedy was tried before Justice Dana T. Smith in July 1907 in Salt Lake City on a charge of threatening to kill her stepfather, W. H. Griffith. On a Friday night, the girl, in a fury, attempted to stab Griffith "with that more or less dangerous weapon of femininity," a hatpin. She told the court between sobs, that her actions were meant as retaliation for his having beaten her. She promised to exhibit better behavior in the future, and was released.[50]

A report in August 1907 noted that an attempted assault on a lone woman on a west side street "adds another case to the long list of attacks on women and children in the streets of New York." According to the story, the attack would have been successful had it not been for the struggle of Adelaide Wilder, a nurse, who fought her assailant with a hatpin, eventually eluded him. Her screams summoned police, who finally cornered and arrested the suspect. At the station house, he gave his name as Pietro Daurie.[51]

The story of a holdup and attempted robbery foiled by a girl with a hatpin was told in police court in Brooklyn, New York, on August 30, 1907, by the woman involved, Kate Murphy, aged 19. She was a ticket seller for the Brooklyn Rapid Transit station at the corner of Myrtle and Knickerbocker Avenues; the would-be robbers were John Brennan and James

Byrnes. According to her account, the men had been hanging around her station for some time. When she went on duty on August 29 her station had about $300 cash on hand and about $1,500 worth of transit tickets. Sometime around midnight they approached her window. They said they were transit inspectors who were there to look at the books. She did not believe them and asked them for some form of identification. After they told her they didn't have any identification with them, she told them to go away and get the proper papers. The two men left on one of the trains. Worried about the encounter and fearing the pair would return, she took the money and tickets and locked them in the safe. A few minutes later her younger sister Margaret arrived with a midnight lunch, which they usually ate together, after which Margaret returned home. Still worried, Kate told her sister to board the next train and go a few stations down the line to where a policeman was usually on duty. She was instructed to tell him the story and, if possible, bring the officer back with her. While Margaret was gone, the pair returned and said they were going to examine the books. They forced open the door of her enclosure. She screamed, but also pulled out two hatpins and held the men at bay until a policeman (who had been close enough to hear her screams) arrived. A moment later, Margaret returned on a train with a policeman in tow. Brennan and Byrnes were both arrested. In court the following morning, Magistrate Naumer said, "Girls with spunk, such as Miss Murphy, [have] shown exactly what this town stands most in need of."[52]

W. C. Buchanan and S. D. Walker were arrested early on the morning of September 27, 1907, in Los Angeles, by Patrolman Bonner. They were alleged to have accosted Emma Larkin and Franz Weingartner on the street when the girls refused to make dates with them. The women were walking along Broadway when the men approached them. Although the women attempted to pass, the men continued to force their attentions.

"Leave us alone or I'll stick a hatpin in you," said Larkin.

"That would be a good thing for you to try," replied one of the men.

"I'll do it," declared Larkin, drawing a hatpin.

The men were alleged at that point to have struck the women. Marks of the blows could be seen on the faces of the victims when they were in the prosecuting attorney's office the next morning. After striking the women, the men ran off, but the women gave chase, finally running into Bonner. They told him their story and he arrested the men.[53]

Della Becker saved herself from an attacker by the use of her hatpin, on the night of October 13, 1907, in Evansville, Indiana. She was returning home when a man jumped out from behind a tree and grabbed her. She jabbed the man in the face with a hatpin, causing him to flee. Later, a man who gave his name as Abe Brown was arrested for the attack.[54]

While Lottie Cannon was returning from church to her home in Beverly, New Jersey, in March 1909, she was stopped by two men who stepped out from behind a tree and tired to seize her pocketbook. "Miss Cannon did not scream nor faint," wrote a reporter, but drew a hatpin from her hat and jabbed the nearest assailant in the arm. With a howl he jumped back and the pair then fled.[55]

Two highwaymen sprang upon Mr. and Mrs. Charles F. Thill in Chicago in August 1909. Mrs. Thill immediately took action, wielding a hatpin; the two would-be robbers quickly turned tail and fled.[56]

As 17-year-old Gladys Green was returning to her Salt Lake City home on the evening of February 13, 1910, she was grabbed by a highwayman, who tried to rip her watch from her wrist. She drew her hatpin and thrust it into his ribs. When she withdrew it there was blood to a depth of two inches on the pin. Yelling in pain, the robber fled the scene. Police were called and a search was launched, but he was not found.[57]

Irene Conway and Agnes L. May were out walking near a New York City subway station near the end of March 1910 when Joseph Peasiana jumped out and tried to rob them. They drew out their hatpins, repulsed him, and then chased him until they came upon a policeman, who arrested the man. The women had reportedly jabbed at him more than once as they pursued him.[58]

Sixteen-year-old Edna Scotton drove a masked burglar away from the family home in El Paso, Texas, on a night in July 1910, before the man had a chance to enter the home. Edna was home alone when she heard a noise at the door and grabbed her tools—a hatpin and a three-pound Indian club—and went to see who was there. When she opened the door to confront the robber she stuck the long hatpin in his side and dealt him a blow with her club. He ran off and was not located when the police arrived and searched the area.[59]

Quick use of a hatpin by Marguerite Le Blanc put to flight a masher whom she jabbed twice, once through the arm and once in the face. She was walking on a street near her home in New York City in October 1909 when a man walked up behind her. He put his arm around her and she "instinctively" used her hatpin. He soon ran off. A number of bystanders who had witnessed the incident gave chase, but the masher got away.[60]

E. L. Dickson was a young man who was arrested on a Friday night in Los Angeles in January 1910 for annoying women in film theaters in the downtown area of the city. When he appeared in police court on January 15, he pled guilty to a charge of disturbing the peace, preferred by a Marcia Taylor, and was sentenced to jail a few days later. According to the police, a number of complaints had been made by proprietors of the theaters located on South Main Street that women in the darkened cinemas were molested by a young man who would sit near them and grab them by the arm and otherwise annoy them. Two plain-clothes policemen were detailed to investigate and traced the masher to the Olympic Theater, where they saw him take a seat next to Taylor. He grabbed the woman by the arm. She moved to a different seat but he followed her and tried to grab him again. Finally, Taylor pulled a long hatpin from her head and told him to move away or she would jab him with it. At the point the police stepped forward and arrested Dickson.[61]

An article published in a Marion, Ohio, newspaper, published on August 16, 1910, asked:

> Why wouldn't a hat pin be a good cure for some of the mashers who disfigure the peaceful face of the Sunday evening streets? One of those nice long affairs with scintillating jeweled heads so harmlessly attractive adorning milady's bonnet, and so nice, and wicked, and sharp when wielded by a determined little hand bent on administering an unforgettable lesson.

The article went on to relate the story of a young woman who, while walking from home to the post office in Marion, ran into a succession of mashers; finally, after several such encounters she pulled out a hatpin and brandished it, causing this latest masher to scamper off. Concluded the article:

> If a refined woman can't walk down the main street of a small city like Marion without being subjected to annoyances from amorous and vulgar loiterers.... How about the hatpin cure?[62]

Josephine Frederick, a ticket seller at a park, was on her way home after a twelve-hour workday, on a streetcar in Alexandria, Virginia, in August 1910. The exhausted woman fell asleep, but was startled awake, only to find that a James Clancy had grabbed her foot. When none of the men in the car would intervene, she drew her hatpin, brandished it, and held Clancy at bay until the police arrived. Appearing in police court before Magistrate Hermann, Josephine Frederick explained what had happened. The magistrate fined Clancy $10.[63]

Mrs. James Chappell, of Ogden, Utah, put three thieves to rout on the street early in the morning of August 7, 1910. They tried to grab a watch and a purse from her as she was walking home. Rather than yield her belongings, she reached for her hatpin and jabbed the nearest of the three men. He uttered a cry of pain, released his hold on her, and fled. Then she turned her hatpin on the other two, who also soon fled the scene.[64]

Attacked as she was walking along a street in November 1910 in the Oakley neighborhood of Cincinnati, Mary Clay, 18, drew a hatpin and jabbed her assailant until he was forced to desist from his attempt at assault. The man had approached her from behind, seized her by the shoulders, and forced her to the ground. Freeing one arm, Mary drew her hatpin and thrust it into his chest. He yelled and released her. She managed to jab him a few more times until he made his escape.[65]

Minnie Pate, a clerk in a downtown store in Oklahoma City, was returning home on foot shortly after dusk on a January evening in 1911. When she was approached by a hold-up man, Pate attacked him with a hatpin. She jabbed him several times before he finally fled the area.[66]

Mistaking a riding habit with a divided skirt for a "harem" skirt, several hundred boys attacked Miss Zurella Stephens of Philadelphia, on February 25, 1911, when she had stopped to water her horse. It was a time when any unconventional attire that might be mistaken for pants on a woman was met with hostility. Stephens rode astride and when she dismounted to lead her horse to water, several scores of boys, mistaking the divided skirt for the harem variety, proceeded to show their disapproval with a shower of stones and mud. Stephens was riding with her friend Sarah Brennan, who was wearing the same type of attire. A stone hit the horse, causing it to bolt, as did Brennan's horse. Those horses knocked a couple of the boys down. Faced with a rough, hostile crowd, Stephens drew her hatpin and held the mob at bay until a policeman arrived on the scene.[67]

Hannah Krotchstil was confronted by a highwayman on April 4, 1911, on Lexington Avenue in New York City. He thrust a pistol in her face, but Hannah did not throw up her hands in surrender. Instead, she drew out two hatpins and began to jab at her assailant. After being jabbed in the arm, the robber took flight. Hannah started off in pursuit, screaming for help as she ran. However, she was handicapped by a hobble skirt and could not keep up with the man. Passersby on the street took up the chase and the would-be robber was finally caught.[68]

Seventeen-year-old Clara Metcalf was attacked in Los Angeles by a villain as she was walking through a park. Clara was accompanied by 16-year-old George Caswell. She drew out two hatpins and jabbed him. Even though he was said to be armed with a revolver, he could not withstand the hatpin onslaught; he turned and fled from the pair.[69]

On a street in Marion, Ohio, on a Wednesday evening in May 1911, around 11 p.m., Florence Lenhart was walking home. She discovered that a man was walking close behind her. He continued to follow her and finally accosted her. She told him to go away after he spoke to her, but he continued to follow. Finally, he grabbed her, placing his hand over her mouth. Florence managed to free one arm, draw out a hatpin and jab her assailant repeatedly. She got her mouth free and started to scream. That brought a passerby to the scene. When the assailant heard someone coming he fled the scene and managed to elude a resultant police search.[70]

Madeline Shamberger used her hatpin on the night of August 26, 1912, on a man giving the name of Oscar Glaus, whom she accused of following her, on the streets of New York City. Patrolman O'Connell was walking his beat when he came across a crowd in the street. Pushing through the crowd, O'Connell found Madeline jabbing her hatpin at Glaus, who was trying to avoid being stuck. As the crowd learned that Glaus had been following Madeline, the men therein started to rough him up. O'Connell had to rescue Glaus, and then arrest him, and then take him to the station.[71]

Using her hatpin as a weapon, Mrs. George Enright of Pound Ridge, Westchester County, New York, went to the rescue of a farmer who was being beaten in a fight with a tramp, on the afternoon of September 16, 1912. She used the hatpin so effectively that the tramp turned from fighting and ran off. Enright had been on her way to New York City in a car driven by Elizabeth Kirwin. Passing through Greenville, they saw two men struggling in a field. One was George Burnett, a farmer with a crippled leg; the other man was described as a tramp. Burnett was calling for help as they struggled. There was no one else in sight so Enright drew out her hatpin and went to his aid. She drove the pin into the tramp's leg again and again until he gave up and fled. Then she helped Burnett into the car and the women drove him home. Reportedly, Burnett had come upon the tramp plundering his tomato patch."[72]

Clad only in night clothes and carrying a hatpin, Miss Agnes Thornton of Bedford, Massachusetts, a coed at Beloit College in Beloit, Wisconsin, routed a burglar whom she found in her room. She chased him through a park and inflicted several stab wounds on him, causing him to cry out in pain and to drop her violin, which he had stolen.[73]

Mary McArdle, a ticket agent of the Brooklyn Rapid Transit Company, told a reporter in November 1912 that she would always keep a stout hatpin within easy reach. She had defended herself successfully with such a weapon when a robber reached into her cage and tried to steal money. The jab in the arm she gave the robber caused him to withdraw it long enough for her to close and fasten her cage window. She picked up the telephone receiver in her booth and called for help. Police officers came and arrested the would-be robber. At the station he gave his name as Joseph Feist, aged 40. He was charged with attempted robbery.[74]

Complaints of thefts from letter boxes belonging to business firms and residential tenants in the same building in New York City had become so frequent in the spring of 1913 that Miss Raener Herold, a bookkeeper for a business in the building, was determined to watch her employer's box. She figured the theft probably followed close on the heels of the arrival and departure of the mail carrier. When she heard his whistle one day she hurried down and spotted the thief stealing from the boxes. Herold grabbed a hatpin and, brandishing it, she told him to wait for the police. He tried to get passed her but she jabbed him and managed to hold him until the police showed up and arrested him; he gave his name as Alexander Farawitz. A fingerprint check revealed him to be a fugitive wanted for bail jumping and a man with a long prison record. The unusual aspect of this case was that Herold got the hatpin she grabbed not from her hat but from the floor, where Farawitz had dropped it. He had used it as a tool to open the letter boxes.[75]

On the night of July 27, 1913, Sadie Haverelkoss held two men in her apartment in New York City at the point of a hatpin until her husband and his brother-in-law turned the men over to the police. The two men, Michael Pavlole and William Stahl, were arrested on a charge of grand larceny. They had tried to steal clothing from the Haverelkoss residence.[76]

Advice for what women should do in the event they were victims in a holdup came, in September 1913, from Alice Stebbins Wells, a high-profile Los Angeles policewoman, and someone with a high-profile media presence at the time. She gave such expected advice as not to wear a lot of jewelry, not to go to bad areas, and so forth. Wells also said, "Scream first. Then use the first weapon to hand. Don't forget the trusty hat pin." She added, "The hatpin is the best weapon and most to be depended on." And, as a final thought: "Don't carry arms—they are dangerous."[77]

The stab of a hatpin, delivered in self-defense by Catherine Hermes, caused the January 14, 1914, death in Milwaukee of Daniel Sweeney, who, one week earlier, paid a fine of $50 and costs for annoying the girl. According to the testimony in police court, Sweeney took the girl to a dance on New Year's Eve and the pair visited several cafés. On the way home, the girl testified, she was forced to draw a hatpin and use it for self-defense. A piece of the pin was removed by a doctor from the man's chest. On the morning of January 14, he was found dead in his bed. Reportedly, an examination showed that blood poisoning and hemorrhage were the causes of death.[78]

A week later the coroner in Milwaukee held an inquest into the death of Sweeney, who had been 22 years old; Catherine was 17. At that inquest, the coroner ruled Sweeney's death was "justifiable homicide." Back on the early morning hours of January 1, he had tried to attack Hermes. She pulled out one hatpin and it broke off with the first jab into the man's body. She then seized another pin from her hat and plunged it into his chest. He then ran off but went to work as usual the next day, although blood still dripped from the wound. Not until well over a week later did he become unconscious and then die.[79]

Rose Hauser, a 20-year-old New Yorker, was being hailed as a heroine in July 1914 because she saved a neighbor, Beulah Reich, from serious injury who was being choked and beaten by a robber in her apartment. Reich screamed when she was attacked and that alerted Rose, her neighbor across the hall. When she heard the yell from her neighbor she grabbed the nearest thing at hand—a pin cushion—and ran to Reich's aid. She grabbed a hatpin out of the cushion and stabbed the man several times; he yelled in pain and finally fled the building. Rose chased him down the street and a crowd soon joined in her pursuit. Eventually, the man was cornered in a basement, where he was arrested by the police. He gave his name as Albert Richardson.[80]

In the middle of December 1916 in Kansas City, Missouri, one film theater there had started a campaign against what it termed "men pests," or mashers. At the end of every show it ran a slide, warning the women in the audience against them. The slide gave notice that "the house" would point out any man found guilty of bothering its women patrons. At the close of the slide was a sentence that read: "Ten dollars reward to any woman who sticks a hat pin in a 'man pest.'"[81]

Bessie Veigler was walking along a street on the evening of December 17, 1916, in Washington, D.C., when a man tried to snatch her purse. She drew a long hatpin, lunged at her assailant and stabbed him in the chest. He fled. Police were said to be on watch at all Washington hospitals, looking for a man to turn up for treatment of a hatpin wound to the chest.[82]

Washington, D.C., in the period covered by this book, always had a lot more female residents than it had male residents, due to the dramatically better employment opportunities for females (in government service there was much less discrimination against women). A brief editorial in a Washington paper in July 1919 declared: "I would suggest that Washington women carry red pepper with them. A little of this thrown in the eyes of a man is about as good protection as you would want. Reinforce the pepper with a long hatpin and perhaps there would be fewer women followed by loafers on the street."[83]

When he appeared in court in New York City on October 24, 1919, Charles Almendinger, 17, told the judge that since October 5 he had held up people in Central Park at the point of a .22-caliber revolver, and, while doing so, he had always worn the uniform of the United States Navy. Of his victims, eleven men and four women, the only one who inspired him with fear, he said, was a woman who drew a hatpin and chased him for a half mile or so. His total take from those robberies was $32.25.[84]

As Anna Welch was walking along the street in Chester, Pennsylvania, in March 1921, a "roughly dressed man" approached her and demanded she give him her purse. She took a punch at him and then drew a long hatpin from her headgear and made a lunge at him. He gave up his attempts and fled.[85]

When a holdup man entered the millinery shop of the Kalichman sisters in the heart of New York City's shopping district in March 1922, Ida Kalichman attacked the bandit with a hatpin and chased him through the streets. A policeman arrested the bandit after being pursued for several blocks.[86]

When a would-be robber invaded a millinery shop run by Ida Kalichman in March 1922 she grabbed a hatpin and chased him out of her shop into the street.

It was reported at the end of 1922 that Boston girls had declared war on "the flirt." Leaders of the movement said there were no dues or membership limitations for this new organization. They had adopted as an insignia a button on which was depicted a lizard impaled on a hatpin.[87]

5

Group Use of the Hatpin

And then there was the group use of the hatpin as a weapon. In these instances, more than one woman acting more or less in concert, but sometimes individually, suddenly turned to their hat fastener in a seemingly unplanned way. Some of those uses could have been construed as good; some of them, bad. A group of a dozen or so excited women held an angry meeting in front of the Charles P. Harris stockbroker office on May 8, 1896, in San Francisco. They had invested money in penny stocks and Harris had gone out of business suddenly. Another employee, Edgar L. Atkinson, had his home besieged by these women later in the day after they had been unable to locate Harris or obtain satisfaction from anyone else. When they besieged the home of Atkinson, they were brandishing their hatpins as weapons, as well as hefting bricks in a menacing way. However, Atkinson was also nowhere to be found.[1]

In Manhattan, Kansas, during the visit of New York State Governor Theodore Roosevelt in October 1900, a large crowd was present. The men had all the good vantage points, although it completely obstructed the view of the women who were gathered in the rear. According to the news account, the women pleaded in vain with the men to get down and let them see, but the men held their positions and refused to move. One young woman then yelled to her companions, "Try your hatpins." In an instant, every woman started forward with her hatpin leveled at the offending men. Those men hesitated for a bit, but finally moved out of the way to let the women see the event. (Of course, this story is almost certainly completely false.)[2]

Western Union messenger boys were on strike in Chicago beginning in September 1902. Girls were hired as replacement workers. At first those girls held the messages (telegrams) in their waistbands. But striking boys took them away and destroyed them so they could not be delivered. Then the boys came to believe the girls were hiding the messages in their stockings. That led to a number of altercations between the boys and the girls, with the latter sometimes resorting to using hatpins in their defense. At least one such altercation made its way into court. John Navansky, 15, was in court charged with attacking Julia Benham, 16. She had several Western Union messages in her stockings. John had grabbed at her hosiery and Julia, seizing her hatpin, stabbed him and kicked him down. He yelled and ran off, straight into the arms of a policeman. Julia testified that she heard a loud cry: "Hey, there she goes! She's got it in her stocking." Then John began his assault on her lower limbs. In court, Judge Tuthill gave John a warning, but nothing else, and then discharged him.[3]

In a separate incident stemming from that Western Union labor dispute 17-year-old Janette Bonneau, another girl hired as a strike replacement, found herself in a struggle with a crowd of striking messenger boys who had surrounded and attacked her. She managed to knock one of her tormentors down then, with a hatpin as her sole weapon; she held his companions at bay until the police arrive. Reportedly, the crowd that had gathered to watch the street brawl had cheered the girl.[4]

During the afternoon of April 27, 1903, two young girls caused terror for a number of women visitors to the Mall in New York City's Central Park by running around, brandishing long hatpins. When the two females came down the center of the Mall, they were described as boisterous— singing and shouting and hurling "vile epithets" at the women (most of whom were with young children). Taking hatpins from their headgear, they approached some women on benches, made stabbing motions and came within an inch or two of making contact with flesh. Finally the police were called, and Patrolman Doyle arrived. He caught the girls after a short chase and arrested them. At the station house they identified themselves as Louisa Grant, 13, and Henrietta Downes, 14.[5]

Annie Clark, forewoman for Nelson Morris & Company, was attacked by picketing girls who were on strike against that firm, while riding a streetcar in Chicago in August 1904. A fight followed in which hatpins were used as the weapons. Clark was said to have been injured and was taken to her home by the police. She was able to recognize several of her assailants and secured warrants for their arrest.[6]

An actress by the name of Gladys Chapman was seized about the waist and "insulted" on the street in New York City on the afternoon of March 25, 1905. During the struggle, she screamed and broke away from her attacker. A crowd ran to the area, as did Officer Willemse. He had to battle through the angry crowd to save the masher from a beating at the

This 1903 illustration came from Charles Dana Gibson, famed for his creation of the Gibson Girl, a representation of the beautiful and independent American woman at the turn of the 20th century. In this scene, several women regard a very tiny man with contempt. The little man is in a begging posture as one of the women apparently gets ready to impale him on a hatpin.

hands of a number of indignant men and women who had witnessed the attack. As Willemse walked away with his prisoner, women were jabbing hatpins into him and men punched and kicked him. At the station the prisoner gave his name as Rudolph Meller.[7]

Every woman compelled to be alone on the streets in the evening in Williamsport, Pennsylvania, was carrying a hatpin "concealed" in her muff or her dress to defend herself from an uncaught masher who had been terrifying women and girls in all sections of the city for a week, or so it was reported in December 1905. The assailant was said to seize his victim, hug her, and then run away. Two such victims were Eva L. Keeler and Nellie M. Perkins, in separate incidents. Wrote the reporter, "The hatpin defense is being generally adopted and it is believed it will prove effective."[8]

A fight that took place on a subway car in New York City, on the morning of March 5, 1906, on an "owl train," came to a head when several women used hatpins, and a score of men swung their fists and blackjacks, causing consternation among the other passengers. About 30 members of a Brooklyn Italian society boarded a Broadway train in Harlem. They had spent the night in New Jersey and were returning home. There were as many women as men in the party, as well as several children. It was evident that at least the men had been drinking excessively. They crowded into one car, sang songs, jostled each other and made much noise, but kept it all among themselves. At a later stop, nine youths, aged about 18 to 20, boarded the train. Pushing and shoving between the two groups led to fighting, and then to a brawl. At least two of the women from the Brooklyn group drew hatpins and started for the other group. Their men held them back. Finally, the motorman managed to push the second group out the door and then closed it before the Italians could follow.[9]

On July 24, 1906, the New York City Police Department received reports of a riot at 59 Bond Street, the premises of a clothing business operated by Samuel and Hyman Cohn (brothers). Men, women and girls were engaged in a battle with hatpins. The police arrived and quelled the crowd, but nobody would talk. The Cohn plant had been the scene of a strike two weeks earlier, a dispute the workers lost. Non-union operators took their places. Union operators who worked in the same building but for a clothing business on a floor below the Cohn plant had been one side of the fight, against the non-union scabs then employed by Cohn.[10]

Anna Aaronson and 11 boys were charged with inciting a riot in the vicinity of Bregstein Brothers garment factory in New York City, on August 20, 1907. Some two weeks earlier about 1100 girls employed there had gone on strike. Their places were promptly filled by scabs. Strikers mounted persistent demonstrations in the vicinity of the plant, causing management to hire a squad of "athletic" young men to escort the scabs to and from work. Among those guards was a man named John Mulligan, a former prize fighter. Mulligan was leaving the factory, escorting a party of scabs on the evening of August 20, when a group of young women "pounced on them." Mulligan said they were striking pickets. As the sides confronted each other, the striking women, on command from their leader, each drew a hatpin. Other strikers joined in, all brandishing hatpins. Mulligan was jabbed a few times in the melee and then he fled the scene. Police soon arrived and broke up the rioters.[11]

John Jones found himself a prisoner by six indignant women on a streetcar in Pittsburgh on October 13, 1907. They attacked him with hatpins and umbrellas and finally pulled him off the car in front of the police station and took him inside, where they had him locked up. When Jones boarded a streetcar that day he found himself on a car with no other men on it at the time. He jostled all the women within reach, or so it was reported. Those women put up with it for some time and then six of them attacked him at about the same time. The conductor did not interfere and accommodatingly stopped the car when they reached the police station.[12]

Ten angry women, each with a hatpin brandished and ready for use, surrounded Henry Gaynor, a chauffeur whose machine had just injured a child. That took place in New York City in September 1908. The angry women said Gaynor had also killed a dog with his machine and they menaced and threatened the man for a time until the police arrived and three officers rescued him. The child turned out to have been only slightly injured.[13]

Annoyed beyond measure by a "Jack the Hugger," who was on the loose in Steelton, Pennsylvania, in February 1909, the Young Ladies Protective Association of Educational Hill had formulated some rules for protection. Each member was to be equipped with a hatpin (at least 14 inches long) and a container of red pepper that could be unlimbered and fired the moment Jack went to work. The members of the group had pledged to use the hatpins and pepper on any Jack who might "make any advance attempt to caress, kiss, hug, fondle, pinch, address, flirt with, wink at, or walk alongside of them."[14]

During a parade in San Francisco on October 23, 1909, police had difficulty in holding back the crowd at Stockton and Market Streets. The advance of the crowd was checked and mounted police were used to keep them back. Cases were reported of women using hatpins on men who were aggressively trying to push forward to get a better view of the parade.[15]

On April 7, 1910, the kosher butcher shops located in the Upper East Side of New York City attempted to resume business. They had been under a boycott by area residents because of the allegedly high prices of their meat. When business resumed that morning, rioting resulted, with the women boycotters scuffling with customers going in and out of the shops. Within a few minutes, the street was blocked with a mob, and police reserves were called out. When those reserves arrived, the women boycotters turned on them, using hatpins, market baskets, bottles, and anything else that was handy. Finally, the street was cleared and a patrol wagon carted off a load of women to the police station.[16]

Militant suffragettes engaged in a physical battle with the police in London, England. An estimated 220 of these women were in court in London on November 22, 1911, to answer to charges of obstructing traffic, assaulting police officers, and malicious destruction of property. The women were sentenced to a night in jail. The prisoners, according to several witnesses, sported blackened eyes and scratched faces. A number of police officers had been stabbed with hatpins; others had eyes blackened, noses bruised, and teeth knocked out by brass knuckles.[17]

Because of the numerous assaults and attacks made upon girls and women in Morrisville, Pennsylvania, in January 1913, the women of that city had formed a hatpin brigade. The hatpins, it was reported, would be "of extra length and quality so as not be break or bend when used on an assailant." The women in the group declared that after those pins were received from the manufacturer they would need no policeman or escort, but "will be prepared to go upon the streets [at] any hour of the night." Each woman was to wear two of those new-style hatpins.[18]

Armed with hatpins and umbrellas, several hundred women fought the police on January 18, 1913, in New York City in one of the riots connected with the garment workers' strike. A lone policeman tried to protect the scabs present and was severely beaten. He arrested one woman before summoning a dozen more officers to help quell the riot. Some 150,000 workers were reportedly involved in the strike.[19]

Although Boston, Massachusetts, legislators had been discussing the advisability of reducing the length of hatpins, in January 1913, the young women of Simmons College were determined to obtain hatpins that were extra long and extra sharp as a defense against pickpockets and mashers. Students had frequently been "insulted" on the way to the dormitories that were located nearly half a mile from the college. A policeman had been stationed in the area to protect the women.[20]

In Columbus, Ohio, on the morning of January 31, 1913, some 20,000 women battled one another and with the police in an effort to get into the tabernacle where the Reverend W. A. (Billy) Sunday, the evangelist, was conducting a revival. Women fought with umbrellas and with hatpins; policemen used their clubs. Women gathered as early as 4 a.m. although the meeting did not start until the afternoon. At 10:30 a.m. the doors were flung open, the crowd surged forward, and the riot broke out. Several police officers were stabbed with hatpins.[21]

Back in London, England, the headquarters of the militant suffragettes in that city was raided by the police in April 1913, and closed, on orders from the home secretary. In the battle to close the office, the police used clubs, and the women fought back with hatpins and umbrellas.[22]

In June 1913, girls employed at the textile factory of J. Gebhart & Company in Hazelton, Pennsylvania, used hatpins as weapons when warned by striking United Mine Workers and other unions to stay away from the factory. One female worker was arrested on a charge of threatening to use a hatpin on a policeman.[23]

Scenes of major rioting unfolded on the streets of Portland, Oregon, on July 17, 1913, when police with drawn clubs charged some 3,000 people, including members of the Industrial Workers of the World (IWW), sympathizers with the striking female employees of the Oregon Canning Company. One woman, Dr. Marie D. Equi, used a hatpin to jab Patrolman Evans as he tried to arrest her.[24]

Famed UK suffragette Emmeline Pankhurst was arrested in London on the afternoon of July 21, 1913, when she was entering a public hall to attend a weekly political meeting. A large force of police officers took hold of her and removed her from the hall. Some of the women trying to prevent the arrest used hatpins as weapons of offense "and several persons were badly hurt," noted a news story. When Pankhurst arrived at Holloway Jail she refused to leave the conveyance and had to be carried in to the building by the police.[25]

Several fights between strike pickets and rag pickers in shops where the workers refused to join the strike, occurred on August 7, 1913, in New York City. One of the most stubborn battles took place in front of a shop in Vestry Street when a large detachment of girl pickets, led by Fannie Lerner, tried to force girls who worked in the shop to join in the demonstration. A fight between the two sides broke out, during which hair was pulled and faces scratched. Hatpins were also drawn. In this case, the workers succeeded in driving the pickets from the area of the shop.[26]

Three women were placed under arrest and further arrests were expected as the result of anti-conscription rioting that took place in City Hall Park in New York City on June 16, 1917. According to a reporter, it was a riot "during which hat pins were used freely on policemen who attempted to break up the small mob." The demonstrators were protesting against conscription and the war. When the police waded into the crowd of some 300 to break things up, the women fought back, using fists, teeth, and hatpins.[27]

6

Accidental Use of the Hatpin

Sometimes, accidental damage was inflicted due to use of the hatpin—perhaps one might term it collateral damage. It was something that was mentioned in media accounts more as time passed and as the hatpin grew in size, and as the fear of the hatpin grew, and as the crusade against the hatpin increased in pervasiveness and volume.

A story out of Atlanta, Georgia, told of how a Joel Williams, about 17 years old, died as a result of being stabbed by a hatpin in the hands of his friend Cora Young, aged 15. This occurred late in July 1890, during a service held at Antioch Church. Williams and Young both attended, sitting side by side. During the service the restless teenagers began to fool around, with Cora prodding Joel with a pin (not a hatpin). Williams put up with it for a few minutes before he finally took the pin from her hand and threw it on the floor. Quietly Cora drew from her hat a hatpin about five inches long and with all her force drove it into Joel's right side just above his hip. The pin penetrated all the way in until only the head could be seen. People gathered around him after his cries and, once they determined the problem, they pulled the hatpin out. The pain then ceased and the pair remained at the church services until the end. As he walked home Joel suddenly became sick, grew weak, and fell to the ground. His younger sister was with him, and tried to help him home. But they only made it a block before she left him on the porch of a house while she ran home for help. The boy's aunt, Polly Pierce, and her husband were sent for; they arrived and carried the boy home. They could find nothing wrong with him, but they put him to bed. The next morning Joel complained of intense pain in his side and back and could only walk with difficulty. His aunt thought he was fooling and would not allow him to stay in the house. Later in the day she found Joel lying under a tree in the yard, groaning in pain. She put him to bed and called a doctor. For some reason the doctor did not respond to the call until the following day. By that time Joel was beyond the doctor's help. Joel lingered until 4 p.m. Sunday (he had been stabbed on Monday), when he died of what an account called "lockjaw." Cora stated she and Joel had been playing "pins" and he knocked the pin out of her hand; she then took one out of her hat. "Just as I struck at him some one pushed him and he fell against me," she explained. "That drove the pin deep into him. I pulled it [out] myself. I had no idea of hurting Joe, because we were playing, and were always good friends. I never knew he was hurt until his aunty told me yesterday."[1]

During the last weekend in July 1891, a huge crowd journeyed by transit to Redondo Beach, California, from Los Angeles. Every available transit vehicle was said to be in use. Vehicles were so full that when a person in the crowd would get his hands to his sides he could not get them up again. According to the account: "One fellow had a lady's hat pin run through his nose. He could not prevent it. The lady thought she was pinning her hat. He lost so much blood that he fainted."[2]

Paul Jones, described as a "prominent" young man of Caldwell, Ohio, was spending the evening of February 10, 1894, with Laura Dumble, daughter of the editor of the *Republican* newspaper. It seems she had a hatpin in her hand and playfully struck Jones with it, breaking the pin off in one of his limbs; the broken part was buried so deeply that it was impossible to remove. A doctor was called but all efforts to remove the broken pin failed. The journalist wrote that the whole incident was "quite mortifying to the young lady."[3]

An editorial on the above event began with a recap of the incident, with the editor commenting that the story illustrated "the great truth that no young lady should go armed with a hat pin. Especially should no playful young lady go thus armed. A playful young lady and a hat pin are more dangerous than a boy with a gun that isn't loaded. It is to be hoped for the sake of the good name of Caldwell's young ladies that the practice of carrying hat pins as a sort of concealed weapon is not general." This editorial was probably meant as satire.[4]

The Reverend S. H. Phillips of Durham, Pennsylvania, 31 years old, died at St. Luke's Hospital in Bethlehem, Pennsylvania, of blood poisoning on July 30, 1895. Six weeks earlier, a Miss Cope, one of his parishioners, for a jest, pricked him with a hat pin in the leg. Blood poisoning followed; to save his life, the leg was amputated. However, Phillips failed to survive that operation.[5]

Two ladies arrived at Wallack's Theater in New York City on a night in March 1899. Part of the settling-in ritual involved them removing "a couple of flaring and towering hats." One woman had a vacant seat in the row in front of her; the other woman sat behind a young man. The first woman impaled her hat with the pin to the back of the vacant seat. The second lady did the same, only to elicit a howl of pain from the man in the seat, who had been impaled on the hat pin that had gone all the way through the seat and into his back. Management soon had the situation straightened out, with apologies from the woman.[6]

At a performance at the Grand Opera House in Indianapolis early in January 1900, a young man entered the auditorium and got himself comfortably seated. A man and woman who arrived after him sat directly behind him. "She wore a hat that was a triumph of millinery and in accordance with the rules of the theater she removed her hat," remarked a reporter. She drew a long hatpin from her hair and thrust it into the back of the chair in front of her, so that it functioned as a temporary hat hook. The man in front suddenly felt a "stinging sensation" but, apart from a brief twitch, pretended there was nothing wrong. The woman was unaware of any problem. That man sat "literally pinned to the chair" throughout the night's performance, too polite to cause the woman embarrassment, or so the story went.[7]

Early in the performance of a play at the Garden Theatre in New York City on the night of March 3, 1903, the players and the audience were surprised by a cry of pain and then a disturbance between two couples. All four were removed to the lobby, where it was determined that the man in front, Philip B. Levy, had been stabbed in the back by a hatpin wielded by a Mrs. Goetz, who had been in the act of trying to pin her hat to the back of the seat in front of her. The hatpin went all the way through, stabbing Levy. Mrs. Goetz was mortified, and after apologies were extended, the incident was put aside.[8]

As the result of being scratched by a hatpin, Howard T. Miller, 20, died in Binghamton, New York, in February 1907. A few days earlier he had been sitting beside a woman on an electric car when she turned her head as he happened to be leaning toward her, and her hatpin accidentally scratched him behind his left ear. Nothing was thought of the injury for several days, when the wound began to swell and blood poisoning developed.[9]

An editorial summarized Miller's death as a consequence of a scratch from a hatpin and declared, "Each woman sticks her hat on her head with at least three pins, and some of them use five or six. They are usually about nine inches in length and often longer, protruding in some cases half a foot beyond the hat or the hair." He thought protective tips should be used on the items. He concluded by asking, "Must man appeal to the law to protect him from these cruel barbs and points?"[10]

An accident befell Conductor Dan Sanford on a Pasadena-to-Los Angeles car which left Pasadena at 1:15 p.m. on December 27, 1908. It was a very crowded streetcar, holding about 130 people. Halfway through the journey, a girl with a Merry Widow hat, which was secured to her head "by huge hatpins," blocked the way of the conductor as he tried to pass through the car. He tried to dodge around it and she, as she saw his attempt, also dodged. It was an unpleasant move for the conductor. One of the hatpins stabbed his nose, from which blood streamed forth. After a long interval he finally was able to stem the flow of blood.[11]

According to a September 1909 report in a New York City newspaper, a "small riot" took place on the subway there, precipitated by a woman's hatpin. It took place on a Broadway rush-hour train that was packed to the limit. The woman with the hatpin—it was said to have protruded a good four inches beyond her hat—found herself swaying with the motion of the car, as did the other passengers. In that swaying, the pin struck the corner of a fellow passenger's eye. Another passenger seized the point of the pin in her hand to try and push it back, but withdrew with a scratched hand. People began then to duck away and the people they bumped into protested.[12]

Because the South Covington and Cincinnati Streetcar Company allowed on one of its cars a woman with a hatpin sticking out far enough to reach the eye of Robert E. Dugan, a music composer, the corporation was made the defendant in a suit for $25,000 in damages, brought by Dugan in January 1911. When the car lurched, in Covington, Kentucky, he said, he was thrown against the woman, whose hatpin stuck into his left eye. Dugan said both his eyes were affected, his sight was threatened, and he was then incapable of earning his usual $3,500-$4,000-a-year income. His action was based on the grounds that the company was negligent in permitting the car to be crowded and to have permitted "such a dangerous projecting hatpin to stand in the car."[13]

Captain Andrew England, described as a well-known sea captain on the New England coast, died in Boston in February 1911 as a result of a jab from a hatpin. "This is the first death recorded in the United States since the long hatpin came into use," wrote a journalist, erroneously. England came to Boston some five weeks before his death, from his home on Peaks Island, Maine. He and his wife were in a crowded trolley car when a woman standing beside him turned her head suddenly. Although he was jabbed by a hatpin, he only received a slight prick to the cheek. He thought nothing of it for a couple of weeks or so, but then his face began to swell and he was taken to the City Hospital. It was too late: he died on February 14 of blood poisoning. Captain England was 67 years of age.[14]

On the afternoon of June 12, 1911, Ruth Feighor was riding on a streetcar, returning to work after her lunch break. Sitting in the seat beside her was Velma Hickman, whose hatpins protruded somewhat from her hat. Feighor had taken note of this, but, in spite of the care she used, a lurch of the car sent the hatpin into her left eye. The pin missed the ball of the eye and there was no serious injury; Ruth was expected to recover fully within a few days.[15]

Vaudeville actor Daniel Mack was attempting to make his way through a dense theater crowd on Market Street in San Francisco on the evening of August 1, 1911, when a woman beside him turned her head. A long steel pin projecting from her hat passed through Mack's right eyelid, through his nose and into his left eye. "You brute? How dare you touch my hat?" the woman cried as she felt a frantic tug on her headgear. Without looking around she wrenched the pin free and disappeared into the crowd while Mack staggered blindly about on the sidewalk. According to the story, Mack was in danger of losing his sight.[16]

A news story published on October 18, 1911, stated: "The murderous hatpin, used exclusively by women," made its presence felt in Pendleton, Oregon, that morning. Ed Davis was a railway employee and while passengers were stepping off a local train, Davis was assisting passengers to alight. One wore a large hat with a protruding hatpin. As she turned her head suddenly, the point struck Davis in the chin, going all the way in to the bone. According to the report, he wiped away the blood "and remarked that the next congressional candidate who wants his vote will have to incorporate in his platform a promise to work for legislation to protect mankind from the dangerous hatpin."[17]

The Reverend Edward Myers was stabbed by a hatpin in November 1911. It took place on a Pullman car as the train was pulling into Baltimore. Meyers was in the same sleeper car as a woman and her companion. When the car lurched, the woman was thrown into Meyers, resulting in his being jabbed in the nose.[18]

Miss Julia Mason of Libertyville, Iowa, was hospitalized in March 1912 as the result of a hatpin jab she received in one of her eyes during a store's bargain-counter rush. Physicians said she had lost sight in that eye.[19]

Jabbed by a long hatpin worn by an unidentified woman in a streetcar in Seattle on the night of May 5, 1912, E. J. Anderson, a well-known businessman, was expected to lose the sight in his right eye, according to a reporter. The car lurched and the women swayed in the aisle, resulting in the point of the pin catching Anderson in the eye.[20]

With respect to Anderson's injury, it was reported that, after the first sharp pain, the victim felt nothing. The woman on the car turned and excused herself, with Anderson saying something to her about it being all right. Nothing happened for awhile, but then the eye began to water. That evening he began experiencing pain, prompting him to be checked in at the hospital, where he was placed under the care of Dr. C. E. Noble. "An ordinance limiting the length of hatpins is urgently needed," Noble was quoted as saying. "The points of the pins should not be allowed to protrude beyond the brims of the hats, or they should be equipped with buttons. So long as some are permitted to wear these dangerous pins, the eyesight of the public will be threatened, especially in crowded cars." A number of Seattle councilmen, reportedly, discussed the advisability of introducing an anti-hatpin ordinance.[21]

Alfred Canancamp was a prosperous farmer who was in a Wooster, Ohio, department store doing his Christmas shopping in December 1912. He had worked his way through a crowd when a woman wearing a big hat with a long pin suddenly turned her head. The pin grazed his eye and passed through the right side of his nose, three inches of it project-

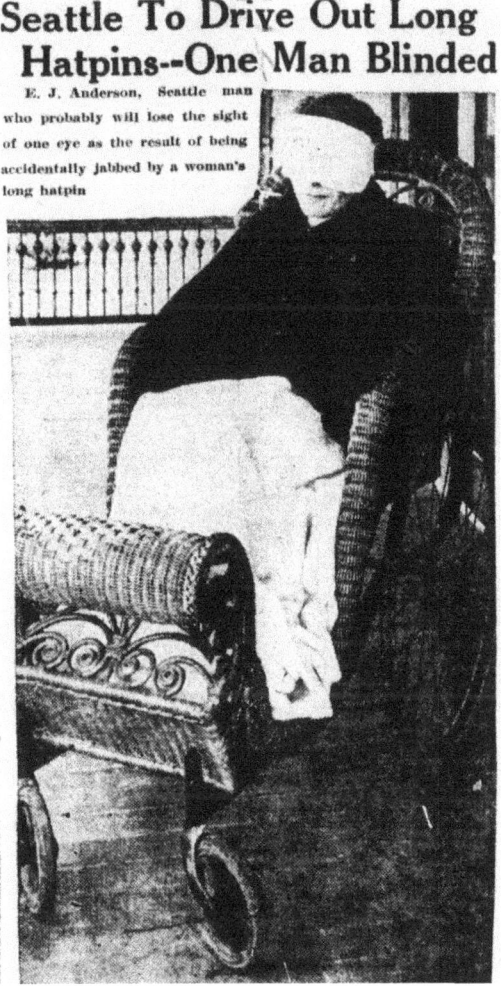

E. J. Anderson, a 1912 victim of an accidental hatpin stabbing in a crowded streetcar, is shown recuperating in the hospital. Such incidents led to pervasive crusades against the hatpin, particularly the long and protruding hatpin.

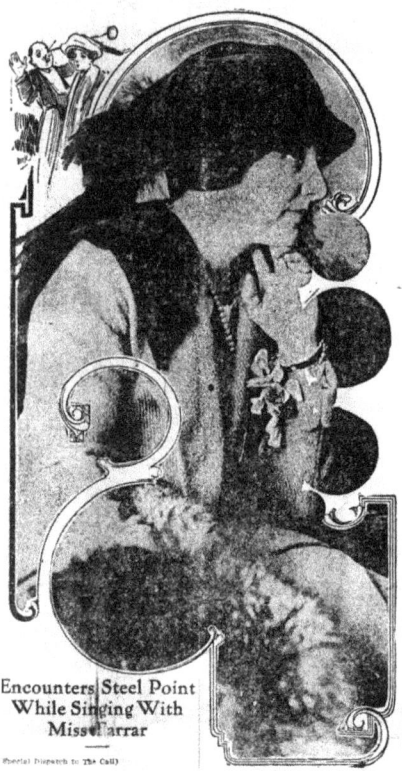

Hatpin Pierces Caruso Tenor Exclaims 'Ouch!'

Geraldine Farrar listening to a talking machine's rendition of a song in her own voice.

Encounters Steel Point While Singing With Miss Farrar

Special Dispatch to The Call

ing from the left side. He was compelled to await the arrival of a physician before the pin could be extracted.[22]

The most famous victim of the hatpin was undoubtedly the noted opera star Enrico Caruso, who had an encounter with the sharp point of a hatpin worn by the opera diva Geraldine Farrar. The incident took place in the first act of Puccini's *Tosca*, which was having its season's premiere at the Metropolitan Opera House in New York City in January 1913. Caruso took Farrar in his arms after the first aria and placed his right arm about her neck, only to impale his thumb on the point of her hatpin. He shook his arm and hand, stuck the injured thumb in his mouth, and then applied his handkerchief to the slight wound. Farrar and the audience laughed, but Caruso only frowned.[23]

While performing onstage in 1913, opera star Enrico Caruso received an accidental jab from the hatpin of his co-star, Geraldine Farrar.

7

The Hatpin Abroad

The problems that existed in America over hatpins ran a similar course in many foreign nations where the crusades against the hatpins and the legislative attempts to control them were pursued with as much vigor as was seen in the United States, and with about the same success rate. Almost no reports surfaced in the American press as to whether or not women in foreign nations used the hatpin as an offensive or defensive weapon, with the sole exception of suffragettes in the United Kingdom being so inclined.

One of the foreign nations that initiated a great deal of activity against hatpins was Germany. An editorial in a Washington State newspaper in July 1909 mentioned the police chief of Hanover, Germany (but did not name him), and said of that individual: "There is a savior of menaced humanity." For some time, continued the editor, women of Hanover had been using very long hatpins and that led to many scratches and punctures inflicted on bystanders. This police chief announced that, henceforth, when an accident occurred to another person through a woman's hatpin she would be subject to arrest and prosecution for assault. The editor believed this "suggests that the American guardians of the public security have not blazed before them a plain path of duty. Perhaps if the Hanoverian doctrine is locally adopted it will be possible to ride in Walla Walla [Washington] street cars without being threatened with permanent disfigurement or total blindness."[1]

In November 1910 it was reported that the police president of Berlin "has declared war on the dangerously protruding hat pin." In proclamations issued that month he called the attention of women to the many recent reports of injuries inflicted by hatpins that projected beyond the rims of women's hats. Especially frequent were the accidents in streetcars "and usually men have been the victims." He called upon women to cease using long pins or turn the points so they would not be a constant menace to the traveling public.²

On March 27, 1911, cards were posted in all the streetcars of Berlin, requesting that women passengers not wear long hatpins. The notice pointed out that those ornamental articles were liable to injure the wearers' fellow passengers. Herr Von Jagew, head of the Berlin police, issued a request to all women not to wear those long hatpins, but the results from that request, said a reporter, have "not been altogether satisfactory."³

The Berlin Elevated Railways Company announced in June 1911 that it had joined with the Consolidated Berlin Street Railways and the prefect of police in the war against the projecting hatpin, posting in its cars an order that women passengers must place a protective guard over the end of the projecting pins. However, in spite of such orders and the warnings, noted a journalist, "No abatement of the menace can be noticed and accidents from this source are constantly reported."⁴

One month later the railway administration of Saarbrücken, Germany, gave orders to its officials that ladies whose hats were attached with long hatpins were to be requested to remove those pins; if they declined, they were to be prevented from traveling in the trains and to be called upon to leave the stations. If they refused to leave, the police were to be summoned and those women were to be arrested.⁵

It was announced, on August 10, 1911, that dangerously protruding hatpins were under a ban by police in Berlin. The police department in that city had announced that a fine of as much as $225 or two years' imprisonment could be inflicted for injuring any person with a hatpin. The victim of a hatpin accident was to be entitled to financial compensation in any amount up to $1,500. Milder penalties were said to have been imposed against the hatpin wearers some time earlier, but they proved inefficient.⁶

When Washington, D.C., police commissioner Rudolph was in Germany in August 1911, one of the things that impressed him the most was the city of Hamburg's hatpin ordinance. While details of that ordinance were not given, the reporter in the U.S. claimed that three eyes had been "sacrificed" by the hatpin in various parts of the nation during the past few days "so it would not be a bad idea for the Commissioner to go out after a similar ordinance here in the District."⁷

Police authorities in Hamburg reportedly issued an order on July 20, 1912, whereby any woman who entered a streetcar with unprotected hatpins was subject to ejection by the conductor. For the benefit of strangers and visitors to the city, the company had provided its conductors with hatpin protectors, which they were then selling to passengers for one cent each.⁸

According to an April 1913 news story, following prohibition of long hatpins "formerly worn" by women, the police were about to open a campaign against projecting feathers and trimmings stiffened with wire or other potentially hazardous material. Many men were said to have made complaints about projecting ornaments and, recently, the eye of a straphanger had been injured by a wired feather protruding from a hat. A prohibition order had not yet been issued but it was understood to be pending. Women were reported to be indignant and stated that they might ignore the proposed order.[9]

Police authorities in Hamburg instituted a regulation, as of October 1913, ordering tramway car conductors, under penalty of losing their licenses, not to allow women with unprotected hatpins to remain in their cars. The police were also ordered to take the names and addresses of women with unprotected hatpins, who were subject to a fine of from $5 to $10.[10]

According to a German newspaper, on November 8, 1913, "The crusade against the dangerous hatpin is raging fiercely in all German public conveyances. Conductors of tram cars, etc., must first of all look at the hats of women passengers before handing them a ticket. If the hatpin is not protected by a safety protector he stops the car and the woman is politely handed out." Related was the story of a woman in Düsseldorf who had been marketing and boarded a tram with her basket. Hardly had she sat down than the conductor looked at her dangerously protruding hatpin and told her she had to get off. Then a bright idea struck the woman. She searched into her market basket for a small potato and stuck it on her hatpin. The conductor was said to have been satisfied.[11]

In Paris, France, according to an August 1909 story, "Official war has begun against the murderous hat pins worn by women." It also stated: "With the advent of the big hat it has become fashionable for a woman to go about the streets with her head bristling on all sides with hat pin weapons of many designs. Sometimes the pins are nearly a foot and a half long and are like thin bladed swords." Numerous reports of accidents had surfaced with most of those taking place in the crowds of people about in the railway stations and in the shops: "Hundreds of persons have been wounded by hat pins, some seriously." A few days earlier, it was said, a man riding in a car lost an eye as the result of a woman's sudden toss of her head. And, a week earlier, a salesgirl was wounded during a buyers' rush. A baby in arms, killed accidentally by a hatpin, was reported to have been the most recent victim. (However, no details of any kind were presented with these "cases.") "The Paris press has begun to make war on the long hat pin, with the result that the police have taken up the matter and are considering a measure to regulate the length. Since June 1 the police have recorded more than fifty accidents due to the pin," concluded the article.[12]

A very brief article that appeared in the American press in November 1910 noted that striking dressmakers in Paris had used hatpins and umbrellas as weapons when they were attacked by the police as they picketed.[13]

The dangers of hatpins in all places where crowds assembled occupied the Paris municipal council during a week in December 1912. Tony Michaud, who introduced the topic, mentioned nine cases of injuries caused by pins protruding from hats. It was pointed out that the mayors of Lyon, France, and several other towns had issued decrees obliging women to protect the points of their hatpins. A Mr. Lepine said he had drawn up such an ordinance for Paris but had not put it into force as he thought that a change in fashions would soon make it unnecessary; however, if the council wished, he would at once issue an order that all hatpin points had to be covered by a protector and he would instruct the police to summon all offenders. The council at once voted that the prefect of police should take action.[14]

According to a January 1914 account, the new police regulations penalizing long hatpin wearers, which went into effect in Paris at the start of that year, were being rigidly enforced. An Englishwoman out walking in Paris was stopped by a policeman who wanted her name and address, indicating the two hatpins that stuck out from her hat unprotected by the required legal guard. She did not speak French and was becoming alarmed until a Frenchman came up to her and handed her two hatpin guards he had purchased from a market stall earlier that day. "Put these on your hatpins and there will be no more trouble," he told her with a smile.[15]

Three months later, in Paris, it was observed that the police prefect in that city had twice issued "stern edicts" against unprotected hatpins, yet the Paris women still disobeyed. On April 6, 1914, the prefect issued orders to guards and conductors on transit vehicles to refuse admission to all women wearing unprotected hatpins. Inquiries from a reporter at the headquarters of both omnibus and railway companies revealed that not a single report of such an exclusion had been made that day, although "there is hardly an omnibus in which a deadly hatpin is not plainly to be seen."[16]

Paris declared war on long hatpins, again, in May 1917. This time it was Mr. Laurent, the Paris prefect of police, who issued the edict. Large placards had appeared in all railway stations of the French metropolis that day, warning the fashionable that long, protruding hatpins were henceforth "without the law. The pins must be either left at home or effectively sheathed."[17]

In Vienna, Austria, the first arrest under a new hatpin law had been made in February 1911, and the prisoner, a young woman, was said to be prepared to take the case to the highest court of Austria. This began when a pedestrian, Richard Englemenn, was scratched on the nose by a hatpin worn by a girl who passed him on the street. He seized the offender—whose name was given as Gretchen Epstein—and took her to the nearest policeman. She was arrested, arraigned, and fined 36 cents, with the alternative of 12 hours in jail. Outraged at this treatment, she hired a lawyer and an appeal was launched. When the case came before a magistrate, Epstein was wearing the hat with the offending pin, the point of which projected. She pointed out that the hatpin did not project beyond the brim; the magistrate countered that a brim that projected so far from the head was in itself a danger to passersby. He added that every woman who wore a hatpin that could possibly endanger her fellow citizens would feel the rigor of the law.[18]

In May 1913, a city official in Vienna issued an order prohibiting unprotected, protruding hatpins on the train. A journalist wrote, "Whether the conductors will prove equal to their new police duties is another question. Probably the fair Viennese will continue to ride on the municipal tramways whether their hatpins be long or short and protected or not."[19]

A February 1911 news story stated that the prosecution of violators of the hatpin regulation had stopped in Budapest, Hungary, but it was not a woman's victory. The city administration, it was reported, found the prosecutions so numerous and costly that the police were instructed whenever they saw a hatpin with an unprotected point to summarily seize it. The officers responded and more than 1,200 hatpins were seized.[20]

At Baden, Switzerland, the local authorities had voted in a new law that absolutely prohibited the wearing of hatpins that protruded farther than one inch from the hat. That was in June 1911. The regulation was said to have arisen from the number of complaints and accidents which had happened recently. The police in Baden were authorized to arrest any woman wearing such a dangerous hatpin and the fine ranged from $2.50 and upward.[21]

In September 1911, the archbishop of Geneva, Switzerland, issued a letter to the clergy of his diocese, in which he said the size of women's hats "is a grave impediment to the proper attention which the faithful should pay to religious functions, as the hats often prevent people from getting a glimpse of the altar or the officiating priest." Even more serious, continued the archbishop, is "the danger arising from the use of stiletto-like hatpins which constitute a source of real peril to the congregation, especially in a crowded church." A journalist commented that this "frank declaration," which followed the bishop of Padua's recent condemnation of modern fashion, was regarded as a reflection of the opinions of Pope Pius X. It was believed that the pope had taken that indirect way of conveying his opinions so as to avoid any criticism that might be leveled directly at the Vatican.[22]

Hatpins protruding from women's hats in Zurich, Switzerland, would cost the wearer 15 cents for every inch the hatpin protruded; it was reported, in December 1911, as stipulated in a recent ordinance issued by that city. As well, the hatpin was to be confiscated on the spot as "the Zurich courts rule that hatpins are dangerous weapons."[23]

A new law from Zurich that went into effect in January 1912 prohibiting women from wearing hatpins whose sharp ends were not protected. This decree was reported to be keeping the police busy: in a single day, 110 hatpin–wearing women were stopped in the streets and their names and addresses taken down. For first-time offenders the fine was $1. That new law was in place, it was reported, as a consequence of the number of hatpin accidents, especially in tram cars.[24]

In London, England, in October 1913, Judge Harrington assessed a woman $15,000 damages for injuring another woman's cheeks with her hatpin; he referred to such implements as "deadly weapons." In this particular incident both women were boarding an omnibus when the accident happened. The court held that it was unnecessary to prove any other negligence than the wearing of a hatpin without a guard. Writers for the two leading law journals in New York City commented on that decision and urged the New York City Board of Aldermen to pass an ordinance prohibiting the wearing of unguarded hatpins in the States; they agreed that the English decision "as a legal proposition is entirely correct." They also suggested that the New York laws permit a hatpin victim to recover damages.[25]

For going about the city of Sydney, Australia, with their hatpins protruding, 60 women—most of them prominent in society—were tried, convicted, and fined on October 30, 1912. The women went to jail rather than pay their fines, declaring they would not submit to "iniquitous and unnecessary legislation." The women asserted that if further arrests and imprisonments were ordered because of the hatpin ordinance they would declare a "hunger strike" in jail.[26]

A syndicated columnist in America by the name of Sophie Irene Loeb commented on the Sydney case in one of her columns. She claimed that the Australian women in question wanted rules for others but none for themselves—a problem she thought existed in general in society. Loeb wrote,

> If your hatpin is too long and there's a possibility of it touching someone in a crowded car get a shorter one or wear an elastic around your hat, my sister Australians. Hunger strikes or rebellion against just rules never got anybody anything but a season of sickness and an awakening to the fact that the display of temper could only be tyranny to one's self.[27]

According to a February 1913 account, Stockholm, Sweden, authorities in the Swedish capital had provided municipal streetcar conductors with point protectors, with instructions to offer them at cost (one cent apiece) to each woman whose projecting hatpin endangered the safety of other passengers. This came about as a result of a series of accidents on the city's transit system. Reportedly, the idea had been a great success, with about 6,000 protectors sold on the first day they were offered. Editorials in German newspapers were in favor of implementing this concept in their cities as well. From Hanover came the complaint that women there paid no heed to the civil injunction found in every streetcar: "Kindly protect your hatpins." The situation was to be so bad in Hamburg that conductors had been especially empowered to prevent women with dangerously protruding hatpins from entering public conveyances.[28]

A relatively long article on the hatpin issue in Europe was published in a New York City paper in May 1913, under the headline, "Europe Fights Long Hatpins." German officials were said to be making the most "heroic efforts to stamp out the practice." In Austria, the Ministry of Railroads had issued an order that women wearing unprotected hatpins should not be permitted to ride on the state railways until they had removed "the perilous pin." The management of the Vienna municipal tramways had gone even further in directing conductors to compel such offenders to leave the car immediately. If they refused, the conductor would call in the police to have them removed by force. In Berlin, the chief of police went a step further, decreeing that the city's women had but two weeks to abolish long hatpins or provide guards. Offenders of the ordinance would be fined up to $15 for each offense and, if they did not pay, they would be imprisoned. At a European conference, the Bavarian Minister of Communications proposed a rule absolutely forbidding long and unprotected hatpins in all international carriages; it was understood that the conference had struck a committee to carry out the proposal. In Portsmouth, England, authorities had posted a request in the tramcars warning women to avoid wearing dangerous hatpins. "So far the notice seems to have had excellent results,"[29] read the account.

8

Agitation, Hysteria, Crusades and Legislation Against the Hatpin

This agitation, hysteria, crusades and the legislative efforts against the hatpin reached a peak in America in the period 1909 to 1912, with particular emphasis on the years 1910 and 1911. But assaults on the fashion item began in earlier years, however, at a much lower level. One of the first such critical attacks on the hatpin was delivered in December 1895 and it came from an unnamed judge in St. Louis. He was cited as saying, "Did you ever realize that in spite of the stringent laws against carrying concealed weapons women are constantly armed with the most terrible weapon—i.e., the hatpin. It is long and sharp as an Italian stiletto, and in spite of recent proofs to the contrary I would rather face a woman with a loaded revolver than one with a hatpin in hand. If women only had the nerve to use it, you wouldn't hear of many assaults upon them."[1]

An editorial cartoon appeared in print in April 1897. It showed two burglars fleeing a house. One burglar said to the other to run for his life. When the second burglar asked why, the first one replied that the lady of the house was coming after them with two hatpins. The headline of the cartoon was "Dangerous Weapons."[2]

An August 1897 report explained that the long hatpin that was being worn that summer by women in London had caused a lot of trouble. London newspapers had started a crusade against the new-style hatpin due to the swarm of accidents that had occurred in public places. The long hatpin fad was said to have started in London. In New York City, women began wearing the long hatpin in the early part of June 1897; that new style of pin was said to be anywhere from one to three inches longer than the old style. Most women used three or four of them to secure their hat to their

8. Agitation, Hysteria, Crusades and Legislation   117

head. As one journalist wrote, "What started the fashion is one of the things no man will ever be able to understand. They are the style, and women will wear them, and that's all there is to it." The journalist added that he hoped the London newspapers would succeed in their crusade against the item; after all, "There haven't been any accidents here [in the U.S.] from the long hatpin yet."³

An article published in California in September 1897 began by declaring: "A crusade has been started against the hat pin, and the evidence advanced regarding it certainly calls for its classification as a deadly weapon." Then it went on to give two examples of lost eyesight resulting from people in separate events in crowded transit cars. (These examples were both from the United Kingdom but that fact was not mentioned in the article, implying that they had taken place in America.) Those examples "show the great dangers of this article of the toilette. It should be retired, if possible."⁴

This editorial cartoon, from April 1897, was one of the first to deem the hatpin a dangerous weapon and to point out the power it gave to women.

Another item from the same time period mentioned the crusade, although this one specified that the accidents resulting in lost eyesight occurred in the United Kingdom. "The loss of eyesight in a male victim aroused more horror in London than loss in a woman," the writer concluded. The victim was attended to by Dr. Edgar Stevenson, of London. He said to a reporter, "I am informed, sir, that the hatpin is an absolute necessity, and that it is quite useless to press for its abolition. Nor, so long as it is not used as a weapon of attack and defense, as in some parts of the Continent, is such an extreme step called for." Stevenson continued, "But I think it may well be pointed out to ladies that they have in their hands, or rather in their hair, a dangerous instrument which might easily be made less formidable to others, by being worn of a moderate length. To use a ten inch pin to attach a hat to a four inch bush of hair seems to me not only full of risk to the public but an ungainly and hideous device that can scarcely be considered to add to the personal attraction of the wearer."[5]

Another editorial in an American newspaper that touched on the London crusade appeared in October 1897: "The hatpin has become the weapon of the women of the Tenderloin district of New York City, and a most dangerous one it is, and the police, who seem to be the chief sufferers, are seriously considering if legislative action cannot be taken to abolish hatpins altogether. They want the carrying of them to be made unlawful, just as it is unlawful to carry concealed weapons." After mentioning the London newspaper crusade, briefly, the editor noted that two notorious women of the Tenderloin district, Mary McGovern and Ellen Lang, had each launched numerous attacks on policemen with their hatpins. The editor added, "There are times, however, when the hatpin as a weapon comes in quite properly and does considerable good. It is when a respectable woman is grossly insulted. As a masher discourager the hatpin is an unqualified success. A determined jab in the arm or cheek or leg with a hatpin in the hands of an insulted woman always convinces the male would-be fascinator that he has business elsewhere which demands his immediate attention."[6]

In March 1898, a newspaper editor remarked that the choice of weapons of personal defense was indicative of the nature of the chooser— the Italian has his stiletto, the Afro-American has his razor. "Simultaneously with the new woman has come the introduction into the armory of the nineteenth century of a new weapon—one unknown and unsung through all the ages of a militant past. It is the hatpin." He added, "The hatpin bears no ascertainable relation to the modern weapons perfected by the other sex.... The glory of its discovery belongs to the new woman alone, unless we prove an analog to the dagger in the garter that protected the honor of the Italian girl of [the] last century." He argued that a weapon was to be judged solely on the basis of the results it achieved. The mass of data in the case of the hatpin was not large but "singularly uniform. When the hatpin starts for a victim it usually runs him to the earth; it keeps in any climate, and is free from all liability to internal explosion. The cost of maintenance is not great, and it is always ready for action."[7]

The first attempt at legislating against the hatpin came in the New York State Assembly. On February 20, 1900, Assemblyman N. Taylor Phillips, of New York, introduced a bill that had as its ostensible purpose

8. Agitation, Hysteria, Crusades and Legislation 119

the protection of the police force of the larger cities of the state. The bill amended the section of the penal code that related to the carrying of concealed deadly weapons to include in the list of banned items "hat pins more than three inches in length." (There were few such implements measuring less than three inches long, perhaps none at all.) Phillips gave as his reason for the bill the fact that "many fine, large policemen have been maimed through the vigorous use of a good strong six-inch hat pin in the hands of an enraged woman whose escapades had brought her into the clutches of the law." He added, with dismay, "Why, they jab them right into a fellow when they get mad and it hurts awfully. It isn't right to allow such weapons to be carried by the ladies." Phillips was greatly incensed about a report that his bill was introduced in the interests of a company that was about to put a new hat fastener on the market: "The idea of such a thing. I wouldn't lend myself to any such scheme."[8]

The introduction of that bill provoked a considerable number of editorial responses. One defender of the Second Amendment wrote, "The right of the people to keep and bear arms shall not be infringed," so long as they wore their hatpins in plain sight. There were laws prohibiting the carrying of concealed weapons, the writer pointed out. The hatpin was visible, at least both ends and therefore was not concealed. Nor could a hatpin be prohibited on the basis of size since the law said nothing about the size of a gun a man carried, so long as it was not concealed. "Let the ladies wear the hat pins, say we," he concluded. "The possession of such a weapon is a notice to the loafer or assaulter to keep hands off. As a rule, a woman will fight only when driven into a corner or in defense of one she loves—and in such cases it is not more than right that she should have an effective weapon within easy reach."[9]

In addressing the New York State Assembly about his measure, Phillips thundered, "Why does a woman want a hatpin at all? I don't wear one, yet if a woman puts on a felt or derby hat just like mine she finds it necessary to perforate it with pins and attach it to herself in a dozen places. There is no more reason why a woman should wear a hatpin than why a man should. I suspect that many of them do it in order to have a weapon handy."[10]

Another comment on the New York State measure came from an unnamed columnist for a Texas newspaper: "It is a funny fact that every once in a while some conscientious legislator gets one or another bee in his bonnet with regard to legislating reform in women's clothes—and gets laughed at for his pains." He reminded his readers that women could not vote and had to submit to being classed with "paupers, idiots, and Indians not taxed, but she will wear just what she pleases." He added, "This particular bill of course has no value except its utter impracticability which makes it funny and fun has a practical value." A pin three inches long "is no hat pin," he argued, and if she drew out her hatpin as a weapon "how could a woman keep her hat on?" In any event it was a measure that was not enforceable. "In truth the bonnet wearers are not worried over the proposed bill."[11]

Yet another editorial on the proposed bill stated that Phillips was being induced to write the bill because of the many cases on record of infuriated females using hatpins "to adjust personal differences, not only with their own, but also with the sterner sex." The editorialist believed that if such charges could be proved to be facts, then hatpins should be "cut down to nothing." He added, "Better give up hat pins altogether and trust native genius to devise something neat and serviceable to hold the hat in place without having the law look upon it as a poignard [long knife], a dagger or a dirk."[12]

In an editorial in a Washington State newspaper published on June 20, 1903, a warning was issued regarding the hatpin. Acknowledging that women had found an effective weapon of defense against the masher, the hatpin, like "all other weapons, may be misused. It promises to become as deadly as the unloaded pistol." After mentioning a woman from Kansas City who had publicly spoken out in favor of the hatpin as a weapon of self-defense, he stated that "some women who never have [the] opportunity to defend themselves against mashers show a disposition to use the hatpin anyway." He worried (citing a case or two), that there were "indications of grave danger that the use of the hatpin as a weapon of aggression as well as defense is apt to be carried too far." Properly employed on mashers, he argued, the "use of the hatpin is a stroke of genius. But the woman who no man would think of mashing has no excuse for using it." A further cause of concern for this journalist was that the "disposition inherent in women [is] to be imitative" and that if "the practice keeps up at the rate that has obtained for the last few weeks it is possible that women may be required to take out a license for carrying hatpins as for other deadly weapons."[13]

Three months later, a different editor suggested that the inventor of the hatpin had created a problem instead of solving one. He mentioned a Chicago case wherein a woman defended herself from a highwayman by the use of her pin and remarked, "If this were the only instance of the employment of the hatpin as a weapon of defense, it would hardly be worthy of mention. And if the hatpin were perverted to this use merely, there would be no problem. But weapons of defense become weapons of offense."

He went on to mention a couple of cases in which women fought each other with hatpins. "But it is the criminal minority who force the peaceful majority to make laws and pass ordinances. And so it is not improbable that the future may witness legislation that shall in a measure suppress the hatpin. Perhaps a special permit will be required to wear it. Perhaps the law will demand that bonnet ties and elastics be restored."[14]

An editor of a New York City newspaper wrote in September 1903: "As things are going, the time is not far distant when it will be necessary to enact a law designating the hat pin as a deadly weapon, and making its possession a misdemeanor, if not a crime. This means a change in the fashion of hats, especially the variety known as picture hats, which will be greatly to the advantage of feminine humanity." He went on to state abolishing the hatpin altogether was "a measure of public safety," and that women would revert to the "excellent custom of our mothers and grandmothers" of holding bonnets in place with ribbons tied under the chin. Perhaps most troubling to this editor was the fact that the hatpin "is dangerously available and convenient as a lethal weapon and females having use for lethal weapons have acquired a fatal facility for its use for purposes offensive and defensive." After listing several examples of ill usage, he wrote of the hatpin in general: "It is long, lithe, elastic, sharply pointed and keenly penetrating. Anyone may with good reason be afraid of it, and women who would prefer not to be classed as dangerous on slight provocation would do well to discard it as quickly as possible."[15]

"Death lurks in the hatpin," or so the American press concluded with respect to the United Kingdom medical press, which had commented upon its "murderous propensities" and the means by which a modern state could protect itself against it. "Feminine fancy has ordained that the skewer-like hatpin is an essential element of cephalic attire, and must be retained. It is an instrument with potential energy for endless damage. Numerous accidents, some of which have proved fatal, have resulted from a persistence in the practice of hat-fixing by this convenient but dangerous article." The writer of this news account also favored a return to elastic or ribbons such as were used in the past, or some other safe means to affix hats to heads. "Unless woman will look to this matter mere man will have to intervene, if only in his own interests and as a means of self-protection," he concluded. "Possibly the plan of licensing might be followed with advantage. Just as a man may not carry a revolver without a license, so a woman may not carry that hardly less deadly weapon, a hat pin, without a yearly license purchased from the state."[16]

According to a September 1904 piece, the modern woman carried about her person "at least two concealed weapons in the form of the newest hatpins. The breadth of the crown of the up-to-date hat has made it necessary to add two inches to the length of the already sufficiently dangerous hat pin, and the result is astonishing. The old-fashioned gold or silver pin of seven or eight inches in length is of no use whatever in securing this summer's hats. The new pin measures ten inches from tip to handle and is made of an inflexible metal to pierce the heavy straws [that is, straw hats]."[17]

When Ella Anderson of Paterson, New Jersey, used a hatpin to successfully defend herself against an assault in November 1904, an editor wrote, "She utilized a weapon of defense that seems to be coming into somewhat general use. The hatpin has long occupied a prominent but inoffensive position, doing its duty where it could be seen by all men, but until recent years content to keep within its legitimate sphere of feminine usefulness." This editor believed that the hatpin would become to modern woman what the spur was to Minerva, or the lance to the ancient Amazon. "It combines within itself all the elements of a defensive weapon. It is always within easy reach, it is an instrument of sharply pointed steel and it can be handled with great dexterity and skill." Henceforth, he concluded, "Let us hear nothing of the defenseless sex. Every woman carries a hat pin and, therefore, every woman is armed. Let her go forth boldly, banishing all timidity, and conscious that before the onslaught of the hat pin all men must quail."[18]

Anne Rhodes was president of the Common Council in New York City and at the start of 1905 she convened her society for its annual moot Parliament. Alderman Edward Addison Greeley reported for the committee on investigation of the danger arising from the hatpin. In the end they carried on a joke debate on the topic, with no specific conclusions being drawn.[19]

An editorial in March 1906 mentioned several horrific examples of related injuries, such as a woman falling from a vehicle and having her hatpin jammed through her skull, leading to her death. "The hatpin is a fiendish implement and gives to the most feminine of women an air of bristly defiance. For its number is legion, it is always found in the plural. One hatpin is not sufficient to anchor the smallest of hats upon the wearer's head." He had observed that most women used many more than one pin "and half a dozen sharp and threatening points are likely to emerge from the feathers and flowers of her hat."[20]

A very brief editorial in October 1906 declared: "A girl, no matter how pretty, who bristles with the points of obtrusive hatpins is a menace to the public welfare and should be legislated against like mobs and invasions."²¹

It was reported in April 1907 that a new reformer had appeared in San Francisco, a man upset at riding streetcars and worrying about being harpooned by women's hatpins. The leader in the new war "against vanities" was Robert R. Russ, a real estate broker in the city. He suggested that the San Francisco Board of Supervisors pass a law limiting the length of hatpins to something less than 18 inches, which "length seems to be the mode. As an alternative, it is suggested that buttons might be placed on long pins after the fashion of protected rapiers." Russ was said to be strongly in favor of a law of protection in this matter. He was not heard from again.²²

One week later the same newspaper reported that a San Francisco woman by the name of Anastasia Carlyle had invented the hatpin shield, and applied for a patent for the device. It was just one of many such devices that sometimes were mentioned in the press. None ever had even the least bit of success.²³

A lengthy article that was originally published in a Chicago newspaper in May 1909 and then reprinted in other publications commented on the benefits of the pistol, the stiletto, and the razor, but "overlapping all three, more difficult to oppose, more intangible than all, the fashionable up-to-date female of today carries an article of self-defense more formidable than any of the above—in the satanic creation of the wicked hatpin. This little article is as cruel and relentless as the cleverest schemes of vice or wickedness could desire, and numberless crimes are laid at its door, yet it has its good points as well, for it has been used for the crushing of evil and also as a powerful protector in the time of need." Should you find yourself in a streetcar or in any assembly where there are women around, he advised, observe their hats: "See if there is not inserted in every bonnet, hat or toque worn by the ladies a most wicked-looking long pin with a very sharp point with which the lady holds her headgear in proper adjustment, but one prick of which could cause immediate danger, putting out the eye, scratching the face, penetrating the bone if enough force were used, or even, like a tiny dagger, sometimes so artfully concealed, could stab one to the heart." According to this piece, hatpins then were about eight inches long, with the fancy ones costing anywhere from $5 to $50 (the fancy ones had gems on the head) down to the ones of plain black wire that sold six for a nickel at the ten-cent store. Mentioned also was the old New York State measure introduced by Phillips as well as the "hue and cry of protest from the ladies all over the land and [how] a delegation of the fair sex assembled at the capitol [building] in Albany to protest against the passage of the measure.

Lillie Devereux Blake, a noted women's rights advocate, denounced the bill as insulting to women's one formidable weapon; the result was that the "hatpin bill" never became law. Then he mentioned the Dolly Tracy case wherein the woman appeared before a judge because she had jabbed a man with her hatpin. The judge ruled in her favor, thus establishing the hatpin as a defensive weapon and giving it a place of legal standing. "From that time, however, there seemed to be an epidemic of casualties and tragedies that could be traced to that one source. Footpads were wounded by these weapons, husband and lovers were stabbed and even men took to using the sharp, cruel instrument in deadly earnest in brawls and fights." In conclusion, "It has been proved conclusively that the 'hatpin weapon' is one of the deadliest and handiest as well as dangerous articles in the hands of an enemy and could easily become murderous as well. Something should be done to prohibit its length or use of a guard should be put upon the point, like a tip on a fencing foil."[24]

"Ridicule never yet killed a feminine fashion, nor yet censure," wrote an editor in a January 1908 piece. "It is therefore vain to attempt to lessen the number of hatpins which are daily brandished by women in public. One sees them in twos or threes, miniature rapiers, flashing the most deadly threats at the human eye," he continued. "Why the hatpin must be of such abnormal length that it protrudes inches of steel—in all eight to ten—on either side of the feminine headgear no man can fathom; he can merely marvel at the recklessness with which women go about armed in this manner." He worried that the alarm about hatpins had been sounded but women went about heedless anyway.[25]

Under the headline, "The Hatpin as a Weapon" an editor on a St. Louis newspaper declared in March 1908: "There has been a steady development of the hatpin as a weapon of defense for several years and it is coming more and more into use." Citing the example of a St. Louis schoolteacher who had repelled a footpad by jabbing him in the face, he declared that example "once again proves that the hatpin must supersede all other means of feminine self-protection." It was a better weapon than a pistol, he argued, since the pistol was "unreliable and ineffective in the hands of women." A woman, he thought, was best in hand-to-hand conflict and the weapons with which she was armed must be those peculiarly suited to her mode of combat. She had, for many generations, been an acknowledged expert with the broomstick and the rolling pin had won unnumbered victories, but "there is a delicacy, a readiness and a deftness about the hatpin that adopt it to the feminine hand more perfectly than those rougher and not so ready instruments." It could be made ready quickly and with a deft motion it was usually unexpected and deceptive to highwaymen or other malefactors. Nor did a woman have to search about in bulky clothing to find the item.[26]

In Salem, Oregon, in 1909, State Legislature Representative Farrell introduced a bill on the morning of January 21, making it a misdemeanor for anyone to sell or have in his possession a hatpin more than ten inches in length. The bill provided a fine from $10 to $100 for violators of the measure or imprisonment from ten days to three months.[27] Farrell explained his reasons for the bill by saying that women were in the habit of wearing extremely long hatpins that were especially offensive to passengers in crowded streetcars and places of amusement; his aim was to eliminate "this evil."[28]

An editor remarked that Farrell's bill was not as foolish as it might at first have appeared: "It would seem that a ten-inch pin would be long enough for all practical purposes and also be of sufficient length to serve as a weapon of defense in times of necessity, while the danger of injuring 'innocent bystanders' would be somewhat relieved." He conceded, however, that "the wisdom of trying to remedy the evil, if it is one, by legislation is doubted."[29]

Several days after the measure had been introduced, Farrell's bill was discussed in the House. Mr. Jaegar, of Portland, said it would not only be ruinous to the jewelry trade but disastrous to prevailing styles. Representative Brady wanted to give the dealers a chance to get rid of the long hatpins they had in stock, and give the women a chance to let the styles change. Much of the so-called debate on the measure was jocular and/or mocking and derisive. In the end, however, the votes of those who opposed the measure were not sufficient and Farrell's measure to "abolish the deadly weapon" passed in the Oregon House.[30]

Mockery of Farrell and his bill was not limited to his home state. Back east in Washington, D.C., a story was published along with an editorial cartoon spoofing the measure. The article asked, How does a woman keep on her head "a thirty-three inch creation of Paris pattern with a hatpin less than a foot long?" That was the question then said to be vexing the legislators in Oregon. Farrell's bill passed in the House by 33 votes. The piece declared that Farrell stood for the protection of the innocent bystander.[31]

A New York City newspaper published its own editorial cartoon spoofing the Oregon proposal. This newspaper jumped the gun by announcing that the Oregon Legislature had passed the law, limiting hatpins to ten inches in length. At that time the measure had only passed the

An editorial cartoon from a New York City newspaper that satirized the proposed hatpin law then being debated in Oregon.

House. That measure does not seem to have ever become law in Oregon; the Oregon Senate postponed the bill indefinitely, which meant death. A few articles did appear in 1909 declaring the bill had been enacted.[32]

An editorial in a Texas newspaper, on February 4, 1909, stated the bill had indeed passed the Oregon Legislature: "A hat pin is a weapon of defense when worn by a lady and the Legislature ought not to interfere. It would be better to give the ladies the right to carry pistols than to take away their right to wear hat pins a foot long." A different editor from a different Texas newspaper stated: "A ten-inch hat pin ought to be long enough to serve the purpose of holding a hat on the head of the average woman, and would doubtless also make a very effective weapon."[33]

Yet another editorial on the issue appeared in various newspapers in March 1909, apparently originating in a South Carolina publication. That account thundered: "What business is it of the Oregon House of Representatives how long hatpins are? The women in that State should not be deprived of some means of defense."[34]

Back in Oregon, it was announced, on February 8, that the hatpin bill had been killed. The Oregon State Senate had postponed indefinitely the bill to limit the length of the pins. According to this article, "The bill was killed by ridicule."[35]

Oregon Legislature Has Passed a Law Limiting Hatpins to 10 Inches Long

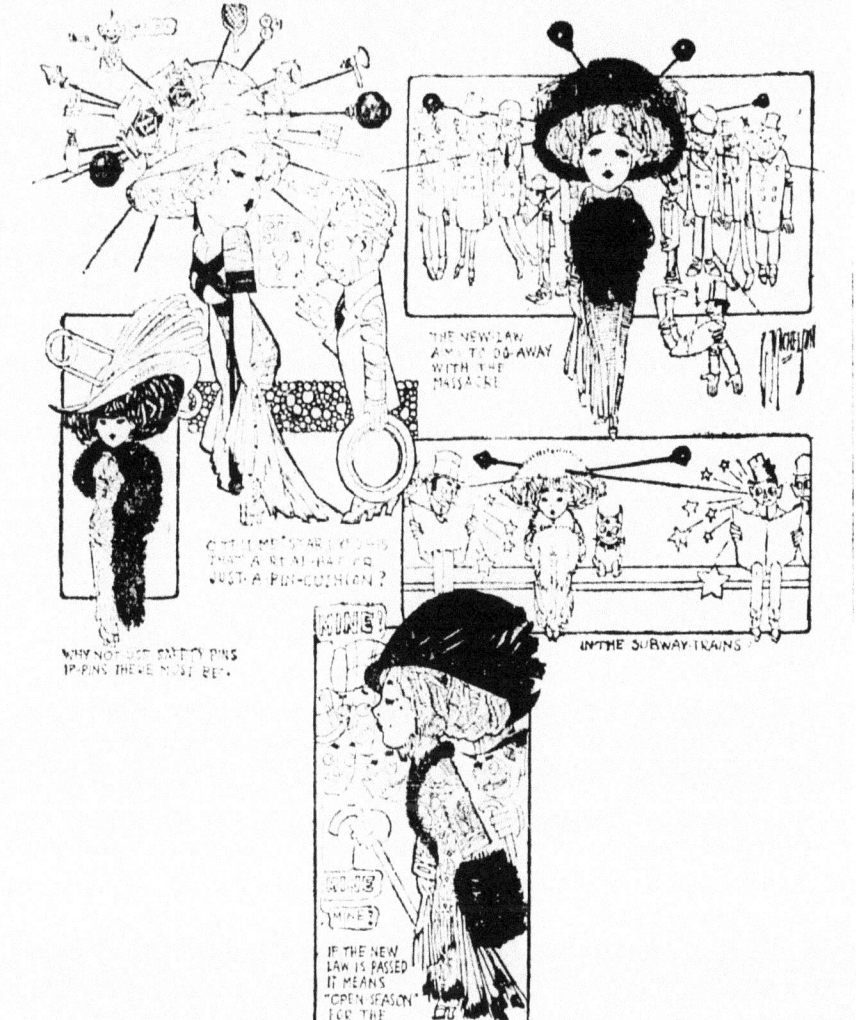

Another editorial cartoon lampooning Oregon's efforts to control the hatpin.

According to several newspaper stories that appeared in October 1909, the state of Oregon had a law in effect that limited the length of hatpins to ten inches. But since it went into effect, in January 1909, according to the story, there had been no arrests, and "women's clubs have derided it in resolutions, and candidates for the next legislature were proposing repeal." A story was related in which a policeman, while riding in an elevator in Portland, was jabbed in the cheek by a hatpin worn by a young woman who was crowded against him in the elevator. He said, "That hat pin is more than a foot long and you are liable to arrest." She replied, "How do you know whether that hat pin is one foot or three inches long? Don't crowd and then you won't get your face scratched; and when you get the evidence you're looking for, you may arrest me." Reportedly, the policeman made no attempt to obtain the requisite evidence.[36]

Another story around the same time also remarked on the failure of the Oregon law and its lack of arrests: "The papers have ridiculed it, the women have openly challenged policemen to arrest them for breaking the law and local statesmen, it is said on good authority, are planning its repeal by the next Legislature." The editor of this piece wrote, "This is as it should be. Such a law is ridiculous, and it is not difficult to gauge the mental caliber of a Legislature responsible for such legislative asininity." He remarked that other legislatures had tried to regulate female clothing. An Illinois solon introduced a bill to prevent women from wearing corsets, Wisconsin tried to eliminate the corset from the female wardrobe, and Kansas tired to regulate the size and adornment of hats. Then Oregon "capped the climax of legislative silliness."[37]

Also in February 1909, an editor on a Nebraska newspaper opined: "There ought to be a law that will prevent a 60-inch woman from wearing a 12-inch hatpin, and jeopardizing the eyes and even the life of everyone within striking reach of her. In the crowded elevated cars it is not unusual to see men frantically bobbing their heads about, in a vain endeavor to get out of reach of the hatpins of the women in front of them." He observed that a campaign against "this murderous but unconcealed weapon" had been instigated by the Berlin authorities; there was also agitation reported in London, England.[38]

Agitation against the hatpin, and in favor of legislation, continued to increase, according to a February 1909 account. Something was going to happen to the hatpin, said one opponent, "Just for fear that the increased length of that necessary weapon, favorite of women, may become a menace to the life and ears and noses of pedestrians and strap hangers, the legislators are getting their pencils out and making laws on the subject." With a mention of the Oregon measure, this journalist observed, "This has tipped off the city dads in a number of thriving metropolitan towns, and ordinances limiting the length of hatpins everywhere from nine to 14 inches are pouring into legislative hoppers." At the time that comment was a fabrication, but legislation would indeed flow, especially in the years in 1910 and 1911.³⁹

An American newspaper columnist named Cynthia Grey mentioned, in a September 1909 article, the war on hatpins in Paris: "In America the press has remained silent, save in the occasional news story of an accident. It's time our press was getting busy. A close observer on crowded city cars will notice how women dodge to keep out of the way of hat pins. Even men keep their eyes wide open." Grey concluded: "Why will women be so foolish? Why can't they wear pins just long enough? Hat pins need only go through the crown to hold perfectly, and yet women jab those long pins clear through and allow them to stick out on the other side—a menace to all who venture near."⁴⁰

A strange story appeared in a couple of small newspapers in February 1910. Supposedly it was a first-person account and was published on the editorial page in the newspaper by a named author (it was rare in this time period for any newsman to get a byline) with the name Alton E. Gasso, likely a nom de plume.

> I was a passenger on a Chicago South Side elevated train the other evening and was standing in the aisle holding a strap when a young woman approached and in the crowd tore my face with her hat pin as she passed. I was very fortunate that my eye was not seriously injured.... The pin projected fully two or three inches over the side of her hat[....] It seems almost incredible that in a civilized community women will wear such dangerous weapons in their hats. If they must wear them, why not have the sharp projecting ends protected by some kind of shield? Would it not be a good thing for the city fathers to take notice of this pestiferous and dangerous menace to life and limb?⁴¹

When the members of the Women's Democratic Club of New

WAR ON HATPIN

And now something is going to happen to the hatpin.

Just for fear that the increased length of that necessary weapon, favorite of woman, may become a

HATPIN STYLES THAT LEGISLATION MAY CURB

This February 1909 piece illustrated a popular and growing sentiment, reportedly, among legislators around the nation—war on the hatpin.

York City met in February 1910, they digressed from their main topic of suffrage to discuss hatpins; two hours of their meeting were devoted to a discussion as to their proper length. Mrs. Margaret E. Fitzgerald declared that the present law, providing for a hatpin of less than nine inches, was dangerous. No hatpin, she said, should extend beyond the crown of the hat.[42]

Harriet Miller, of the Women's Democratic Club of New York, was not afraid of subway crowds, according to an account: "She makes a defensive armor of hatpins for herself, and thus accoutered she flings herself gaily into the struggling throng." As she explained, "I fix them with the points sticking out fore and aft then when men lean against me as they do when you're sitting in a cross seat, you know, I just toss my head back and forth, and generally they don't lean any more. I must admit it doesn't always work, though." She related this tidbit to an interested audience at the club's meeting, held at the Waldorf-Astoria Hotel. Margaret Fitzgerald, a school principal, arose to say she was sorry that any member of the club should use the hatpin as a weapon. She was also sorry to see the club taking the question of hatpins "somewhat flippantly." She argued it was a serious issue: "I seldom enter a car that I do not see some woman's hatpins protruding from her hat in a way that's a public menace." Mrs. John S. Crosby, president of the club, related that a day earlier she had to ask a woman in the seat next to her to please push in her hatpin. A member reminded the club, erroneously, that there was a law forbidding the wearing of hatpins more than nine inches long. The club resolved to try to secure an amendment to the law, making it a crime to let the point of the pin protrude beyond the hat.[43]

In February 1910, the San Francisco Board of Supervisors received a lengthy correspondence from someone wanting protection from long hatpins. It was a letter to the board that was only signed with the initials J.M. He (assuming J.M. was a male) complained that while leaving a theater along with other patrons he had been accidentally jabbed in the face by a hatpin. As well, he claimed that this particular hatpin protruded "about five inches from the body of the hat." He ended his complaint by saying he hoped "a provision covering the nuisance may soon be appended to our municipal ordinances."[44]

Shortly thereafter it was reported that the letter from J.M. "failed to arouse a responsive feeling in the breasts of the city fathers." It was also reported that the city fathers "sympathize with the writer, who complains that his ear was impaled by a spike protruding from a lady's hat. If they dared, they would legislate against the favorite weapon of women. But they

8. Agitation, Hysteria, Crusades and Legislation

do not dare." Recently those supervisors in San Francisco had decided that smoking should be permitted in the streetcars in that city. After sessions with the wives, daughters and delegations from women's clubs, the supervisors decided that they were not so insistent for the repeal of the antismoking ordinance that then prevailed on the cars. "Profiting by that experience, the board has concluded to officially ignore the hat pin," concluded the story.[45]

An editor on a Washington, D.C., newspaper, at the end of February 1910, offered the thought that there was a time when the only man interested in women's hats was the one who had to buy them—and his principal concern was cost. "But times have changed and so have hats, and so have men's ideas of them. The subject has become one which affects mankind. Needless to say, it is the size of the hat which has brought about the transformation." He argued that the state had the right to regulate the size of hats and hatpins: "We do not undertake to say that it will do anything of the sort, but we lay down the postulate that it has the authority. Man in his meekness marvels, but he hasn't got the nerve to act." And that lack of nerve existed despite stories about accidental stabs, jabs and scratches on crowded transit vehicles and in other places where people congregated. "Man has endured these and other trials with exemplary patience, but he had nourished the belief it was impossible that hats would get larger—that the worst was over," he wrote. Yet he had to admit that recent fashion shows had indicated no such hope for the near future: hats were still growing.[46]

On the evening of February 28, 1910, the Chicago City Council deliberated on the following question: "Are women's long hatpins which menace the noses, eyes and faces of other people a public nuisance?" And the other issue raised was: "Ought women, despite the danger of hatpins, to be allowed to wear them for self-protection?" Alderman Herman J. Bauler introduced an order, requesting the corporation council of the city to draw up an ordinance restricting the length of hatpins worn in public places. "We have an ordinance prohibiting the wearing of large hats in theaters," he said. "I am going to teach the women of Chicago that they must stop wearing hatpins a foot and a half long. Some of the pins stick five and six inches beyond the brims of their hats." During the council session, a delegation of women were in the gallery. One yelled out to Bauler, "Doesn't your wife wear long hatpins?" Said Bauler, "No, you bet she doesn't. She wouldn't do such a thing. Oh you women of Chicago, don't you ever consider when you get into a crowded street car with your long hatpins that you are endangering the faces of all us men?" For that the women in the gallery had an answer in the form of a prepared statement that was read out, and signed by May E. Davis. It stated that on behalf of herself and thousands of other women in Chicago who were occasionally on the streets after dark, that

> a hatpin is a woman's weapon of defense. She is not permitted to carry a revolver or other weapons. I always feel safe going home at night with a hatpin available. Before leaving a street car I always get a hatpin ready in my hand until I am safe within my home. It has proved its need. Thousands of other women can speak from their experiences of how a stout hatpin has been an effective defense in time of danger.

At the end of the council session Bauler's resolution was referred to a committee.[47]

A separate newspaper picked up the same story from the wire and printed it as above, except for the addition of one sentence: "The council chamber rang with applause from the women's gallery after the reading of the letter."[48]

Also covering the debate was a newspaper from Washington, D.C. That account asked the reader, "What matter if they are a public nuisance? Has that got anything to do with it? No one but a man would ever have framed such a query, and no body but one composed entirely of men would ever have seriously considered it. No wonder, the suffragette." Then the article dealt with the second question that had been posed in Chicago, the self-defense idea. "Why, certainly," the writer affirmed. "It keeps men at a safe distance. A foot and a half long! Pshaw! The longer the better. These are Chicago women, you know." Also weighing in on the subject was the Reverend Burrell, of Berwick, Pennsylvania, who complained for a bit about big hats and then declared, "But to be serious, these big hats have their proper uses, apart from that of adornment, even as the hat pins, as a part of the system of defensive as well as offensive warfare, in street cars and other crowded places. Do you know why a cat has whiskers?"[49]

Early in March 1910, it was reported that many letters and stories of injuries incurred by the "menacing pin" were being received by many aldermen in Chicago, with Bauler being one of the main recipients of such items. As he stated, "I am glad that the canvass of judiciary committeemen shows them in favor of the ordinance for sheathing the hatpin." He added, "If the committee stood otherwise I am sure the men of Chicago would be tempted to take the matter into their own hands. They are beginning to feel the necessity of the measure. At first it was taken as a sort of joke, but now the seriousness of the thing gets on them." He then recited to the reporter a few of the accidents that had come to his attention.[50]

8. Agitation, Hysteria, Crusades and Legislation   133

On March 7, 1910, it was reported that women's long hatpins were declared to be a "public nuisance" and an "anti-hatpin" ordinance was ordered drawn up by the judiciary committee of the Chicago City Council. That action followed a week's "crusade" against long hatpins that culminated on March 7 in a public hearing. The ordinance would stipulate that hatpins worn in public places "shall not extend more than one-half an inch beyond the crown of the hat." It was to be drawn up by the corporation council and to be presented in the near future for action by the full city council. Present at that public hearing, according to a news account, were nine aldermen, three or four lawyers, and a score of protesting women. "We want to protest right here, against this attempt to regulate women's attire," declared attorney Francis Hinckley (male), representing the women. "It does not become the city of Chicago to try to dictate what its women shall wear." May Davis, one of the women present, added, "That's right. These hat pins are woman's only defense. You must not dictate to us women." Responded Alderman Cermack, "Well, you women want to regulate what we men drink, don't you?" Amid a chorus of boos from the women, Bauler stepped forward to describe what he called "the truth of the whole matter": "I don't believe there was ever a time in history when women have shown so much eccentricity in their personal adornment as at present."[51]

There was much national media attention to the Chicago fracas. Often the headlines were incendiary and/or false, even when the text was faithful in reporting on the subject. A Seattle newspaper declared: "Hatpins Barred by Ordinance."[52]

One of the other comments made by Bauler during the public meeting, with respect to women's attire in general, was:

> We have had the tight skirt, the sheath gown, the Marcel wave and now comes the yard-wide hat with its remarkable accessories. In addition to ribbons, laces, wire flowers, vegetables, animals and birds, women's headgear is armed with the deadly 'snickersnee' [a knife resembling a sword].... If women care to wear carrots and roosters on their heads, that is their own concern and it cannot be interfered with by the city, but when it comes to wearing swords they must be stopped. The hatpin may be the only weapon woman has to ward off attack, but let her wear it sheathed in her belt. Hidden in a mass of plumage or hair, it comes under the designation of concealed weapons.[53]

An editorial from a Washington State newspaper began by saying that some of the women who wore projecting hatpins doubtless still considered the agitation against them as a joke. Albert Putnam, a street railway conductor in Springfield, did not. While collecting fares one day, a week earlier, a woman passenger turned her head quickly and drove the point of her 18-inch pin clear through his ear. At least one woman in Chicago had reportedly had an eye put out by such a pin under similar circumstances. One writer admitted that people took greater risks everyday from other things than hatpins, "But that is not the point. The hat pin risk is stupid, needless and reckless. It imperils eyes, and one single human eye is worth more than all the dagger hat pins in the world." In conclusion, he declared, "No woman with any regard for other people's rights would wear one. No woman who does wear one is entitled to any complaint if the city finds a good legal means of stopping her."[54]

One newspaper published a story of the controversy on March 8 and after a reading of the full quote from Bauler there were more boos from the women at the hearing. Another newspaper delivered an even-handed argument, albeit with an inflammatory headline: "To Put a Ban on Deadly Hatpin."[55]

"Funny though the suggestion may be that women should be deprived of their personal liberty by regulations governing the length of their hatpins, the question has some claim to the serious consideration given to it by the municipal lawmakers of Chicago," started an editorial in a New York City newspaper. Opposition to the regulation was to be expected, although "some of the arguments used in support of the right of women thus to arm themselves might be cited as evidence of a lack of logic on the part of the sex using them." Of course, he continued, it "is all very well to declare

This March 1910 ad drew attention to the dangers of crowded transit vehicles—dangers that came from those deadly hatpins. Note the ad on the transit car wall for artificial eyes.

that man has no right to dictate what women shall wear, and that on general principles any attempt on his part so to dictate would be futile, but public policy always comes before individual rights." While he agreed the streets of Chicago could be dangerous, he pointed out that "the intimation that every woman in the course of a year has many occasions to use the deadly instrument in her hat for self-protection will hardly bear analysis. Not one woman in a thousand, pursuing the even tenor of her ways, would have the slightest legitimate reason for so using a hatpin, and one of the attorneys for the article in question was clearly uttering the call of anarchy when she said, 'I intend to violate this ordinance if it becomes a law.'" Then he cited an incident that took place only a day or two earlier in New York City, where a woman who resisted arrest drew her hatpin and tried to use it on a court officer. It was an odd example to raise when the topic was accidental jabbing from protruding pins in crowded places. Felonious women had been regularly attacking people in the judicial system for an estimated two decades and yet it hardly ever drew any comment. "And why is it any more legitimate for a woman to carry a deadly weapon secreted in her hat than for the Italian to wear the hardly more dangerous stiletto secreted in his clothing?" he wondered. Yet again, it was a poor example. The stiletto was concealed; the hatpin was not. Accidental jabbing could not occur from a truly concealed weapon. "It might be imagined that until hatpins acquired their present alarming proportions women moved about in constant terror, while now, by a simple twist of the wrist, they became invincible." As a final thought, he acknowledged that enforcement of such a measure would be drastically different from passing it.[56]

On March 11, 1901, in Chicago, the draft of the ordinance to limit hatpins was completed by Assistant Corporation Counsel Hayes and was expected to be introduced to the full council within a few days. It made the person an offender if the point of the pin protruded more than half an inch from either side, top, back, or front of the hat, regardless of whether the pin went through or upon the hat. The maximum penalty for violation of the ordinance was a fine of $50.[57]

"Purse snatchers take notice. Chicago has just passed an ordinance prohibiting the use of large hat pins," began a sarcastic editorial comment on the new ordinance. "Any woman found on the street hereafter with a hat pin in the millinery more than two feet long is subject to arrest and the electric chair, and this is your chance, purse snatchers." That is, since women could no longer defend themselves with such restrictions on pins, the city would be a paradise for muggers. The editor went on to suggest that all railroads would run reduced rates to Chicago so all muggers, burglars, and so forth, could get to Chicago more easily "to reap the harvest that awaits them."[58]

On the evening of March 14, 1910, somewhat surprisingly, the Chicago City Council decided that it would be "inexpedient" at that time to regulate the length of women's hatpins by law. "Scores of women who had argued that hatpins were women's only means of defense when going home on dark nights filled the galleries to-night when the measure came up," a report noted. At one point during that meeting Bauler declared, "Now gentlemen, this long hatpin nuisance has been thoroughly thrashed out and we are all agreed that it shall stop." That comment drew a female chorus from the gallery: "Shame! Shame!" Somebody moved the proposed ordinance be "published" and the motion carried before Bauler realized what had happened: "The action means defeat for the measure for the present at least."[59]

Just as suddenly and surprisingly, the Chicago City Council overturned its decision. On the evening of March 21, 1910, the council passed, by a vote of 68 to 2, an "anti-hatpin" ordinance. "It was passed in spite of many hisses and boos from the gallery where a crowd of women had gathered to protest against the measure on the ground the city had no right to attempt to regulate women's apparel and that long hatpins often formed woman's only weapon of defense." With the passage of the law it was then a misdemeanor for any woman to wear a long hatpin in public places in Chicago. Any woman caught wearing one that protruded more than half an inch beyond the crown was liable to arrest and a $50 fine.[60]

Under the measure, the maximum fine was $50; the minimum fine was left to the discretion of the judge. The fine, remarked a reporter, was the "price of two good hats." Such protruding pins could not be worn on any public street, alley or other public thoroughfare of the municipality or in any elevated car or in any public elevator without the offender being subject to arrest. To avoid any charge of legal discrimination against women, when Hayes drafted the bill he worded it in such a way that referred to any person being in breach of the measure by wearing protruding hatpins.[61]

Enthusiastic about the passage of the measure, one editor wrote: "The men of Chicago have risen on their hind feet in rebellion against the long hatpin." He did not accept the claim women made for the need of the item for self-defense: "The man who essays too great [a] familiarity with the girl on the street not only lowers himself to a level below that of the ordinary cur, but makes it necessary for other and perfectly respectable men to act as involuntary pincushions on street cars."[62]

8. Agitation, Hysteria, Crusades and Legislation 137

The official wording of that Chicago ordinance read as follows: "No person, while on the public streets or in any street or elevated car or public elevator or other public place, shall wear any hatpin, the exposed portion of which shall protrude more than one-half inch beyond the crown of the hat, in, upon or through which such pin is worn."[63]

On March 22, 1910, Chicago's Mayor Busse signed the hatpin ordinance. It was a law that made no provision for protectors, or guards, over the exposed points. That is, if the pin protruded more than one half of an inch it was in violation of the measure, even if that point was blunted by a guard. The law was to take effect on April 1, 1910.[64]

When a Louisville, Kentucky, newspaper editor addressed the Chicago law, he wrote: "Here in Louisville the various ugly styles of hats are so wide that there is no danger of the lengthiest hat pin protruding over the edge."[65]

A Shreveport, Louisiana, reporter gave the usual recap of the Chicago law and then added his own thoughts: "It may be ungallant to say that such hat pins should be repressed, but in all candor, it was senseless to excuse such a monstrosity simply to be polite. There should be a limit to all things."[66]

The first arrest under the Chicago hatpin ordinance was made on April 2, 1910, when Mrs. Maude Collins of Brooklyn, New York, alighted from a train at the LaSalle Street crossing and bumped into John F. Slater. The hatpin, described as 15 inches in length and sharp, reportedly jabbed him in the cheek.[67]

Upon being jabbed, he gave a yell and a nearby cop arrested Collins and took her to the Harrison Street police station. According to a reporter, "She was

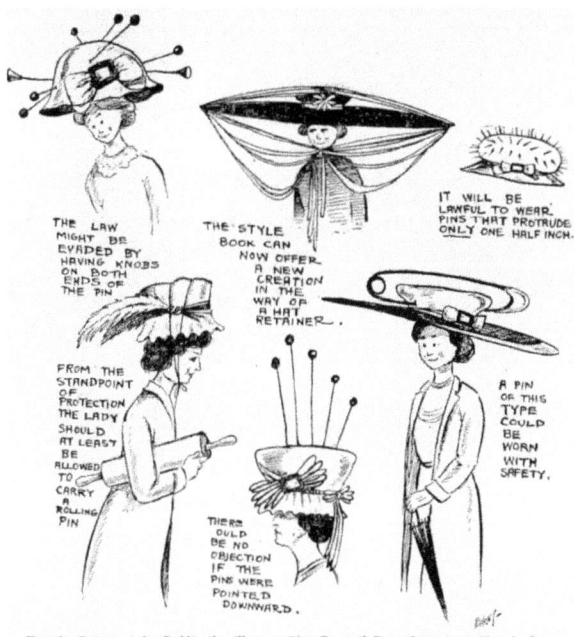

A March 1910 cartoon lampooning the Chicago hatpin ordinance.

indignant when Judge Gemmill fined her $1 and costs. The police kept the hatpin."[68]

An editorial cartoon on the Chicago ordinance show a man giving his mother-in-law a long hatpin as a present while holding a newspaper in such a way that the woman could not see it. The headline in that newspaper announced that the hatpin law was being enforced and that a woman had been arrested.[69]

One editorial on the topic began: "The long hat pin ordinance is not directed against a style of dress, but against a public nuisance. It has been shown that painful wounds and even loss of sight have resulted from the maintenance of this nuisance. The style might be harmless if each of its devotees could be assigned to a ten-acre lot and duly surrounded by a barbed-wire fence, but when they throng the streets and street cars of a great city it is dangerous." This Chicago editor wrote optimistically that the women would hopefully have the "good sense" to see "that there were excellent reasons why an effort should have been made to abolish the nuisance, and that it is their duty to put the long hat pin out of business."[70]

In late June 1910, another editor with a Chicago newspaper wrote that since Chicago had enacted its law "reports of action against the dangerous hatpin have been coming from all parts of the country, and a startlingly large number of serious accidents from long hatpins have been recorded [but no details were given]." He concluded, "At first sight the agitation may seem ludicrous. In the light of actual hatpin casualties and the menace of frenetic females armed with deadly weapons, the argument

More spoofing of the Chicago ordinance. In this cartoon a man hands his mother-in-law a present, a very long hatpin, knowing it is illegal and hoping it will lead to her arrest.

of those who would prohibit hatpins of undue length seems well founded."⁷¹

An announcement from Chicago in June 1912 related that the city was to have a "beauty squad" of women in the police department. Chief McWeeny of the Chicago Police Department made the announcement after he learned that the policemen of his city were "too bashful" to enforce the hatpin ordinance. "I will organize a 'beauty squad' of twenty attractive society and club women of Chicago to aid in the enforcement of the new ordinance," said the chief. "It appears that the great majority of policemen are too bashful to enforce the ordinance which provides that the women's hatpins shall not protrude more than half an inch from their hats."⁷²

Apparently it all began that month when Mayor Harrison, of Chicago, decided he wanted to crack down on "naked" hatpins; that is, to enforce the existing ordinance, then a little more than two years old. He got in touch with McWeeny and called his attention to that section of the city code and said, "I have received so many complaints from persons who have been impaled by these females of fashion that I have determined to go after them. The fine mentioned in the ordinance is anything up to $50." He added, "I have been a victim of the hat pin fad myself. I was standing on Madison street one day talking to a friend when along came a fashionably dressed woman. Her hat pin protruded fully three inches beyond the crown and when she passed me I received a wound in the cheek." He continued; "I am heartily in favor of enforcing the ordinance. The question at present is—how? I will have to provide my men with rulers and then so many of them are bashful that it will be hard for them to do the work. If the women would only wear corks, or chewing gum or small potatoes on the point that would satisfy the law all right."⁷³

And from that came the idea of a beauty squad. When Chicago's society women were queried about the idea it was greeted with little enthusiasm. Said Mrs. Andrew J. Graham, "I'm afraid I wouldn't make a very good police woman. I do think it ought to be enforced, though, and most women think the same way, I am sure. But ought we not to go after the manufacturers who make the long hatpins? They are the ones at fault, for a woman would never think of asking the length when purchasing a pin." Miss Marian Kaufman was aghast at the thought she might be appointed as a "copess." She said, "I'm sure I don't want to be a police woman. I do think the ordinance ought to be enforced." Mrs. Clifford C. Chickering, described as prominent in all the affairs of the Friendly Aid Society, was out of the city but it was reported that Chief McWeeny might appoint her to his squad in her absence.⁷⁴

William Luthardt was secretary to Police Chief McWeeny and the organizer of the beauty squad. Strolling on Chicago's streets with a reporter, Luthardt said, "I never thought much of Kipling but the female of the species on the east side of State Street in certainly deadlier than the male. Madison and State is really Chicago's death corner." The two men were on the busy State Street at 10 a.m. when the shopping district was full. His purpose was to see to what extent the old Herman Bauler law was being disregarded and to establish the present average length of hatpin extending beyond the crown of the average hat. He said one was seen protruding "six dangerous inches. The average was at least three inches." Luthardt pointed out a well-dressed woman emerging from a limousine and heading for a department store entrance, and said to the reporter, "She is wearing two pins, both of them sticking out at least five inches. She is a menace to mankind. There, what did I tell you?" He then added, "They ought to wear numbers. They are just as bad as automobiles, and exceeding the one inch limit is just as bad as exceeding the speed limit. Our 'beauty squad' will soon set things right, though. We shall arm our 'lady patrolmen' with wire clippers and stars. Those who defy the law will have the choice of arrest or amputation of the hatpin. And the women will do it, too. Our office has been bombarded with requests by members of the deadly sex who are anxious to stamp out this pest." With respect to women using guards on the points, McWeeny observed that objections had been made to the cork, chewing gum, and so forth, because none of them were "artistic or beautiful."[75]

Mayor Harrison issued an edict on December 3, 1913, against horizontal "plumes, aigrettes, pompoms" or other devices on women's hats which might injure sensitive portions of man's facial anatomy. If necessary, it was said, the mayor favored an ordinance similar to the one that compelled women to remove their hats in theaters.[76]

According to J. C. C. Alter of the Salt Lake City weather bureau, in an interview conducted in March 1910, one of the greatest evils of the city that had not as yet been called to the attention of the public, was the fact that women were allowed to run around the streets of the city "guarded on all sides by long, sharp-pointed hatpins." He believed the attention of Salt Lake City lawmakers should have their attention called to "the evil" and that they take immediate means to do away with the problem. He then offered his opinion on the proposed ordinance in Chicago: "I believe that such an ordinance would be of great benefit to Salt Lake. Big hats are bad enough, but when it comes to the long, spear-like hatpins, the line should be drawn." Alter fumed, "Men's eyes are always in danger when walking down the street. Some of the hatpins now being worn are fully five inches longer than necessary. A limit on the length should be placed and the councilman who will introduce such an ordinance in this city is pretty certain to be elected for years to come." When he had recently been to the theater, Alter added, he said he was struck by the array of long hatpins in view: "They were actually wicked-looking instruments that are enough to strike terror into the heart of the bravest of men." Alter said he was considering the launching of a petition to be delivered to his local city council, and thundered in conclusion, "Do we, the men of Salt Lake, have to stand for all that? Are we to be harpooned in the back every time we go to the theatre? Are our eyes to be constantly endangered while walking down the street? ... Now is the time for action. Two years from now we will not have our eyes left to write petitions."[77]

On the West Coast in March 1910, a Los Angeles newspaper editor opined: "Hats that are stylish are much smaller than the monstrosities worn by many of the beautiful women of Los Angeles. Hat pins, however, are longer than ever, and if the hats continue to diminish, the headgear soon will resemble a pollywog skewered on a knitting needle." He hoped the big-hat craze would soon disappear from Los Angeles: "A big hat protected by a big hat pin is bad, but a small hat armed with a big hat pin is hadesian."[78]

Chicago's crusade against the long pin habit was reported to be the inspiration for Councilman Rubens of Indianapolis, Indiana, to express the emotions that he had held bottled up since the time he visited an amusement park in Atlantic City, three summers earlier. When he was on one of the rides there, he received a jab from a woman's hatpin. Thus, on March 10, Rubens announced he had prepared an ordinance for his city that would reduce the length of hatpins or cause guards to be placed over their points. A poll of the council members, reportedly, indicated that the ordinance would be passed. Speaking to a reporter, Rubens pointed to a mark on his upper lip and said, "Well, that is my hat pin mark. I was riding in one of those whirling tubs in Atlantic City three years ago and when the tub gave a lurch a woman's hat pin went through that lip."[79]

Several weeks later it was announced that the difficulty of enforcing the hatpin ordinance in Indianapolis, which set a fine for wearing a pin that protruded a half inch beyond the brim of the hat, had been solved, reportedly, by Mayor Shank and Police Superintendent Hyland, insofar as determining liability under the law was concerned. The police were to be provided with a small silver ruler about two inches long and marked in inches, halves, quarters, and eighths, so that the exact length of the pro-

HOME-MADE SUGGESTIONS FOR GUARDS ON HATPINS

MISS SISSIE SINKERSLINGER, OUR COY LITTLE WAITRESS IS PROTECTING THE PUBLIC'S LAMPS BY WEARING A "HAM-ON-BUN" AT THE END OF HER HATPIN.

PROF. PLUMPEN-BRAINY, THE E. MINENT SUFFRAGET HAS SHEATHED HER PIG STICKER IN AN OLD PIPE

MISS FLOSSIE FLUFFEN-DIMPLES HAS BLOSSOMED OUT IN A NEW LID WITH A PET POODLE ON THE END OF HER TRUSTY BLADE

MRS KITTY KOD-LIVER. THE PILL PEDDLER'S WIFE IS OBSERVING THE LAW AND ADVERTISING HER HUSBANDS BUSINESS BY WEARING A CORK ON THE END OF HER CHEESE KNIFE.

MAMMY LOTTA KOLLOR IS WEARING A JUICY PORK CHOP ON THE TIP END OF HER BAYONET – THE WORLD OF SCIENCE OWES THIS INVENTION TO JACK JOHNSON'S FERTILE BRAIN.

An ordinance was introduced recently in Indianapolis to have guards put on hatpins.

More editorial spoofing of a hatpin ordinance. This June 1910 cartoon satirized the measure that had recently been passed in Indianapolis.

truding end could be determined when an arrest was made. Councilman George C. Rubens was the author of the hatpin ordinance in Indianapolis and it was reported to be in force in that city, in October 1910.[80]

An editorial cartoon appeared in the middle of March 1910. It mentioned no specific city or ordinance, but was a general lampoon of the long hatpin and the call for its reform.[81]

A Washington, D.C., newspaper published a piece on March 16, 1910, that featured two separate accounts of eyes being jabbed out by hatpin wearers. In Brussels, Belgium, it was reported, a court had awarded $2,000 to a man who was blinded in one eye by a woman's hatpin. He was standing on the platform of a streetcar which stopped suddenly with a jerk, causing the hatpin to pierce his eye. Damages were assessed equally against the woman and the streetcar company, with each ordered to pay $1,000 to the victim. The other account was from Lafayette, Indiana. It related that Dr. James D. Hillis, city health officer in that community, was then in a hospital there suffering from an injury caused by a hatpin that may have cost him an eye. Hillis had visited a local vaudeville theater and in the crowd he was shoved against a large hat worn by a woman in front of him. She turned quickly and the point of a hatpin caught him squarely in the left eye, tearing the eyeball. The incendiary headline of the piece was "Two Eyes Jabbed Out by Hatpins in Crowd."[82]

That same newspaper ran a story the following day under the headline, "Hatpins Must be Abolished." It was a reprint of an editorial from a Baltimore newspaper. The writer of the piece said the origins of the hatpin were shrouded in the mystery of antiquity, but that we "can easily trace its

8. Agitation, Hysteria, Crusades and Legislation   143

development from the early Victorian period to the Merry Widow era. [The Victorian era ran from 1837 to 1901; the Merry Widow era began in 1907.] Within the memory of men now living it has grown from little more than a spiked hairpin into the length and keenness of a rapier." It all came about when women discarded the "modest little bonnet" that tied under the chin "for monumental headgear" for which she needed something to "nail" the hat to her head. "As long as it stuck to millinery and society the hatpin was

Yes! There Should Be a Reform in Hatpins

This March 1910 editorial cartoon spoofed the hatpin without mentioning a specific city. It definitely favored reform of some kind.

safe. But when it ventured into other fields the challenge came quickly. Out in Chicago women have been roaming the streets, crowding the bargain counters, and thronging the parks." The editor mentioned that several highwaymen had been beaten back and more had been wounded from a jab by a hatpin-wielding women: "These attacks have spread alarm among politicians." With respect to the Chicago measure this editor believed it would mean that the "streets shall be made safe for the men." He added, "Chicago places it with the dumdum bullet, the poisoned arrow, and the Black Hand bomb," in terms of it being a dangerous weapon.[83]

Still in March 1910, a Seattle, Washington, editor commented on the issue: "The hat pin, the delight of women, but the very essence of fright for men, has come under the ban of public opinion, and will hereafter he decried." He noted it was regretful to the average woman because of its protection properties but, he said, the condemnation was not upon the hatpin itself but its length that caused the turmoil. He thought "with an inch or two cut away there cannot be such an objection on the score of danger. The evil complained of having been removed, the hat pin will continue to serve the useful purpose for which it is intended."[84]

Another editor declared that it was to be expected that the recent actions of the Chicago City Council upon the matter of hatpins would lend a new impetus to the suffrage movement: "Women who have not been in sympathy with the present-day demand for suffrage are aroused by this infringement upon their liberty to wear such articles of apparel as they find desirable." Those women may not have been in sympathy with the desire for the voting privilege, but "they are not going to be told what they shall wear to fasten their hats with, or how long it shall be." This editor wondered how the Chicago city fathers had gotten as far as they did: "How it ever escaped the censorship of the wives and progressed so far is the mystery. He added, "It is argued that a pin twelve or fourteen inches long is a dangerous weapon, particularly when it protrudes five or six inches beyond the hat brim. A little matter of a third of a yard of pointed steel is not enough to arouse fear in the breast of a man who conducts himself discreetly. It is woman's only weapon and the suffragettes are finding them useful in more ways than that of holding their hats in place." Another motive was given for its use: "Women who want a large share of a street car seat find long hatpins the most useful means of obtaining it. One sticking well beyond the wearer's head warns away unpleasant intrusion or near association. Crowding becomes uncomfortable.[85]

An ordinance to regulate hatpins was introduced in the Omaha City Council around the middle of March 1910. It was a measure designed to regulate the length of hatpins, but, reportedly, women opposed to the measure "swooped down" on the council members and "shamed those politicians to the extent that as of March 21 the council had decided to let the hatpin ordinance die.[86]

One champion of the long hatpin was Major Richard Sylvester, superintendent of police in Washington, D.C. He believed that Washington women could jab holdup men and mashers with long hatpins all they wanted to in his city and no one in Congress would rise up and cry outrage. In discussing the nationwide agitation against long hatpins, Sylvester noted there were 16,000 more women than men in Washington (job opportunities were much better for women there because the civil service jobs with the federal government were more available to them), and, "Such predominance of the gentler sex can have but one result. Numbers of women are obliged

8. Agitation, Hysteria, Crusades and Legislation 145

to go about the streets at night without escorts and numerous instances have come to the attention of this department where women, assailed by marauders at night, have used hatpins with telling effect. Of course there always will be isolated instances of accidents, but it seems to me that when all is said and done on this subject, the hatpin's value as a weapon of defense to a woman so far outweighs all arguments as to its danger, that this department does not feel justified in issuing a restrictive order." He added, "As long as women must go about the streets, otherwise unarmed, so long will we feel reluctant to take from them a 'concealed weapon' that serves them so effectively."[87]

Sylvester's remarks were reprinted in several newspapers. After recapping those remarks, the editor of one paper commented, "So now, gentlemen who may be visiting the Capital City had best be careful, or a stiletto under the fifth rib may wake them to the fact that the Washington ladies have police authority for stabbing."[88]

A brief, reprinted editorial from a Philadelphia newspaper in March 1910 mentioned the Belgium case, wherein compensation was ordered, and declared: "It is quite time to take some drastic steps to limit the length of these iniquitous spikes, that in crowded cars menace our eyesight and lacerate our faces. The women might just as well carry porcupines on their heads."[89]

According to a statement made on March 26, 1910, by Salt Lake City police chief Samuel H. Barlow, there would be no boycott against long hatpins in Salt Lake so long as the "present mammoth" type of headgear continued to be worn. Barlow could see no reason "for the agitation which is sweeping over certain parts of the country," and which resulted in the Chicago measure. In Salt Lake City, he explained, there had been little, if any, agitation against the wearing of long hatpins, but even if there were, Barlow said, he could see no reason why they should be considered dangerous. Barlow added that, as in Washington, D.C., there were more women than men in his city; he then cited Sylvester and his remarks as being reasonable. Barlow ridiculed the idea of Chicago passing such a law as it had enacted. Mrs. C. H. McMahon was the president of the State Federation of Women's Clubs in Utah. She said she had given the hatpin agitation little consideration, but, in her opinion, the Chicago ordinance must have been passed by a lot of unmarried men not familiar with modern styles of women's headgear. Said McMahon, "Until the long hatpin is worn with a smaller sized hat I do not think the objection is well taken," which produced that Chicago law.[90]

Following the crusade in Chicago it was reported, on March 27, 1910, that a movement had been started in Lynn, Massachusetts, to make it a misdemeanor for any woman to wear a hatpin that protruded from her hat more than one inch. Councilman Edward J. Moran Jr., introduced an order in council, providing a $10 fine for such an offense.[91]

Robert Bailey, elevator operator at the State House in Indianapolis, Indiana, was jabbed in the face by hatpins on two separate occasions on April 1, 1910. Hundreds of women were there to attend the teachers' convention and they crowded into the elevator to such an extent that Bailey could hardly manage his car. One hatpin was bent against his cheekbone and the other gashed him a little farther down on the face. Complained Bailey to the Indiana governor, "I have been ducking and dodging all morning to save my eyes and I've got two wounds that brought the blood. Why, some of the hatpins are two feet long if they are an inch."[92]

An ordinance regulating the length of hatpins and barring those that protruded more than two inches beyond the crown was expected to be introduced in the Seattle City Council later that day by Councilman Revelle. The measure provided for a fine and imprisonment for violators. Corporation Counsel Calhoun, who prepared the bill, believed it was fully within the police power of the city to regulate the length of the hatpin.[93]

As expected, Revelle introduced his bill on the evening of April 4, 1910. The reporter who wrote the story speculated that Revelle must have been jabbed in the past and that he "couldn't figure out how long that hat pin that pricked his cheek was, but he knew it was too long. How much too long he couldn't tell, but it ought to be cut off, so he slipped the ordinance to the council and decided to let the committee [on health and sanitation] to which it was referred figure on how long the hat pin ought to be." As introduced the bill read: "The hat pins shall be limited to ____ inches in length"; it also stated that "any person violating the provisions of this ordinance shall be deemed guilty of a misdemeanor and shall be punished by a fine of not more than ____." As to the length that should be entered into the bill, J. N. Denney, chairman of that health committee, admitted he wanted help badly.[94]

A Seattle reporter interviewed Miss Ethel Ponderford, described as "one of the prettiest and fluffiest stenographers" in the area. She was asked to comment on the bill to regulate the length of hatpins. She said, "This thing of a bunch of men trying to get down and figure out how long a woman's hat pin should be is driveling rot. One woman wears a hat with a crown 16 inches wide. The crown of another woman's hat is 6 inches in width." She added, "No, young man, you tell that health and sanitation committee and Mr. Thomas P. Revelle to keep on figuring on the best way

8. Agitation, Hysteria, Crusades and Legislation 147

to catch rats, real rodents, and the women of Seattle will be able to look after the false hair, boughten [false, store bought] curls, hair rats and hat pins." She concluded: "Now, I never heard of any man getting stuck on a woman's hatpin, but if there is any danger, the council might ordain that the hat pin shouldn't stick out more than an inch beyond the crown. But, really, the best way for men to avoid trouble would be to keep their distance."[95]

Agitation in Seattle picked up again, in May 1912, when a local resident by the name of E. J. Anderson was accidentally jabbed in the eye and was then in danger of losing his sight. Seattle councilman Max Wardell, it was reported, would introduce a bill into the Seattle City Council in the coming days to limit the length of hatpins worn by women in the city and with a provision that a safety device had to cover the point. The proposed bill was reported to be the outcome of an agitation that had begun a week early right after Anderson had sustained his injury.[96]

The Wardell measure went nowhere, but agitation surfaced again in Seattle in May 1913. A delegation of women representing the Federated Women's Clubs intended to pack the Seattle City Council chambers on May 28, when the public safety committee was slated to take up the measure introduced by President Hesketh on May 26. The women themselves proposed the measure and they were said to be ready to fight for it. If the measure became law, women who allowed their hatpins to project more than one and a quarter inches from the crown of the hat would be subject to a maximum fine of $100 and a jail sentence of up to 30 days.[97]

On the morning of May 28, the Seattle Public Safety Committee recommended the hatpin ordinance for passage. The women who had vowed to appear in droves failed to show up. Present were the members of the committee: Aldermen Haas, Wardell, and Hesketh, and some reporters. The session was half over when Mrs. Minnie Dahnken appeared and was welcomed as an expert on the dangers of hatpins. But it developed that Dahnken was not present as a representative of the Federated Women's Clubs but to sell little flags for the benefit of the Women's Relief Corps of the G.A.R. She sold flags to everybody and, observed a reporter, "Mrs. Dahnken wore a long hatpin with an unprotected point."[98]

Seattle's hatpin ordinance was passed unanimously by the city council on June 2, 1913, and went into effect on July 4, 1913.[99]

A woman wearing a hatpin projecting more than one inch beyond the hat would be subject to arrest in the District of Columbia if a bill introduced into the House of Congress on April 4, 1910, by Representative Harry Coudrey of Missouri, was enacted into law.[100]

With respect to Coudrey's bill, the District of Columbia commissioners declined to be interviewed by the press on the subject until their report on the measure was submitted to Congress. It was part of the protocol to first report to the members of the House and Senate Committee on the District of Columbia. The reporter of this piece wrote: "It is believed the Commissioners, aided by the Corporation Counsel and feminine advisers, will arrive at a wise and judicial decision."[101]

An editor with a Washington, D.C., newspaper remarked that Coudrey had introduced a bill "to curb the long hat pin evil" in the District. He "must not be credited with being in full possession of the courage of his convictions, no matter what may be the verdict on his judgment." The women, he believed, may "be expected to protest indignantly that there is no such evil, on the ground that it is well known and generally accepted that any idiosyncrasy of headgear in which they wish to indulge is but the manifestation of that sweet whimsical uncertainty which makes women so beloved by men." He also believed hats were "appurtenances for the heightening of feminine charm," and that Coudrey would have his hands full in trying to convince people on the merits of his bill. "There are two issues which it is particularly dangerous for men to raise in his dealings with women. One is that delicate uncertainty pertaining to her age. The other is that which reflects in the slightest degree upon her hat. Mr. Coudrey has seen fit to ignore one of these cardinal principles of male conduct. Woe betide him! The rest of the sex sympathizes with him, but that's about all he can expect."[102]

As an aid in arriving at a decision, the District commissioners had delegated Dr. William Tindall, secretary of the board, to purchase a hatpin of "standard length" so they could study the item. Tindall did so, returning with a hatpin that measured 10.25 inches in length. He gave it to Commissioner Judson. As well, it was reported that the Corporation counsel was then engaged in a study of the statutes relating to hatpins, extending "back to the days of Cleopatra and Helen of Troy."[103]

For days Corporation Counsel E. H. Thomas was engaged in studying those statutes and it was said that his opinion would bode ill for Coudrey's bill. His opinion was that the commissioners were authorized to enact such "usual and reasonable regulations for the protection of the lives, limbs, health, and comfort and quiet of the residents of the District of Columbia as in their opinion are necessary." In other words, it was the belief of Thomas that the hatpin issue should be left entirely in the hands of the commissioners and that Congress should not be called upon to decide the "momentous questions." While the board of commissioners had not then completed its official report, it was understood that the board would conclude the proposed legislation was unnecessary.[104]

A report from a Honolulu newspaper in April 1910 declared that the city "will soon be the scene of a hatpin crusade," and that the "deadly weapon" would soon be on the way out. "It is expected that there will be considerable opposition to the passage of an anti-hatpin ordinance and it is even feared that should the bill become a law an effort will be made to break it in the courts. For that reason the framers will take no chance and the bill will not be introduced until its supporters are certain that it is puncture proof." At first it was thought, the account continued, that the use of hatpins could be stopped under the concealed weapon law, but it was pointed out that even the biggest hat failed to conceal a hatpin. Rumor had it that Daniel Logan, nestor of the board of supervisors, would be the official to introduce the bill. "Whether women will have to go back to the old-fashioned sunbonnet with homely tie strings under the chin, or whether some philanthropist will invent a new fastener for feminine headgear, is not yet determined. But the slogan of the antis is 'The hatpin must go.'"[105]

Humorous comments on the issue were profuse. A May 1910 piece by an author listed as "Amere Man" presented a supposed conversation between a husband and wife on the topic. Appearing with it was an illustration that showed the wife in the process of attaching a 42-inch hat to her head with two 48-inch hatpins.[106]

A second article that month contained several photos and illustrations of what might happen in San Francisco if the police arrested wearers of hatpins. This was the result of an ordinance that read: "It shall be unlawful for any person in the city of San Francisco, not being a public officer, to wear or carry concealed about his or her person any pistols, slingshots, brass or iron knuckles, sand club, dirk, house knife, iron bar or other dangerous or deadly weapon." And that was because an Eastern judge had decided that women's hatpins, particularly those of the style then in use were "dangerous or deadly weapons" and should come under the supervision of the police. The reporter wondered if that ruling should be accepted by the local, San Francisco, police. This ordinance provided that, on payment of a fee of $3 in San Francisco and $2.50 in Oakland, a written permit could be granted by the mayor for a period not to exceed one year to any peaceable person to carry a concealed and deadly weapon upon his or her person. The penalty for violating the measure was a fine not exceeding $500 or one day's imprisonment for every $2 of such fine imposed.[107]

A June 1910 article discussed the social etiquette involved in whether a man should keep his hat on or take it off in an elevator: "Now the fem-

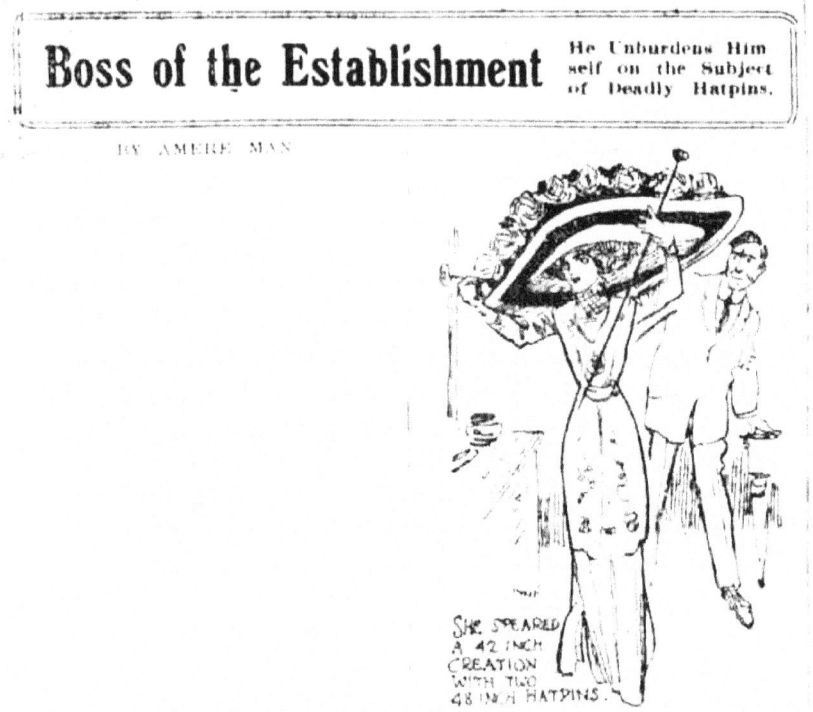

"Amere man" unburdened himself in May 1910 with respect to his wife and her predilection for a 42-inch hat attached to her head with two 48-inch hatpins.

inine hat is large and its saw-tooth edges threaten to decapitate, but the man who would dodge it finds a worse snare in the pointed hatpin. Gentlemen, your headpiece held before you as a shield in the correct and reasonable disposal of the summer hat, while elevating. It is the one protection for modern man against this feminine foible."[108]

A reporter named Barbara Boyd produced an article on the subject that was published in June 1910. In it she mentioned the Chicago ordinance and also cited various museums in Paris and London where women's strange fashion items from the past could be viewed. The viewer of today could be smug by being far removed in time from such fashion items and noting such a lack of sense in dress. "Yet in this twentieth century a city's representatives must pass a law to prevent women from jabbing any inoffensive person who may happen to be near them with pins which they carelessly permit to protrude from their hats to a dangerous extent." Boyd went on to say, "Ever since women [have] taken to wearing large hats and lengthy hatpins accidents from the protruding ends of the hatpins have been

8. *Agitation, Hysteria, Crusades and Legislation* 151

These images illustrated an article in May 1910, in which the journalist speculated what would happen if the police in San Francisco arrested the wearers of hatpins.

numerous.... These are actual facts, as the records of hospitals show. The very fact that a law has had to be passed shows how numerous and how serious such accidents have been." She argued that no "thinking" woman wore such hatpins, only the unthinking ones. "And while women carry dress and conduct to an extreme that either is ridiculous or must be legislated about, just so long will it be extremely difficult for the workers for women's progress to make headway. The woman who unthinkingly or carelessly does the things that bring ridicule or criticism upon her sex is retarding if just so much the coming of the many good things that the pioneers in women's advancement are trying to secure," she added. The woman who carelessly let the point of her hatpin stick out two or three inches might not think it a matter of much moment, but "she is one of the many who are causing a law to be passed that will be regarded by future generations in the same that we now look upon the foolish and freakish dress of bygone ages." Boyd concluded, "It is to be hoped no other city will need to pass the law Chicago has had to pass, and that even in that city the mere passing of the measure will have worked a cure and that there will be no violation of it."[109]

An article that appeared originally in a millinery trade journal was reprinted in a Washington, D.C., newspaper in July 1910:

> The men are always thinking about what we women wear. I don't think it's anybody's business, so long as our clothes and hats are modest. What do you suppose we are in business for? Styles must change in hat pins as well as they must in the hats themselves. If they remained the same the year around we would have to close up shop. I suppose they're a lot of old, sour bachelors, who haven't anything to do but waste the government's time. Always picking on the women. I never saw the like of it.[110]

In New York City in August 1910, a new police magistrate placed himself on record as being in favor of legislation that would compel women to cover the sharp ends of their hatpins with some device to prevent casualties. The magistrate, M. S. Hermann, was, noted a reporter, a bachelor. Two very long and very sharp hatpins were brought before him in court on August 16. "Are those stilettos?" he asked the female defendant. "Why must you wear such dangerous adornment?" She replied, "That is the style, and I must keep up with the style." Hermann responded, "It is all wrong. Men have a right to use their hands to protect themselves from being stuck when they get near such pins, and then they are arrested for assault or for being disorderly. I invariably let them off. Why don't you cork the ends?"[111]

According to a reporter with a Los Angeles newspaper, on September 21, 1910, Police Chief Galloway advised women under attack by a man to "stick them with hatpins." Galloway believed hatpins were effective weapons when they were attacked by robbers or by men intent "on worse crimes."[112]

In Pittsburgh, the mayor of the city referred the task of preparing the "hatpin ordinance" that was to be submitted to the city council in the coming days, to city comptroller Justice Morrow. He consulted a number of "legal lights." They opposed the bill as written, but most of the lawyers thought a prison penalty might be attached for violators instead of a $10 fine. The measure proposed that any woman in public wearing a hatpin more than nine inches long be subject to arrest and fine. Women in the city held "indignation meetings" in streetcars and at the theater matinees. Two enterprising jewelers hung out signs, advertising "Hatpins clipped and resharpened without charge," but up to the end of that day neither had a single customer. Police Superintendent McQuaide, of Pittsburgh, refused to commit himself as to whether he favored equipping the police with pliers to snip off hatpins that were over the prescribed length. According to the reporter, "It is practically certain that the measure will be enacted."[113]

Miss Ethel Violet Kinston, of Moberly, Missouri, who had been studying and traveling in Europe for the previous decade, was then a freshman (and the lone female student) at the School of Law at the University of Missouri in Columbia. She had spent some time in England in the spring and summer of 1909 and observed the "outbursts of the English suffragists" and that the idea of emphasizing principles with hatpins did not shock her as much as it did some Americans. She said, "When men defend their rights they use any sort of weapon they choose and are called heroes for it, but just let a woman use a hat-pin in fighting for hers and they are horrified. It may be very nice to sit down and be a lady, but that is not the way to accomplish things."[114]

Philomena Kiernan was riding in a crowded streetcar in New York City in November 1910. Another passenger, Hugo Bauer, found the point of her hatpin too close for comfort and chided her about it. A disturbance ensued and resulted in the case taken to court, at the insistence of Kiernan. The case was heard before Judge House, who sentenced Bauer to pay a fine of $5 "to teach him to mind his own business." When an outraged newspaper editor summarized the case, he described Kiernan as the "wearer of the eye-destroying hatpin." He then grumbled, "Women's rights have been vindicated by the majesty of the law. A woman can wear a murderous hatpin in a crowded street car, and it may menace the eyes of a mere man, but he must grin and bear it; he is not a censor of the fashions, and if he murmurs he will be arrested and fined."[115]

In an effort to curtail what was called "the long hatpin evil" in Philadelphia, an ordinance was introduced in the city council on December 1, 1910, providing that no person upon the public streets or conveyances shall be permitted to wear a hatpin, the exposed point of which extends more than one-half inch beyond the crown of the hat. A fine of $50 for each and every offense was provided for in the proposed ordinance. It was introduced by Councilman Schmucker, who declared that, with the new-style hats, the lives of riders on streetcars and pedestrians in crowded streets were imperiled by the "immense hatpins."[116]

Reporting on that Philadelphia measure at the end of December, a journalist declared Schmucker, whose "only claim to fame is his prosecution of the feminine stiletto, is the hero of his sex." In that vein, the writer continued: "Wherefore that portion of Philadelphia's male population, who sometimes during their careers have been haplessly impaled upon the needle-like points of the external feminine's hat fastenings, have arisen to call him blessed." When he introduced his measure, Schmucker admitted he represented not his ward "but the whole race of masculine humanity." He introduced it because he had a friend who almost had his eye jabbed out by a hatpin. He also declared "the hospital records are blood stained with the history of similar outrages." However, the bill was not then law. Most of his colleagues on the city council were married or had girlfriends. "These individuals first applauded the bill and hailed Schmucker as the modern Hercules. Lately, however, they have been turning sheepish eyes towards him and cold shoulders." According to the report, there were opponents predicting that the bill would never become a law.[117]

And, indeed, that proposed hatpin ordinance in Philadelphia did not pass. The committee on law of the Philadelphia City Council defeated the proposal by seven votes to three. According to one story, the measure was "laughed to defeat." In the words of one journalist: "The member who had the parting shot at it said he thought the big hatpins were merely a passing fad, and better they might enact a law making women wear rubbers for the sake of their health, or a bill to stop business men eating hasty lunches—also a health measure." Amid the laughter, the bill was defeated.[118]

An editor argued in December 1910: "Some legal restrictions should be imposed upon the size of hatpins that women wear." He felt women blindly followed a fashion without taking a thought as to its consequences. "Hatpins have kept abreast of the size of hats, and no matter how huge the headgear there is a pin big enough to protrude several inches beyond the brim of the hat." Describing the average wearer, he went on to state emphatically: "With exasperating indifference the wearer makes her way through crowds, every movement of her hat threatening the face and eyes of all near her. It is a wise man who steps out of crowds." He argued that "it is useless to request women to wear guards over the points of their hatpins, for they wouldn't do it; but legal steps should be taken to require it, and to restrict the size of the pins. I do not make this suggestion in any spirit of jest. As a matter of fact, the very method which woman has adopted for holding a hat on is ridiculous." In conclusion, he asked rhetorically, "Why can't a woman's hat fit and stay on her head like a man's without the necessity of jabbing through it with a pin three feet long, to the peril of other people when she gets under way?"[119]

Columnist Cynthia Grey had, as a subhead of her December 1910 article, "Woman's Cruel Weapon—the Hatpin." She argued that, in Paris, women wore hatpins to suit their hats, simply because public opinion wouldn't let them wear the longer pins. There were many arrests and prosecutions before French women came to their senses, however. "In America women go about with the sharp points of hatpins projecting anywhere from one to four inches—a menace to all who come near them," Grey wrote. "There's no question about it—women who wear these murderous stilettos, called hatpins, ought to be arrested." Grey concluded: "I have seen many a man dodge from side to side in a street car until in sheer desperation he gave up and fled—from a hatpin."[120]

It was reported, on December 28, 1910, that women in Kansas City, Missouri, had to "muzzle" their hatpins or they would become lawbreakers liable to a fine of from $1 to $500. The upper and lower houses of the municipality's city council passed a hatpin ordinance on the evening of December 27; there was reported to be little objection to it in either house.

8. Agitation, Hysteria, Crusades and Legislation

Most of the aldermen who voted against the ordinance were bachelors. Mayor Darius Brown, for one, indicated he would sign the measure into law. The most enthusiastic supporter of the bill, however, was Alderman John Ward, survivor of a collision with a long and pointed hatpin: he bore a scar as proof of that encounter. How the pins were to be muzzled was not stated in the ordinance; it was something that the women would have to figure out for themselves. Dr. C. A. Jackson introduced the ordinance, saying that the pin point had to be protected or, wrote a journalist, the "poor, helpless men will have to wear screens over their faces."[121]

An editorial on the Kansas City measure read: "This is a good ordinance for the benefit of unprotected mankind." And according to Jackson, "My motives are purely humanitarian, with the emphasis on 'man,' if you want to put it that way. I have treated several cases of wounds in the face and around the eyes from hatpin jabs and several of my friends have suffered."[122]

The lower house of the city council of Kansas City passed the protected hatpin ordinance on January 9, 1911, over the veto of Mayor Darius A. Brown, by a vote of 13 to two. The ordinance, which provided that anyone wearing a hatpin with an unprotected point would be guilty of a misdemeanor and liable to a fine of from $1 to $200, originated in the lower house. The mayor vetoed the measure on the ground that it was trivial. Dr. Jackson was displeased by the mayor's action and made a speech on the subject on January 9 in the council chambers:

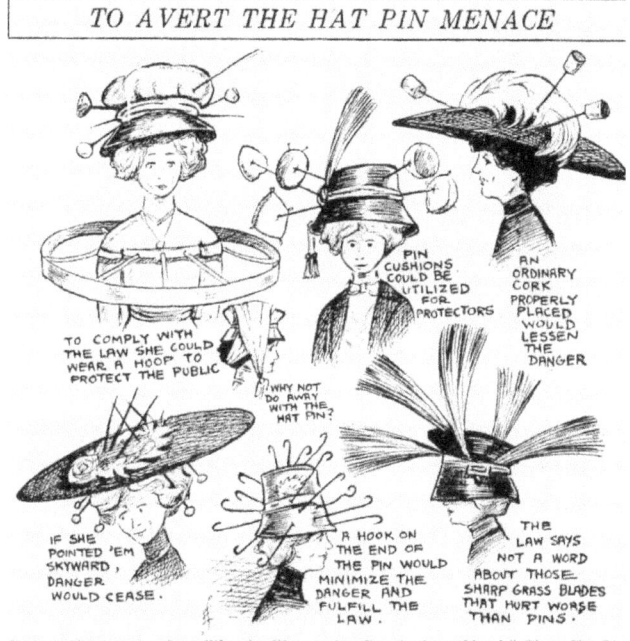

This December 1910 editorial cartoon spoofed the Kansas City measure that required dangerous hatpins to be "muzzled."

"I introduced the ordinance in all seriousness. People should be protected against the harmful point of the hatpin. Within the last two months I had occasion to treat several men who had been injured by them. One man sustained a serious injury to his cheek and another lost an eye."[123]

A story about the Kansas City measure in a Seattle newspaper read: "The long hatpin convicted of murder and other crimes, is legally barred from Kansas City." Hereafter hatpins were not to be worn without some type of protector over the point. The upper house of the city council asserted the belief that the law would prevail over fashion by passing the ordinance on March 27, 1911, over the mayor's veto. It had been two months since the lower house passed the measure. It was then law.[124]

On the last day of 1910, an article published in a Tulsa newspaper covered the passage, noting, "The hat pin is the peril of the hour!" He blamed Paris for the big hats and big hair of modern women the world over. He then lamented, "The joys of street car riding have vanished. With every lurch of the car there is a puncture for some poor man's physiognomy. They confront him on every side during his homeward trip. They prick him right and left.... Each turn of the pretty strap-hanger's head by his side is recorded by a long red line drawn catty-cornered across his face. His ride is one long, demonic journey of torture." Physicians, the readers were informed, said that the hatpin was as much to be dreaded as anthrax, with several fatal cases of tetanus having been caused by a pin jab "and there have been innumerable cases of blood poisoning resulting less seriously." Claiming a lot of women (that is, advocates of women's rights) sided with men on the issue, Mrs. Rachel Foster Avery, former president of the Pennsylvania Suffrage Association among them. As she affirmed, "The excessively protruding points of hatpins are menacing and ridiculous and [...] the authorities have a perfect right to legislate against them."[125]

In Pierre, South Dakota, Representative Stuverud, of Codington, thought hatpins should be eliminated and that he should be the one to do it. The puzzle, for him, was whether to classify them as dangerous weapons with a penalty to fit such an offense or to put them in the class of hardware or millinery. Stuverud's motive for introducing this bill was personal. As he was working his way through the crowd in the South Dakota Legislative building lobby on the night of January 7, 1911, he came into contact with a pin he described as "about so long" while holding his arms out wide, and from which he received a long scratch. He said he was ready to introduce legislature to require such articles of wearing apparel to be properly muzzled at the point or relegate them into lawful "outer darkness" unless they could be rendered harmless.[126]

8. Agitation, Hysteria, Crusades and Legislation 157

On January 11, his hatpin bill was referred to the Military Affairs Committee of the South Dakota Legislature. On January 15, there was a reported "talkfest" over the hatpin measure in the House, but the bill went down to defeat after the committee report was adopted.[127]

After Representative Stuverud had been going around with a long scratch on his face, and hearing endless comments intended to be humorous about it, he finally determined that he would "fix" the hatpin. He kept his word when he introduced House Bill Number 54. He acknowledged his bill would make him unpopular with women, but, he insisted, his bill was a good one and that it should pass. The bill read as follows: "It should be unlawful for any person in the state of South Dakota to wear any hat pin, or other sharp pointed and dangerous contrivance for holding the hat, or hair, of a greater length than seven inches, or any such contrivance with the sharp end exposed in such manner as to be dangerous to the public." The second paragraph of his bill was actually a "big hat" measure. It read "It shall be unlawful for any person to wear any hat, bonnet or other head covering in any public audience within doors, or to wear the hair in any manner or fashion in any such public audience within doors as shall obstruct the view of the speaker or actor addressing such audience, from persons sitting in the rear of any such audience."[128]

Alderman Drescher presented a resolution on January 10, 1911, at the New York City Council, for the curtailing of the length of women's hatpins. The resolution provided that the pin should not extend more than a half inch beyond the crown of the hat unless the point was so guarded "as to render contact with it entirely free from danger." Penalty for violation of the measure was the usual $50. This bill went to the Committee on Laws and Legislation.[129]

In commenting on the New York City measure, one editor of an out-of-state paper wrote that New York would join other cities "in the crusade against the hat pin evil."[130]

In January 1911, an artist for a New York City newspaper sketched the inside of a subway car during a busy time to show the hatpin menace.

On the afternoon of January 26, 1911, a public hearing was held in the New York City Hall before the Committee on Laws and Legislature. One reporter commented that if this meeting was any criterion there would be a riot in the Board of Aldermen when the Drescher hatpin ordinance came up for debate. From the attitude of certain aldermen, continued the journalist, it would appear that they were opposed to an ordinance that would inflict a fine on a woman wearing a hatpin that protruded unprotected in a public place. Other aldermen were said to be ardently in favor of the ordinance. At the public hearing in question, half a dozen clubwomen argued for its passage: "But the most passionate and eager leaders were the dozens of inventors and dealers who were on hand to exhibit safety devices ranging from a cork to impale on the sharp end of a hatpin to a scheme for anchoring the hat to the hair on the inside of the crown with a sort of celluloid anchor attached to a piece of rubber." Alderman Downing (described as a bachelor who had never been jabbed) downplayed the idea that hatpins as worn then were dangerous. Alderman Campbell agreed. The number of women who appeared and argued in favor of the bill were said to number six or seven. Alderman Drescher opened the hearing with the following comments: "I want my efforts in this direction regarded seriously by my colleagues and not in the spirit of fun as a certain few are inclined to treat some of the matters presented to this board." Downing suggested it would be wrong to try to force women to adopt a different style; he suggested hatpin reform could be brought about through a campaign of education. Mrs. James McCullough said, in her opinion, that such a campaign was not necessary, that women had to be forced to abandon "dangerous hatpins." Downing was cynical about the amount of damage supposedly done and wanted to see the scars. All the women present admitted they had never been jabbed, but all claimed to have had close calls. Campbell argued it was not possible to be jabbed—that a wide brim on a hat nullified a protruding hatpin and that one could not be stabbed by a hatpin unless one got closer to the end of it than the broad brim would allow. The women unanimously disagreed with him. No one appeared in opposition to the ordinance. Once everyone there who wanted to speak on the issue had done so, the inventors were allowed to display their stuff. And, said a reporter, "They charged out of their seats like an attacking army. They were loaded down with sample hats, sample devices and literature."[131]

Another newspaper account in a New York City publication covered the same meeting as noted above and declared it was a big enough assembly to have two rows of "girls." (The term "girls" was used repeatedly in the piece to refer to the women who had come to debate the proposed measure.) That ordinance read, in full,

> That no person shall while upon any public street or thoroughfare or in any public street car, elevated train, subway train or elevator, or in any other public place, wear a hatpin or similar device, the exposed point whereof shall protrude more than one-half inch beyond the crown or other portion of the hat upon, in or through which such pin is worn unless said exposed point of the hat pin shall be so guarded by device or otherwise as to render contact with it entirely free from danger. Any person offending against the provision of this ordinance shall be subject to a fine of not more than $50.

Said Mrs. Cartwright, "I very much regret that the ordinance has to be introduced by a man." With respect to the inventors at the meeting, this article stated: "Everybody who ever patented anything that has to do with a pin or a hat, men and women, crowded around the committee to demonstrate and to sell their wares. No oratory to equal it ever has been heard, even in the Aldermen's chamber."[132]

An editorial on that ordinance said the public hearing drew upwards of 100 people and one of them, a female, was quoted as saying, "This whole thing can be settled in five minutes. All women want this law." The editor thought that was perhaps too sweeping a conclusion, but that it was "essentially true. Such women as do not wish the ordinance are too careless of their own safety as well as that of others to be worth counting in the mat-

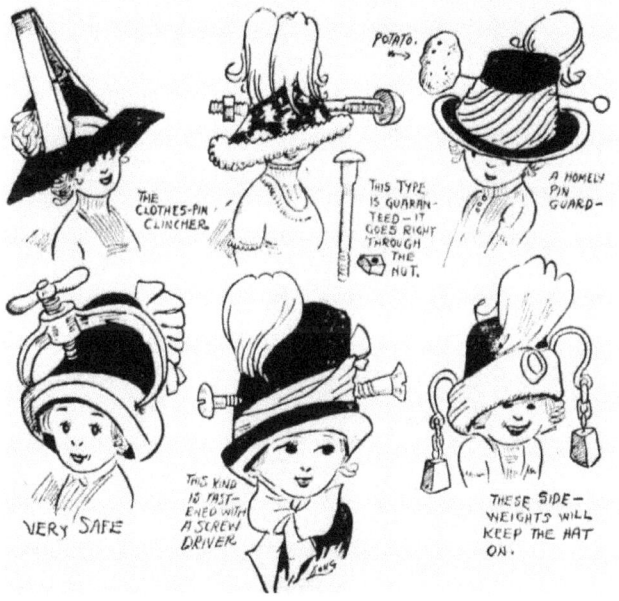

A January 1911 cartoon from New York with humorous suggestions on how women could avoid completely the use of the deadly hatpin.

ter. Virtually the whole community approves the measure." He then offered the thought that the curious point in all this was that a law should be required: "The evil is like the old one of wearing hats at the theatre. That custom discommoded women more than it did men, for a man could often see over a hat that completely barred the view of a woman. Yet the ladies held to the habit until compelled to abandon it. It appears that in all matters of reform no one wishes to begin. Laws are required to make them start even."[133]

On January 31, 1911, it was reported that the proposed hatpin ordinance in New York City had been defeated in the Board of Aldermen on that date: seven committee members voted against; three voted in favor. Before that vote, Alderman Frank Dowling spoke against the ordinance and declared that all the militia of all the States, the U.S. Army and all the battleships of the U.S. Navy could not enforce such an ordinance.[134]

When the Board of Aldermen voted it was 37 to 20, a vote not to interfere with the length of women's hatpins. The law committee had brought in two reports: that of the majority, signed by seven members, advocating the pigeonholing of the proposal with the minority report, signed by three members wanting the ordinance passed. Alderman Walsh (described as being married 40 years) declared, "I don't think it's up to us to regulate women's dress, and anyway the hatpin is a great weapon of defense." One alderman who opposed the measure said of the women who showed up at the hearing (and who supposedly all favored the bill) that they were "of the sort who are always showing up at hearings."[135]

In New York City, the aldermen may have given up the fight against the hatpin, but the women had not. At an assembly of the Women's Health Protective League (16 attended) held about a week after the aldermen had given up, Mrs. Ralph Trautman told the women that Mrs. Cartwright was not discouraged, adding, "In fact, if it is necessary, she is going to carry the matter to Albany, for we must have a law. Women cannot be controlled without it. Why, I was in a store the other day, and a woman came along with a great pin sticking out, so that the floorwalker was afraid. But when he asked her politely to please remove it, she snapped, 'If you don't like it, get out of my way.' Now, you see a woman like that can be reached only by law."[136]

A hearing took place in the New York City Aldermanic Chambers on February 10, 1911. It lasted for three hours, during which time the city fathers examined all sorts of safety devices for the hatpin. Representatives of 116 women's clubs, reportedly, appeared at the hearing against the hatpin.[137]

Another plea for "legal protection" against women's long hatpins was made at a meeting of the New York City Board of Aldermen on the afternoon of October 3, 1911, by A. F. Jones, a member of the firm of Moran and Jones, who wrote in support of a proposed ordinance to limit the length of the "weapons." He stated, "Having this week had my face cut with a protruding hat pin I add my protest against the prevalence of carrying these exposed weapons and hope you will put through the contemplated ordinance relating to them. Dr. H. Everett Russell and others had previously complained of the hatpin but the aldermen refused to reconsider their action of a previous meeting. Said Alderman Drescher: "The majority of the Aldermen seem to fear to interfere with the foolish fashions of women so I shall wait until more people are stabbed or who lose their eyes from hatpins when the ordinance will have to be passed. Maybe the new Board of Aldermen will help me." (When that new Board was installed the following year, they did not reconsider the old pigeonholed measure.)[138]

In Boston, at the end of January 1911, State Representative Newton of South Boston held up an 18-inch-long hatpin for the edification of the Legislative Committee on Legal Affairs. He said, "If I should walk down the street carrying a fishknife as long as this I would be arrested as a dangerous character." He appeared before that committee in support of legislation to limit the length of hatpins. The bill that Newton advocated provided a fine of $20 for any person wearing a hatpin, the exposed point of which projected more than half an inch beyond the crown of the hat. "It does not seem to make any difference whether a girl wears a cartwheel or a little ding-dong affair of a hat on her head," he added, "the pins are just as long as she can get them, and it is time something was done to put an end to this murderous practice."[139]

In the Massachusetts House on February 1, 1911, the Committee on Legal Affairs reported leave to withdraw a bill to regulate the length of hatpins. Representative William Newton had introduced it "and was bitterly fought by the women of his district."[140]

The wearing by women of hatpins that were a menace to the traveling public had to stop in Massachusetts, at least that was the conclusion of a legislative committee that, on January 28, 1913, recommended the adoption of a state law, making it a misdemeanor for a woman to permit the pointed end of a pin to protrude more than a half inch from the side of her hat, unless the end was covered with some device rendering it harmless. According to the article, "The most serious argument against the legislation was that women sometimes were compelled to draw their hatpins and use them as weapons."[141]

An editorial, from a Washington paper, with respect to the Massachusetts committee recommending a hatpin law stated, "The law is a good one. Already similar laws are in force in many European cities, where they are quite popular—popular with the men for obvious reasons, and even with their ladies because they have brought into use such cute and pretty point guards." He thought the law proposed for Massachusetts might be popular in that state; "It certainly will be popular with the men, and until women suffrage comes in, it is safe to predict the re-election of those legislators who are sponsors for the bill. Perhaps such a law or ordinance in this city [Washington, D.C.] might be a popular one, but as to that, we prefer to express no opinion."[142]

According to an announcement made in March 1913 on behalf of Governor Foss, of Massachusetts, he would sign the bill regulating the length of hatpins. The measure would go into effect on April 12, 1913. The bill read, "It shall be unlawful for a person to wear in public a hatpin which protrudes more than one-half inch beyond the crown of the hat, unless the point thereof is protected in such a manner as to be incapable of causing injury to others. Violation of the provisions of this act shall be penalized by a fine of not more than $100 for each offense." Foss signed the bill into law on March 10.[143]

Reportedly, the Massachusetts politicians had that measure under discussion for more than two months and it "had provoked heated arguments in committee in which men and women took part. Attempts to restrict the length of the pins failed and the manner in which they were to be rendered harmless was left to the discretion of the wearers."[144]

In Boston in April of 1913, the question arose of what constituted the crown of the hat, as distinguished from the brim, rim, edge, border, and so forth. A reporter observed, "The Police Commissioner is reported to have already declared that no one on his force can prove what constitutes the crown of the feminine headpiece. A newspaper woman boasts she wore extra long hat pins all the afternoon parading the shopping district and no policeman questioned her.[145]

A few months later, in June, an editor asked rhetorically, Wasn't Massachusetts going too far in passing a law that no woman should wear a hatpin that projected more than a half an inch. The law seemed to serve a useful purpose, he wrote, but "the real objection to this particular law is that it is not adequate for the purpose. The first day after it went into effect we are informed that 90 percent of the women in Boston were permitted to wear hat-pins in the usual manner, apparently because no member of the police force had courage enough to make an arrest." Satirically, he suggested the state should pass a law requiring that every woman who wears

8. Agitation, Hysteria, Crusades and Legislation

a hatpin should take out a license and be required to wear a number on her back, granting her the privilege.[146]

On February 3, 1911, it was reported that Nebraska "at last" was to join "the great hat pin crusade": a bill on the topic was expected to be introduced at the next session of the Legislature, which would prohibit long and unguarded hatpins. According to the article, the bill was not going to be a copy of measures introduced in other states, not an imitation at all but one that "springs from the serious moral sense of Hatfield of Lancaster," a Democrat. Representative Hatfield declared he would introduce the bill at the request of the streetcar patrons of Lincoln. The bill read "that hereafter in this state it shall be unlawful for any person to wear a hat pin over seven inches in length; provided, however, that this act shall not apply to wearing of hat pins over seven inches in length when worn with the point thereof protected with a muzzle or guard. That any person violating this act shall be guilty of a misdemeanor and punished by a fine of not less than $1 or more than $25."[147]

In Sacramento, California, Assemblyman Kennedy introduced a bill prohibiting the wearing of exposed hatpins, in February 1911. He brought with him to the assembly a large collection of hatpins, some of which, he said, were taken from women by men who had been stabbed by them. One such hatpin was 18 inches long. Kennedy planned to exhibit them when his bill came up for passage.[148]

Kennedy's bill came out of committee on the morning of February 17 with a favorable report after the measure had been amended by the committee so that it was practically the Wisconsin law. It provided that no person in a public street or place or on a public conveyance, streetcar, train or elevator, could wear a hatpin, the point of which protruded more than a half an inch beyond the crown, unless the point was guarded with a safety device.[149]

At the first night session of the California Assembly that year, Kennedy's hatpin bill was passed by a vote of 46 to five, on March 3, after an "amusing debate in which the members had fun with Kennedy and his measure," according to one account. Representative Ryan took the matter very seriously, though, and remarked, "If you go into a streetcar in San Francisco you practically take your eyesight into your hands."[150]

Ever since February 1911, when Miss Persons addressed the Women's Equal Suffrage League of Montclair, New Jersey, and emphasized her belief that women would not be worthy of the privilege to vote until they made manifest their common sense of curtailing the length of their hatpins, local jewelers had a rush of orders for short hatpins and were being "overwhelmed" with the work of shortening existing hatpins. One jeweler said that a few hours after Persons made her address there was a run on his shop for short hatpins. Said a reporter, "He hadn't any stock, but he got busy shortening what he had." Then came a rush from women wanting hatpins to be shortened. Leaders of Montclair society were prominent in those throngs, it was reported.[151]

Reportedly, a law forbidding hatpins that project "beyond the headgear and threaten to disfigure the faces of bystanders" was being prepared in Hawaii at the insistence of Speaker Holstein. "It ought to be enacted, as such laws have been in some of the States and, in the form of ordinances, in several cities," he exclaimed. "Morally speaking, a man has as much right to wear spurs at a ball as a woman has to wear projecting hatpins in a crowd; but men wouldn't think of such a thing. It is only women, slaves of fashion, that lack consideration for others and have to suffer law's restrictions of costumes as they did in regard to theater hats."[152]

A crusade against long hatpins gained a strong supporter in Providence, Rhode Island, in March 1911, in the form of State Representative John B. Leclerc, of Woonsocket, who, after being wounded by one of the "dangerous weapons," announced he would introduce a bill in the Legislature limiting the length of the item. While riding to the State House, Leclerc was stabbed in the face by a long pin protruding from the new spring headgear of a female passenger on the streetcar. It got him in the nose and he bled freely.[153]

If a bill introduced on the evening of April 3, 1911, in the New Jersey Legislature by State Assemblyman McGowan, becomes a law, women permitting more than two inches of the sharp end of a hatpin to be exposed in any public place would be liable to a fine ranging from $5 to $25. The bill was introduced at the request of one of McGowan's acquaintances whose friend was injured by a protruding hatpin.[154]

Nothing happened with McGowan's bill, but a hatpin law did go into effect in New Jersey, on April 3, 1913. Under its provisions, all hatpins or other devices of apparel capable of inflicting "lacerations upon the flesh of another person must be provided with tips or guards." Governor Fielder signed the bill into law on April 3. It provided for a fine of from $5 to $20, with half of the fine going to the person making the complaint. In the words of one journalist, "This is calculated to set a lot of people on the job of hunting down unprotected hatpin wearers."[155]

The day after the New Jersey law went into effect, a reporter asked the rhetorical question as to whether or not that law was being obeyed in Jersey City that day; "the answer was a loud and decided NO!" The women of the Garden State still "wore them brazenly and openly, and declared they hadn't been the least bit afraid of an arrest." Then the reporter commented on the "mean, spiteful feature of the law," referring to half the fine going to the person making the complaint. No arrests, though, were made on that first day. Stores in many New Jersey towns put the latest models of hatpin guards in their windows and prepared for a brisk trade but, reportedly, virtually none were sold. Said one woman to a reporter, "I'd like to stick a hatpin in the man who is responsible for the law." (He was James P. Kirkpatrick, of Jamesburg.)[156]

A story that appeared in April 1911 and told how a long hatpin "tore

An April 1913 editorial comment, in cartoon form, lampooning the New Jersey measure.

out the eye of a railway guard" as a woman rushed by him on her way to catch a train featured an illustration and declared that "such comparatively minor incidents as this cartoon depicts are of daily occurrence."[157]

An editorial cartoon on the hatpin controversy appeared in a newspaper in June 1911. It depicted several women, one of whom says that her friend Vera always uses such "dangerously long hatpins." Her listener replies, "Yes, but she's careful to sterilize them."[158]

In August of 1911 an editor declared that most efforts at passing legislative measures to limit or regulate hatpins that women could wear "have been laughed out of being, but it is not entirely a laughing matter, after all." He felt that the city or state had no business in trying to regulate women's (or men's) fashions, yet it was different when it came to the issue of safety. The woman who looked out for the comfort of others would not wait for the law to tell her how far from her head she could extend her hatpins. "Common sense and modesty will regulate that, and perhaps it is this fact that deters law-makers from unbending their dignity to deal with the menace," he opined. "Unreasonably long hatpins should be discarded—here is where the 'rule of reason' can be legitimately invoked."[159]

Another editor stated at this time: "Women who will wear such decorations are either thoughtless or careless. These long pins came in with the wide hats, and so long as the brim rendered them harmless, nobody cared. But they sur-

An April 1911 drawing of the deadly hatpin at work in its favorite location—an overcrowded transit vehicle.

8. Agitation, Hysteria, Crusades and Legislation 167

vive the broad brims and reappear in tiny turbans—and become a menace to humanity. Not a few cities prohibit their use; all cities should follow suit."[160]

In an editorial printed in a newspaper of September 1911:

> In nearly every state and in most large cities efforts have been made to pass laws against the use of long hatpins. The fatalities from these instruments have been many and serious. They have put out eyes, scratched faces, made dangerous wounds, and added a new terror to life. The inclination has been to ridicule any effort to regulate them, because fair woman is supposed to be allowed to do anything or wear anything that fashion may impose upon her. But this is a real terror and it is to be regretted that solemn reformers have not been able to handle it with better results.[161]

A five-panel hatpin-related comic strip appeared in September 1911. It depicted a woman at a mirror busy fixing her hair as she told her cat Pete that there was somebody at the door and to see who it was. Pete leaned out of the window to see who was there. However, he leaned out too far and fell out the window, disappearing from view. The woman looked down and observed that Pete had fallen right on the caller's hat. The last panel showed Pete having returned, only now he was covered in bandages. As to the identity of the visitor, it was Mrs. De Rigger wearing the hatpins the woman had given her the prior Christmas.[162]

Another editor that same month argued that American efforts to regulate the length of women's hatpins "are the extreme of silliness" when compared with the drastic measures adopted by the railway administration of Saarbrücken, Germany. He noted that a few communities in the United States had fixed upon the length hatpins should be, but so far as was known there had never been an attempt to enforce those ordinances, probably "for the reason that American women are considered able to regulate such matters for themselves." Concluded the editor, "Thus it is made manifest that Germans are bold where Americans are timorous."[163]

In October 1911, a different editor remarked, "Whatever may be said

This comic strip from September 1911 reinforced the idea that hatpins were very dangerous indeed.

in favor of 'milady's' hat ornament, a great deal of damaging testimony can be brought against it, and it is reasonably certain that if it was an adaptation of 'mere' man it would long ago have been forced into the 'has-been' class. But women, with her supreme power, and her hat pin, make a combination difficult to defeat."[164]

In New York City, in November 1911, the delegates of the State Federation of Women's Clubs adopted a resolution condemning hatpins. The resolution, offered by Mrs. Eugene J. Grant, read, in part: "Resolved, that this convention condemns the use of hatpins that project beyond the crown of women's hats."[165]

One editor believed that the hatpin would go, if it went at all, through the fact that it became unfashionable: "This is the point of view of Queen Mary of England, who has joined the crusade against it." The hats that she had taken with her to India were to be held in place by means of an elastic coming down under the back hair in the old-fashioned style.[166]

In another report on Queen Mary, she was cited as having said that long hatpins were "unjust to others, risky to oneself." But this editor did say that while Queen Mary had given up hope of having the women of her country abide by her decisions in matters of dress "she still makes an occasional protest against certain fashions."[167]

In March 1912, it was the Cook County League of Women's Clubs in Illinois which spoke out against the use of long hatpins. The group was well aware an ordinance against the hatpin had been passed in Chicago, but they complained that "it hasn't been enforced." Therefore, the members of those clubs were resolved to protect their husbands and children "and a militant campaign for law enforcement by women was planned" at a meeting of the league. Each of the league was to carry a card and a cork with them. The cards were to be handed to every offender who fell under the "censuring eyes" of the organization. It was decided to purchase thousands of corks, which were to be distributed among the women of Chicago, with the request that they would be given to those who were seen wearing long hatpins. Accompanying the corks were cards bearing the inscription: "Please use this cork on the point of your hatpin. Don't you know that you are endangering the eyesight of those with whom you come in contact? Why don't you stop wearing long hatpins?"[168]

George Lord, of Detroit, represented his state of Michigan at Lansing in the State Legislature. During his time there, he wrote a measure and presented it to the Legislature. The measure, if passed, would make it a felony for any woman to appear in public in the state of Michigan wearing a hatpin that was more than ten inches long, and provided for a fine of

$500 or two years' imprisonment, or both. That proposal came as an amendment to the statute forbidding the carrying of dangerous weapons. Reportedly, he thought it would be taken as a joke, but it became a law. An editor commented, "It was an evil day when women first desired the use of hatpins of the elongated variety." Such hatpins, he added, were "an abomination on the face of the earth."[169]

An editor with a Washington, D. C., newspaper commented in March 1912 with respect to the Michigan law: "The deadly hat pin has been classed and characterized as it deserves by the Michigan legislature. That body rushed through and gave immediate effect to a bill which prohibits ten-inch hat pins, slingshots, razors, and other deadly weapons." He went on to say that it was impossible to state, without reference to the complete text of the bill, what "elements of the facetious may be embodied in this bill, but the fact is that it may well be taken in all seriousness." He added, "The ten-inch hat pin is the most subtle of all the weapons of the armory. It flaunts itself abroad with an apparent innocence and candor which would deceive the very elect. The victim scarcely realizes that he had been wounded until he is on his way to the eye-infirmary." As well, he thought it was time to pass a few more laws such as the one passed in Michigan, with the provision that such acts should have immediate effect.[170]

Also in March 1912, the New York City Department of Health was asked by a number of women to begin a crusade on "long and dangerous" hatpins. As a beginning, the health commissioner was asked to have printed notices that could be passed out in subway trains and surface cars warning those who wear them of the menace they were to other people. The women interested said that many thousands of the slips could be circulated to good effect in that way and many of those women promised to pass out such notices.[171]

The Era Club of New Orleans was described as the biggest woman's club in the South. On March 27, 1912, it lobbied the New Orleans City Council for an ordinance against long hatpins. That council was asked by the women to bar pins that protruded through the crown of the hat.[172]

It was reported, on May 15, 1912, that thereafter any woman in New Orleans who wore a hatpin protruding more than one inch from the crown of her hat would be subject to arrest, according to an ordinance that was passed by the New Orleans City Council.[173]

In December 1912, State Commissioner Newman, of New Orleans, told a delegation of women representing the Era Club to hold a conference and adopt some plan for the enforcement of the ordinance prohibiting the wearing of hatpins that protruded more than one-half inch and report to him at the next meeting. Newman said the subject of arresting ladies who violated the hatpin ordinance was a serious one and that he would be loath to instruct police officials to call a patrol wagon and herd these ladies off to jail; such a state of affairs would hardly be tolerated in New Orleans. Newman suggested that club members meet and make some suggestions for enforcing the ordinance, which provided a penalty of a fine from $5 to $25, or a jail sentence of up to 30 days.[174]

In March 1913, the police in New Orleans reportedly received special instruction to arrest any women found violating the city's hatpin ordinance that had recently passed. The ordinance provided that no hatpin was allowed to protrude beyond the hat unless the point was covered. The penalty was said to be a fine of from $1 to $10, or imprisonment from six hours to five days.[175]

On April 2, 1913, Miss Edna Lichtenstein had the distinction of being the first person arrested for violating the Newman hatpin ordinance. On a Wednesday morning, acting under instructions of Police Superintendent Reynolds, Corporal Eugene Casey and Patrolman Claverie made affidavits against eleven women who wore protruding hatpins. The policemen had large crowds following them as they worked. Casey, noted a reporter, in "a most dignified manner took every precaution so as not to leave the impression that it was a joke, at the same time being careful not to offend any of the women he approached." He would say, "I beg your pardon but I must call your attention to the fact that you are violating the law by permitting your hatpins to project out more than an inch. Now would you kindly give me your name and address." According to the reporter, all the women thus approached took the matter good-naturedly and cooperated. Nearly all the women against whom affidavits were made were "known in social circles." Casey met two females who were visitors to the city and ignorant of the law. They were cautioned and permitted to go. "At no time during the morning's work of enforcing the Newman ordinance was any unpleasantness experienced," the account stated. "The women resigned themselves to their fate smilingly."[176]

At Baton Rouge, Louisiana, State Representative Alphonse Dupont, of Terrebonne, was reported to be going after hatpins. He gave notice that he was preparing a bill for introduction in the State Legislature fixing the size and prescribing penalties. No details of his proposal were then available but it was said that he planned a "drastic measure" that would place the burden of responsibility for violation not so much on the women who wore the long pins but on those who sold pins above the size to be prescribed in his act.[177]

8. Agitation, Hysteria, Crusades and Legislation 171

On the floor on the Louisiana State Senate on July 6, 1912, State Senator Vincent stated, "The hatpin is woman's weapon of defense; it's like her tongue. I am afraid of both, and the man who doesn't want to get 'stuck' had better get out of the way. I'm opposed to the Dupont hatpin bill." Other state senators agreed with Vincent and the bill providing that points of pins should be either protected or shortened was sidetracked indefinitely.[178]

A hatpin bill did pass in Louisiana, but it took two years. It was introduced in 1912, went through a House committee, passed the House, was considered by the Senate committee and was finally voted down in the Senate. It was resurrected in 1914, went through both houses and finally became law, one of about 50 measures that passed during the first 50 days of the Legislature's session. One commentator remarked, "As a joke, the woman's hatpin bill is a screaming success. As a subject for serious legislation it is mere piffle." Bemoaned was the fact the Legislature wasted its time on such trivialities while more important measures were ignored or postponed. He concluded, "As an instance of the utter futility of Legislature and legislative sessions, it may be pointed out that, through its governing body, the great State of Louisiana has at last succeeded in passing a law which regulates the use women make of hatpins to keep the seasonal monstrosities they wear fastened to their hair ... for the Legislature to waste its time on such legislation, however, is supreme folly." Violation of the law was a misdemeanor punishable by a fine and/or jail time.[179]

Mary Swain Wagner, the president of the American Suffragettes, declared war on hatpins, in Milwaukee, in April 1912. She said she was going to have a bill introduced in the legislature: "I know it will take about three minutes to get a unanimous vote on the subject. It is all one's life is worth, or one's eyes to get into an elevator or streetcar, especially with the short women, who always have the biggest hats and the longest pins." She added, "I think they ought to be compelled to wear a cork on the end of the hatpin or else cut them off—or out."[180]

During that same month, the Woman's League of Chicago adopted a "safety plan" regarding "sharp pointed and dangerous hatpins." The plan was to use corks on them. The first person to put the plan into operation was Carrie Bryan, who, according to a news story, ought "to be granted a Carnegie medal as the heroine of the age. Surely the dangerous and deadly hatpins have long been an annoyance to the race. They have often lanced the cheeks of men and youth. Surely no one will grieve when their pestiferous points are sheathed. It is a thousand wonders that the humane society has not corked hatpins long ago."[181]

In May 1912, it was reported that the women of Muskogee, Oklahoma, had declared the long hatpin to be a menace and had gone on record against it. The long hatpin would thereafter be taboo to this group and—if the plans of the Women's Federated Clubs were carried out—it would be a violation of the city laws to wear a hatpin that protruded more than one inch from the crown of the hat. The organization passed resolutions for a safe and sane hatpin. Copies of the resolutions were presented to the Muskogee City Council, and the council was asked that an ordinance be passed making it a violation of the law to wear long and unshielded hatpins. The group promised that at the next council meeting any woman would be welcome to present to urge the council to pass an ordinance. A member of the federation declared that women were continually asked for reform measures; she believed that reform should begin at home.[182]

The hatpin came under fire from the leading club women of Cincinnati in June 1912, when a resolution was passed at a meeting during which the members demanded that a ban be placed on long pins. That resolution came about after several hours of discussion following a report made to the meeting that only several hours earlier a man's face had been badly lacerated by a pin protruding from a woman's hat in a crowded streetcar.[183]

Declaring long hatpins to be as unsanitary as un-muzzled dogs, the San Francisco Board of Health in June 1912 was reported to be considering an ordinance prohibiting them. A special "hatpin nipper," to arrest non-complying females, was also provided.[184] After considering the question at length, the members of the San Francisco Board of Health received the proposed hatpin measure at its meeting on June 25. The ordinance that was recommended for passage prohibited any person from wearing a hatpin that projected more than 1.25 inches from the crown of the hat; it further provided that all millinery fasteners of the pin variety had to be enclosed in a protective sheath if protruding. Enforcement of the proposed new city law would be left in the hands of the regular police. Violation of the measure involved a fine of $10 for each offense, a jail sentence of 20 days, or both.[185]

The Klimm hatpin ordinance, originated and drafted by Frank J. Klimm of the San Francisco Board of Health, was recommended to that city's board of supervisors on July 2, 1912, by a unanimous vote of the members of the board after they had engaged in a discussion as to whether regulation of hatpins was within the jurisdiction of the committee. The arguments of Klimm that the ordinance was designed to prevent accidents and possible fatalities as the result of infections arising from wounds by hatpins and therefore within the province of the board swayed the members. Said Klimm: "Many sad accidents can be prevented by the prohibition of

8. Agitation, Hysteria, Crusades and Legislation 173

exposed hat pins in public places. Such laws have been enacted and enforced in London, New York and Chicago, and San Francisco should not be dilatory in keeping up with the times and protecting its citizens from the menace of the hat pin." A violation of that measure constituted a misdemeanor, punishable by a fine of from $10 to $25 or by a jail sentence of two to ten days, or both.[186]

As far as Klimm was concerned, any hatpin that protruded more than 2.5 inches from the crown of the hat was unsanitary. He proposed that a sanitary hatpin ordinance be drafted and that an official hatpin "nipper" be appointed. Commissioner Klimm was said to have gotten his idea from Chicago, where "the long hatpin has been legislated out of business." There, he explained, hatpins were more like stage swords and daggers, decorated with jewels on one end and blunt on the other. In presenting his case, Klimm reasoned, "You've muzzled the dogs, why not nip the hat pins?" Klimm said that, if necessary, he would present a history of the long hatpin to the committee, showing that it was not until the Merry Widow hat was created (in 1907) that long hatpins came into existence and that since that time "according to the hatpin statistics [no such thing existed] many have been injured by absurdly long hatpins."[187]

An editorial noted that San Francisco's attempts to pass an ordinance governing the length of hatpins and observed that "many of the leading club women are very indignant, saying that it is not a fit subject for legislation." The editor added that it should not be necessary to pass such legislation "but unfortunately it is. Ladies should have enough regard for the safety of others to themselves insist that hat pins be not long enough to become dangerous, but unfortunately they are not." He continued, "It should not have been necessary to pass ordinances to compel ladies to remove their hats in theaters, but until such legislation was passed it frequently occurred that people attending theaters would pay for seats and not be able to see a thing that was occurring on the stage." However, he did admit that selfishness was not confined to women. It was, for example, necessary to pass a law against spitting in public places.[188]

According to an August 21, 1912, story, the "doom of the deadly hatpin" was sealed by the San Francisco Board of Supervisors Public Welfare Committee when it recommended a hatpin ordinance to limit the protruding point to a distance of no more than one inch beyond the crown of the hat. The ordinance suggested by the Board of Health would have limited to the projection length to 1.25 inches but the committee members, after a brief argument, cut the length down to one inch.[189]

Armed with two hatpins for display purposes, Supervisor Payot, of

San Francisco, convinced his colleagues on the board of supervisors, on September 4, 1912, that such items as he displayed were a menace to mankind and should be suppressed. They were. The ordinance was passed and would go into effect as soon as it was signed by the mayor. According to this piece, the projection length was limited to one-half of an inch, when the point was unguarded. Any length was okay if the point was sheathed. Payot told the supervisors: "This ordinance is to protect men from injury." He explained that the major department store people had informed him that they would gladly cut all hatpins down to the required length if their patrons so desired.[190]

Realizing the danger "mere man constantly runs of being impaled on the business end of the average hatpin worn in public places by the fair sex," read a report, the California State Board of Health, on July 6, 1912, adopted a resolution condemning the long hatpin. The group also declared that hatpins should not protrude more than one inch beyond the hat. The board planned to send its recommendation to the next session of the California Legislature.[191]

Members of the Badger California Club met at Hermosa Beach on August 29, 1912, and adopted a resolution asking the Los Angeles City Council to make it an offense for any woman to wear a hatpin that protruded more than one inch beyond the crown of the hat. It was planned to present the resolution to the council in a few days.[192]

In reply to a letter from a man suggesting that a police regulation should be enacted prohibiting the wearing of hatpins with unprotected points, New York City mayor William Gaynor sent the following reply: "I fear I have no power to prohibit the ladies from having stick pins in their hats. Suppose you apply to the Board of Aldermen? They seem to be able to do almost everything. I must confess that I never saw any one hurt by a lady's hatpin, but since you say so, and since the Prefect of the Rhone Department [France], as you say, has issued an edict against ladies hat pins, I suppose they must do much slaughter. But is it altogether seemly for a man to get his face so close to a lady's hat pin as to get scratched? Shouldn't such a fellow get scratched?"[193]

In Los Angeles, the board of public utilities and members of the city council were said to be about to declare war, in November 1912, upon "these instruments which have scratched and maimed the male beauty on crowded streetcars." President Foulkes, of the board, promised that he would urge the incorporation of a clause in the proposed anti-smoking ordinance compelling women to wear guards on their hatpins. "Many complaints are received daily of men who have been scratched while riding on crowded cars," said Foulkes. "If we are going to protect women by the abolishing of smoking on streetcars I believe we should reciprocate by protecting the men from hatpins." Mayor Alexander, of Los Angeles, was said to look favorably upon the proposal. Asked if he favored protection from hatpins, the mayor replied, "The hatpin is a dangerous weapon. I am a protectionist." Charles Wellborn, a member of the public service commission, was also enthusiastic over the proposed reform: "Many a man takes his life in his hands when he gets on a streetcar."[194]

Taking their cue from the opponents of anti-streetcar smoking measures who would retaliate by prohibiting long hatpins in the cars, club women of Los Angeles began in November 1912 a campaign against the "protruding eye menace." One of the leaders among those club women was Mrs. Morgan Jones, who stated, "We intend to continue our campaign until we accomplish the desired results. What we want is at least a restriction on hatpins. The long pin is merely a fancy, and unnecessary."[195]

On the recommendation of its committee on legislation, the Los Angeles City Council, on November 20, 1912, instructed the city attorney to prepare an ordinance regulating the use and length of hatpins. The order was adopted, said a journalist, after "determined resistance by several women's organizations."[196]

Contending that "constant tickling" was as exasperating and menacing as the pricking by hatpins, Los Angeles city councilman Topham had a proposal before the city council early in December 1912 to amend the hatpin ordinance so as to curtail the size of millinery plumage. Topham wanted sweeping feathers banished, declaring that they worried everybody in their vicinity.[197]

A fine of $500 or six months in jail was the alternative offered violators of the proposed Los Angeles ordinance governing the length of hatpins, drafted on December 4, 1912, by the city attorney. The legal distance that pins could protrude from the crown of the hat was fixed at one inch. Longer shafts had to be covered by a guard. The measure was slated to go to the city council within the week.[198]

On the morning of December 10, the Los Angeles City Council voted by an "overwhelming" majority to pigeonhole the proposed ordinance for regulating hatpins.[199]

That the hatpin was a deadly weapon was the ruling of Recorder Keefer in Atlantic City, New Jersey, in November 1912, when he imposed a fine of $2.50 on May Clark, who drew one on her husband, Samuel Clark, and threatened to use it. "Hatpins are very dangerous, more so than some revolvers," said Keefer, without a smile.[200]

An editor on a Washington, D.C., newspaper, writing in January 1913, mentioned the hatpin law in Michigan, where pins were limited to a length of ten inches and that it was a felony to wear one "just as it is to carry a concealed weapon." He continued, "It seems a pity that the time of legislatures should have to be taken up with a measure limiting the length of hatpins, yet at least one State, Michigan, has deemed it wise." He felt that "the subject is not altogether deserving of the light treatment some of the legislators are inclined to give it. Only a few weeks ago, a man in Boston died from the scratch of a hatpin, and a serious accident is liable to overtake anyone in a crowded car so long as women thoughtlessly persist in wearing hatpins that protrude several inches outside the crown of their hats, as many of them still do." He added, "These perilous pins, of course, are relics of the time when hats were of the washtub style. Hats have been reduced in size but too many pins have not."[201]

Los Angeles women would have to depend upon their prowess in wielding a hatpin in protecting themselves from holdup men in that city, according to Police Chief Charles Sebastian. Mrs. William Kent was granted a permit to carry a revolver, on January 28, 1913, but later that day Sebastian revoked it, declaring that it was not the policy of the police department to allow women to carry revolvers or other weapons classified as "deadly."[202]

A hatpin ordinance became a law in Milwaukee in March 1913. It was passed by the Milwaukee City Council and Mayor Gerhard Bading had given the measure his official approval. That bill read: "No person in any public place, or a place where the public is allowed to congregate, shall so wear any hatpin that the exposed point thereof projects more than one-half inch beyond the crown of the hat, in, upon or through which such pin is worn; provided, however, that the above provision shall not apply if the point of the hatpin is covered with a suitable and effective guard." Punishment for violation of the ordinance was a $1 fine for each offense.[203]

A humorous editorial cartoon spoofing hatpin guards was published in March 1913. It read that Mrs. Jusserand, wife of the Russian ambassador to the U.S., was setting an example to the rest of Washington society by having the points of her hatpins sheathed.[204]

Connecticut's House of Representatives passed a bill on March 20, 1913, fixing a fine for wearing exposed hatpins that had the point projecting more than one-half inch beyond the hat. That law provided for the first offense a fine of not more than $7 and, for each subsequent offense, not more than $100, or imprisonment for not more than 30 days, or both.[205]

A general article by Frances Shaffer, published in April 1913, declared in its subhead, "Laws Brush Aside Ant Hills While They Let Mountains Stand." She said she was conflicted as she read all the laws and ordinances passed to protect pedestrians against the hatpin—on the one hand was the truth that several inches of sharp steel protruding could do a lot of harm: "And it is only fair to protect the public. But there also stands another truth: Our cities are menaced with evils far greater than any ever wrought by that harmful little weapon, that is not meant to be harmful at all." Overall, if such measures had to be taken, she wished "that it had been women who had taken the initiative, for it is one of the little things that do not speak so very well of woman's claims to thoughtfulness."[206]

This satire, from March 1913, speculates on what it would look like if various hatpin guards become all the rage.

The editor of a newspaper in Opelousas, Louisiana, wondered, in May 1913, if his city could not follow the example set by New Orleans on the hatpin question: "New Orleans has a law on hat pins, why can't Opelousas have the same law? At the same time it would be better if such a law would be passed by the Louisiana legislature."[207]

In 1913, one Mrs. Viola Brophy gave a would-be masher a black eye in New York City and had him arrested. She told a reporter that "any woman annoyed on the street should not hesitate to defend herself. She should use her fists or her finger nails or her hat pin or any weapon that's handy. She should strike and strike to hurt. And she should have her man arrested and appear against him in court."[208]

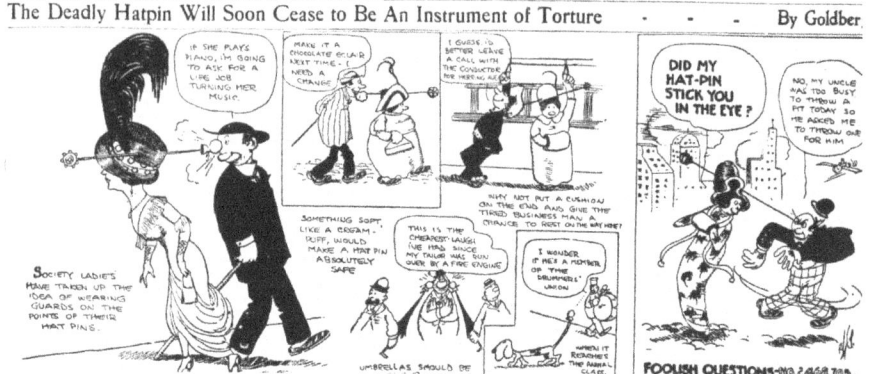

Various humorous comments, in cartoon format, about the hatpin as an instrument of torture.

"Desiring in every possible way to protect the life and liberty of the thousands of visitors from every civilized nation of the world who will be in Tulsa" attending a farming congress slated from October 22 to November 1, 1913, the city commissioners were reported to be framing an ordinance that would prohibit women from wearing hatpins over eight inches in length. According to the story, "The ordinance also regulates the kind of trimmings on the hats and their general circumstance and diameter." That ordinance would only be in effect during the time the Congress was in session; Tulsa women's groups were said to be thoroughly in accord with the idea. Under that proposed ordinance, no hat could be more than 24 inches in width (diameter) and any fancy trimmings on those hats had to extend upward instead of outward.[209]

An old joke about hatpins resurfaced as an illustration in newspapers in October 1913. In the illustration are two strap hangers in a car. The man asks the woman to be a little careful with "those infernal hatpins of yours. I don't want to die of blood poisoning." She replies; "Oh, there is no danger of blood poisoning, I assure you, sir; my hatpins are sterilized."[210]

In March 1914, syndicated columnist Sophie Irene Loeb devoted one of her columns to the topic of the long hatpin. "Every woman knows the dangers of the long hatpin, but how few correct it," she lamented. Loeb went on to relate that a New York City alderman told her that when the controversy of hatpins was up before a committee some time earlier, the very woman whose protests were the loudest against that abuse wore the longest hatpins in the room. Not until it was brought to her attention did she realize it and make haste to offer the excuse that she had forgotten it was there and meant to change it. After she mentioned the law prohibiting the long pin in Switzerland, she stated that it might be the right solution in that country, but "must we always make laws as the only way of defending the rights of others? It is not the wish of the average woman to annoy her neighbor, but rather a thoughtlessness that causes her to disregard those about her." Loeb related that not so long ago the large hat nuisance in theaters and other public places was evident everywhere, and not until every woman realized the injustice that she inflicted on others by wearing one was that abuse corrected. "It is but a slumbering conscience that must needs be awakened into activity. Of course we must keep our hats on, and though there have been many devices for that purpose, the old-fashioned hatpin seems to fill the bill best for most of us," she concluded. "We should make such endeavor to render ourselves less obnoxious by reducing the hatpin to a size that will eliminate its dangers."[211]

The hatpin as a source of danger was made the subject in a bulletin issued by the *Journal of the American Medical Association*, in the spring of 1914. It read: "Everyone knows that a hat-pin point protruding several inches beyond the brim of a woman's hat is a source of danger to anyone in close proximity to the wearer of the pin." After the piece went on to explain the potential damage a scratch to the eye could cause, the piece stated: "It ought not to be necessary to pass laws to prevent such accidents, but as the number of such cases does not decrease it would seem to be desirable to make the wearing of shorter hat pins obligatory."[212]

Over the years many laws against the hatpin had been passed, by cities

An October 1913 illustration to an old joke that surfaced from time to time in this era.

and by states. Many more had been proposed but never made it into law, and were often ridiculed out of the house. Those that were passed were almost universally ignored by law enforcement officials. American women were indeed disarmed; their hatpins were taken away from them, but not by men. Big hair and big clothing and big hats all were erased by the fashion industry. In 1928, the *Journal of Commerce* estimated that in the 15 years to that date the amount of material required for a woman's complete costume (not including stockings) had declined from 19.25 yards to 7.0 yards. Petticoats disappeared, as did corsets. Gigantic hats did not go well with a slimmed down wardrobe style. Not content with the freedom of short and skimpy clothing, women also sought the freedom of short hair. During the early years of the 1920s the bobbed head became increasingly frequent among young girls. In 1918, the bobbed head had been regarded by the proprietor of the Palm Garden in New York City as a sign of radicalism. In the latter years of the 1920s, bobbed hair became almost universal among girls in their 20s, very common among women in their 30s and 40s, and by no means rare among women of 60. Not only was the hair bobbed but in most cases it was cropped close to the head, like a typical man's haircut. Women universally adopted the small cloche hat which fitted tightly on the bobbed head, and the hatpin faded quickly away. Once women adopted shorter hair they could wear hats as a man did, just pulled down on the head, no fasteners of any kind needed.[213]

So then, it could be said, with respect to the eradication of the hatpin: Man proposes; Fashion disposes.

Chapter Notes

Chapter 1

1. "The theater hat." *Austin Weekly Statesman* (TX), December 24, 1891.
2. "The theater hat." *St. Paul Globe*, December 28, 1892.
3. "The theater hat." *Evening Star* (Washington), October 27, 1894.
4. "Large theater hats must go." *Los Angeles Herald*, January 31, 1895.
5. "The theater hat." *St. Paul Globe*, February 16, 1895.
6. "High hats in theaters." *Marietta Daily Leader* (Ohio), March 25, 1896.
7. "The theater hat in Ohio." *Evening Star* (Washington), March 26, 1896.
8. "Aiming at theater hats." *Evening Star* (Washington), January 20, 1897.
9. "The high hat ordinance." *Kansas City Journal* (MO), January 23, 1897.
10. "Anti-hat ordinances galore." *Kansas City Journal* (MO), January 23, 1897.
11. "Not milliners." *Wheeling Daily Intelligencer* (West Virginia), January 27, 1897.
12. "No hats in theaters." *Baxter Springs News* (Baxter Springs, Kansas), February 13, 1897.
13. "Theater hat ordinance." *Evening Times* (Wash), February 26, 1897.
14. S. C. Schenck. "Theater millinery." *North Platte Semi-Weekly Tribune* (NE), February 19, 1897.
15. "High hats at theaters." *Record-Union* (Sacramento), March 17, 1897.
16. "Hats off in church." *Kansas City Journal* (MO), July 4, 1897.
17. "Written at random." *Paducah Sun* (KY), January 22, 1898.
18. "Answers to correspondents." *San Francisco Call*, February 5, 1901.
19. No title. *San Francisco Call*, May 22, 1901.
20. "Delegate Kinney would bar high hats from theaters." *St. Louis Republic*, January 15, 1902.
21. "Of hats and plays." *St. Paul Globe*, December 2, 1903.
22. Cholly Knickerbocker. "The mode of the moment in hats." *Washington Times*, November 24, 1907.
23. "Many more Merry Widows and Broadway must be widened." *Los Angeles Herald*, March 22, 1908.
24. "Advantages and disadvantages of the new hat." *Bisbee Daily Review*, May 2, 1908.
25. "Bigger closets needed." *Sun* (NY), October 4, 1908.
26. "Cermak to the rescue with bill limiting specifications for hats." *Rock Island Argus* (Illinois), April 24, 1909.
27. "Real reason for the anti-big hat bill." *Morning Examiner* (Ogden, Utah), April 25, 1909.
28. "The law against hats." *Rock Island Argus* (Illinois), April 26, 1909.
29. "Throttle is open." *Rock Island Argus* (Illinois), May 8, 1909.
30. "Legislator wars on freak hat." *Albuquerque Citizen*, May 10, 1909.
31. "Freak hat legislation may cost him his job." *Tacoma Times*, May 11, 1909.
32. No title. *Intermountain Catholic* (Salt Lake), May 15, 1909.
33. "Express rates on high hats to be subject of dignified inquiry." *Los Angeles Herald*, January 28, 1910.
34. "Rebellion against tyranny of big lid." *San Francisco Call*, January 30, 1910.
35. "Size of women's hats." *Washington Herald*, February 12, 1910.
36. "Pinless hat offers solution of long hatpin controversy." *Salt Lake Herald-Republican*, April 3, 1910.
37. "Size of women's hats." *Washington Herald*, April 11, 1910.
38. "Mysterious fire gets skyscraper." *San Francisco Call*, May 6, 1910.

39. "Policeman took off her hat." *Sun* (NY), October 3, 1909.
40. "Regulating size of women's hats." *Washington Herald*, July 25, 1910.
41. "Hats on or off in church." *Washington Herald*, July 25, 1910.
42. "Hats are out of order in woman's clubs." *San Francisco Call*, November 28, 1910.
43. Frances Marshall. "Fashion's latest word in smart creations." *Washington Herald*, November 22, 1914.
44. "Tailored chapeaux of velour and felt will do away with hatpins." *Washington Times*, September 25, 1915.
45. Irene Bordoni. "Irene Bordoni describes her favorite hat." *Ogden Standard*, September 27, 1917.

Chapter 2

1. "The souvenir pin craze." *Lafayette Advertiser* (Louisiana), October 28, 1893.
2. "Fads in hat pins." *Evening Star* (Washington), November 1, 1895.
3. "More hatpins than ever." *Minneapolis Journal*, August 11, 1905.
4. "Fancy hat pins." *Evening Star* (Washington), May 27, 1906.
5. "Another triumph for the big hat pin." *Salt Lake Tribune*, June 15, 1906.
6. "Fancy hat pins are now all the rage." *Minneapolis Journal*, November 4, 1906.
7. "Fashionable hat pins." *Washington Times*, December 30, 1906.
8. "Complains of short hatpins." *Rich Hill Tribune* (Rich Hill, MO), December 12, 1907.
9. "Great variety of hatpins demanded by fashion causes comment." *Washington Times*, February 12, 1909.
10. "The hatpin craze. *Carlsbad Current* (New Mexico), February 19, 1909.
11. "Holds the hatpins." *Daily News* (Newport News, VA), May 15, 1909.
12. "Rhinestone hatpins." *Wenatchee Daily World* (WA), February 4, 1910.
13. "Long hatpins are imported as needles." *Deseret Evening News* (Salt Lake), July 26, 1910.
14. No title. *Omaha Daily Bee*, October 3, 1910.
15. "Wex Jones news of tomorrow." *El Paso Herald*, October 6, 1910.
16. Keith O'Brien (ad). *Salt Lake Tribune*, July 18, 1911.
17. Julia Bottomley. "The panama hat." *Baxter Springs News* (Baxter Springs, Kansas), July 20, 1911.
18. Ethel Lloyd Patterson. "Women's fall hats so small shoe horns needed, not hatpins." *Evening World* (NY), August 2, 1911.
19. "Hat pins." *Tulsa Daily World*, December 21, 1911.
20. "Dangerous hatpins will go." *University Missourian* (Columbia, MO), March 18, 1912.
21. "Hatpin menace to go." *Sun* (NY), November 17, 1912.
22. "Clever device for keeping a hat on without the aid of hatpins." *Denison Review* (Iowa), January 20, 1915.

Chapter 3

1. "Mortally hurt by a hat pin." *Sun* (NY), November 12, 1887; "Killed by her hat pin." *Wichita Eagle*, November 18, 1887.
2. "Killed by her hat pin." *Los Angeles Herald*, December 26, 1890; "Killed by her hat pin." *Critic* (Washington), December 26, 1890; No title. *New York Tribune*, December 26, 1890.
3. "Killed by her hatpin." *Abbeville Press and Banner* (SC), March 6, 1895.
4. "Hatpin in her head." *Evening Times* (Washington), September 10, 1896.
5. "Hatpin enters woman's scalp." *San Francisco Call*, December 8, 1901.
6. "Deadly hatpin again." *San Francisco Call*, October 17, 1904.
7. "Car sinks hatpin into her skull." *San Francisco Call*, May 2, 1908.
8. "Hat pin killed Mrs. MacDonald." *Daily Capital Journal* (Salem, OR), July 2, 1910.
9. "Scratched by her hatpin." *New York Tribune*, September 19, 1910.
10. "Hat pin caused death." *Evening Standard* (Ogden), September 16, 1912.
11. "Woman stabs a prison matron." *Evening World* (NY), January 5, 1893.
12. "Tried to stab a policeman." *Evening World* (NY), January 7, 1893.
13. "Tried to stab a policeman." *Evening World* (NY), December 30, 1893.
14. "Used a hat pin." *Kansas City Journal* (MO), June 23, 1895.
15. "Becky Fream arrested." *Sun* (NY), July 24, 1895.
16. "Jabbed a cop with her hatpin." *Sun* (NY), December 4, 1896.
17. "Hat pins a favorite weapon." *Sun* (NY), December 5, 1896.
18. "The man-eater sent up again." *Sun* (NY), January 18, 1897.
19. "Surprise, wrath and profanity." *Sun* (NY), February 15, 1897.
20. "Stabbed with a hatpin." *Evening Times* (Washington), March 7, 1898.
21. "With her hat pin." *Daily Public Ledger* (Maysville, KY), December 9, 1898.
22. "Hatpin in policeman." *Evening World* (NY), January 26, 1900.

23. "Stabbed with a hat pin." *St. Paul Globe*, March 8, 1900.
24. "Hat pin for weapon." *St. Louis Republic*, August 22, 1900.
25. "Detective stabbed by woman." *New York Tribune*, September 1, 1900.
26. "Women prisoners mutiny." *New York Tribune*, December 28, 1900.
27. "Vicious woman stabs officer with hatpin." *Seattle Star*, March 25, 1901.
28. "Hatpin Curtis is sentenced." *Seattle Star*, April 5, 1901.
29. "Woman made a scene in court." *Evening World* (NY), July 23, 1901.
30. "Crowd tries to rescue prisoners." *New York Tribune*, August 6, 1903.
31. "Stabbed with a hatpin." *Alexandria Gazette* (VA), March 30, 1904.
32. "Stabbed cop with hat pin." *Evening World* (NY), March 31, 1904.
33. "Attacks rubber company man." *New York Tribune*, October 24, 1904.
34. "She jabs policeman with her hat pin." *St. Paul Globe*, November 5, 1904.
35. "Girl attacks cop with wicked hatpin." *Evening World* (NY), March 7, 1905.
36. "Fought like a tigress." *Minneapolis Journal*, April 20, 1905.
37. "Hatpin Minnie busy." *Evening World* (NY), September 26, 1906.
38. "Police fear hatpins more than revolvers." *Spokane Press*, October 26, 1906.
39. "Officer insulted her." *Deseret Evening News* (Salt Lake), June 30, 1908.
40. "Is stabbed by negress." *Ogden Standard*, July 7, 1909.
41. "Police matron's work." *New York Tribune*, July 11, 1909.
42. "Woman uses hat pin on officer." *Omaha Daily Bee*, August 22, 1909.
43. "Jennie used her hat pin." *Daily Capital Journal* (Salem, OR), September 1, 1909.
44. "Patrolman is stabbed with long hat pin." *Seattle Star*, November 5, 1909.
45. "New hatpins as weapons are deadly." *Seattle Star*, November 29, 1909.
46. "Hatpin nearly ends life of detective." *San Francisco Call*, May 15, 1910.
47. "The hatpin used with deadly effect." *Arizona Republican* (Phoenix), June 15, 1910.
48. "Tries to stab man with her hatpin in court house hall." *Evening World* (NY), January 17, 1913.
49. "Button protests police officer." *Salt Lake Tribune*, April 13, 1913.
50. "Stabbed with a hat pin." *Springfield Daily Republic* (Ohio), May 8, 1888.
51. "Pricked by a hat-pin." *St. Paul Globe*, October 21, 1891.
52. "She broke up the meeting." *Sun* (NY), April 21, 1894.
53. "That hat pin stabbing." *Sun* (NY), October 22, 1895.
54. "Live topics about town." *Sun* (NY), October 25, 1895.
55. "Stabbed him with a hat pin." *Guthrie Daily Leader* (OK), December 11, 1895.
56. "War on a boat." *Evening Times* (Washington), June 19, 1896.
57. "Used a hat pin." *San Francisco Call*, March 30, 1897.
58. "Another bad case of hatpin." *San Francisco Call*, July 19, 1897.
59. "A woman's weapon." *Los Angeles Herald*, July 19, 1897.
60. "Jabbed with a hatpin." *Sun* (NY), September 21, 1897.
61. "A salesgirl goes crazy." *New York Tribune*, September 21, 1897.
62. No title. *Sun* (NY), September 22, 1897.
63. "Stabbed with a hat pin." *St. Paul Globe*, October 12, 1897.
64. "Recovering from the hatpin wound." *Sun* (NY), October 15, 1897; "Take the pin from his lung." *Omaha Daily Bee*, October 16, 1897.
65. No title. *Princeton Union* (MN), October 14, 1897.
66. "Maidens fight over a young man's hand." *San Francisco Call*, July 23, 1898.
67. No title. *San Francisco Call*, July 26, 1898.
68. "She used a hat pin." *Scranton Tribune* (PA), September 23, 1898.
69. "Red pepper and a hatpin." *San Francisco Call*, February 2, 1899.
70. "Overstepping the bounds." *San Francisco Call*, February 3, 1899.
71. "Attacked by female bandits." *Times* (Washington), October 5, 1899.
72. "Stabbed with a hatpin by a jealous woman." *San Francisco Call*, March 25, 1900.
73. "Drummer jabbed with hatpins." *Deseret Evening News* (Salt Lake), October 9, 1901.
74. "She used a hatpin to restore peace." *Evening World* (NY), March 21, 1903.
75. "Stabbed him with a hat pin." *Times Dispatch* (Richmond, VA), March 22, 1903.
76. "Crowd's enthusiasm causes president to mount railing." *St. Louis Republic*, May 1, 1903.
77. No title. *St. Louis Republic*, May 2, 1903.
78. "Hatpin fight in car." *New York Tribune*, May 31, 1903.
79. "Kills woman with hatpin." *Times Dispatch* (Richmond, VA), June 30, 1903.
80. "Hatpins weapons of women robbers." *Evening World* (NY), July 31, 1903.
81. "Crowd tries to rescue prisoners." *New York Tribune*, August 6, 1903.
82. "Stabbed with a hatpin." *Daily Journal* (Salem, OR), August 22, 1903.

83. "Jealous woman attacks her rival with hatpin." *Rock Island Argus* (Illinois), June 1, 1904.
84. "Says woman robbed and then beat him." *Evening World* (NY), May 1, 1906.
85. "Woman in crowded car stabbed with hatpin." *San Francisco Call*, July 11, 1906.
86. "Hatpin wound is fatal." *Rock Island Argus* (Illinois), December 17, 1906.
87. "Low life murder." *Watchman and Southron* (Sumter, SC), December 19, 1906.
88. "Suspected of murder with hat pin." *Deseret Evening News* (Salt Lake), December 29, 1906.
89. "Charge model with crime." *Evening Statesman* (Walla Walla, WA), January 1, 1907.
90. "Fined $10 for her bit of fun at the Gotham." *Evening World* (NY), January 16, 1907.
91. "Hat-pin battle aired in court." *Deseret Evening News* (Salt Lake), July 15, 1908.
92. "Actress in fight stabs with hatpin." *Los Angeles Herald*, April 22, 1909.
93. "Accused of trying to stab him with hatpin." *Paducah Evening Sun* (KY), July 19, 1909.
94. "Women use hat pins to check train rush." *Seattle Star*, August 4, 1909.
95. "Eva Tanguay is arrested." *New York Tribune*, March 2, 1910; "Stage hand is punctured." *New York Tribune*, March 4, 1910.
96. "Hatpin leads to divorce." *Bemidji Daily Pioneer* (MN), March 23, 1910.
97. "A hatpin baffled workmen." *New York Tribune*, July 2, 1910.
98. "Girls use hatpins to check linemen." *Washington Times*, November 24, 1910.
99. "Girl, in unwritten law case, wields hatpin in courtroom." *Los Angeles Herald*, December 1, 1910.
100. "Fined for using hatpin on trolley conductor." *Washington Times*, January 11, 1911.
101. "Woman used hatpin in effective way." *Salt Lake Tribune*, June 4, 1911.
102. "Fight with hatpins." *Evening Standard* (Ogden), August 14, 1911.
103. "Women fought with hatpins." *New York Tribune*, February 24, 1912.
104. "Attacks lawyers with hatpins." *Mathews Journal* (VA), August 1, 1912.
105. "Maid attacks Mary Pickford with a hatpin." *Seattle Star*, August 2, 1912.
106. "Many women held as shoplifters; all deny guilt." *New York Tribune*, December 15, 1919.

Chapter 4

1. "They used a hatpin." *Evening World* (NY), August 11, 1891.
2. "The hatpin." *Red Cloud Chief* (Red Cloud, Nebraska), October 25, 1895.
3. "New use for hat pins." *Perrysburg Journal* (Ohio), May 15, 1897.
4. "Robbers routed by a woman." *Salt Lake Herald*, January 10, 1898.
5. "The hatpin's new renown." *San Francisco Call*, January 11, 1898.
6. "The deadly hat pin." *Scranton Tribune* (PA), January 14, 1898.
7. "Brave Barbara Stack." *Rock Island Argus* (Illinois), February 5, 1898.
8. "Routed men with hatpins." *Evening Times* (Washington), May 2, 1900.
9. "Hatpins as weapons." *St. Louis Republic*, June 19, 1900.
10. "Hatpin." *Seattle Star*, January 31, 1901.
11. "Uses her hatpin to capture Negro." *St. Louis Republic*, February 17, 1901.
12. "Fair Miss sits on a burglar." *San Francisco Call*, March 18, 1901.
13. "Kissers routed by sharp hatpins." *St. Louis Republic*, April 28, 1901.
14. "Beware of the hatpin." *Salt Lake Herald*, May 23, 1902.
15. "Hatpin for her weapon." *Valentine Democrat* (Nebraska), July 3, 1902.
16. "Sallie Slick and her surprising Aunt Amelia." *Times* (Richmond, VA), July 13, 1902.
17. "Used her hatpin." *Minneapolis Journal*, September 8, 1902.
18. "Hat pin a legal weapon for women to employ." *St. Louis Republic*, September 16, 1902.
19. "Arrival of the hatpin." *Daily Ardmoreite* (Ardmore, OK), September 18, 1902.
20. "Justifies use of hatpin." *Florida Star* (Titusville, FL), October 10, 1902.
21. "Put to flight with a hatpin." *St. Paul Globe*, November 11, 1902.
22. "Young woman used hatpin on an offensive masher." *St. Louis Republic*, April 20, 1903.
23. "To stop the goo-goo habit." *Indianapolis Journal*, April 26, 1903.
24. "Stuck hatpin into a masher." *Evening World* (NY), May 27, 1903.
25. "Girl's hatpin routs masher." *St. Louis Republic*, May 31, 1903.
26. "Judge says women have right to wield hatpins." *Washington Times*, September 8, 1903.
27. "Brings a robber to grief with a hatpin." *St. Paul Globe*, September 8, 1903.
28. "For and about women." *Omaha Daily Bee*, September 13, 1903.
29. "Hatpin saves her honor." *Norfolk Weekly News-Journal* (VA), November 13, 1903.
30. "Used hatpin on assailant." *Salt Lake Herald*, January 12, 1904.

Chapter Notes—4

31. "Woman's handy weapon against thieves." *New York Tribune*, February 7, 1904.
32. "A dangerous woman." *Barton County Democrat* (Great Bend, Kansas), March 11, 1904.
33. "Used hatpin on negro assailant." *St. Louis Republic*, July 11, 1904.
34. "Hat pin and yell save her." *Omaha Daily Bee*, November 6, 1904.
35. "Girl puts ruffian to flight with hat pin." *Minneapolis Journal*, November 14, 1904.
36. "Woman drives off robbers with hatpin." *Minneapolis Journal*, February 3, 1905.
37. "Wounds thug with hatpin." *San Francisco Call*, July 25, 1905.
38. "Hatpin foils bandit." *Minneapolis Journal*, August 15, 1905.
39. "With hat pin girl fought hiwayman." *Washington Times*, October 23, 1905.
40. "Hatpins saved girls their money." *St. Louis Republic*, December 30, 1905.
41. "Girl uses hatpin with telling effect." *Washington Times*, January 23, 1906.
42. "Stabs hugger with hatpin." *Los Angeles Herald*, January 26, 1906.
43. "Woman used hatpin." *Gainesville Daily Sun* (Florida), March 9, 1906.
44. "Hat pin, woman's weapon." *Minneapolis Journal*, May 18, 1906.
45. "Things heard and seen." *Evening Star* (Washington), June 16, 1906.
46. "Woman hat-pinned burglar." *Evening Star* (Washington), June 1, 1906.
47. "Used a hat pin in justification." *Times Dispatch* (VA), July 4, 1906.
48. "Woman routs robber with her hatpin." *Los Angeles Herald*, January 7, 1907.
49. "Girl with hatpin, battles 5 thugs." *Minneapolis Journal*, December 16, 1906.
50. "Threatened to use hatpin on stepfather." *Salt Lake Tribune*, July 29, 1907.
51. "More attacks cause lynch spirit to rise." *Albuquerque Citizen*, August 6, 1907.
52. "Hatpin foils men." *Washington Herald*, August 31, 1907.
53. "Girls chase assailants." *Los Angeles Herald*, September 28, 1907.
54. "Defend honor with hatpin." *Spokane Press*, October 14, 1907.
55. "Hat pin thrust makes 'em howl." *Washington Times*, March 2, 1909.
56. "Woman with hat pin routs two highwaymen." *San Francisco Call*, August 27, 1909.
57. "Uses hatpin on holdup." *Salt Lake Herald-Republican*, February 14, 1910.
58. "Girls capture highwayman." *New York Tribune*, April 3, 1910.
59. "Girl, hatpin and club rout bold burglar." *El Paso Herald*, July 11, 1910.
60. "Stabs a masher with her hatpin." *Washington Times*, October 18, 1909.
61. "Man routed by hatpin held in City Hall." *Los Angeles Herald*, January 16, 1910.
62. "How about the hatpin as a teacher for mashers?" *Marion Daily Mirror* (Ohio), August 16, 1910.
63. "Catches Masher with hatpin." *Alexandria Gazette* (VA), August 23, 1910.
64. "Woman wields hat pin." *Salt Lake Herald-Republican*, August 8, 1910.
65. "Punctures assailant." *Democratic Banner* (Mt. Vernon, Ohio), November 4, 1910.
66. "Hatpin to the rescue." *Daily Ardmoreite* (Ardmore, OK), January 12, 1911.
67. "Jeered her harem skirt." *New York Tribune*, February 27, 1911.
68. "Hatpin for defense." *Bennington Evening Banner* (VT), April 5, 1911.
69. "Hatpins help girl rout an assailant." *Salt Lake Tribune*, April 23, 1911.
70. "Bold attempt at assault." *Marion Daily Mirror* (Ohio), May 4, 1911.
71. "Hatpin routs mere man." *New York Tribune*, August 27, 1912.
72. "Woman's hatpin stops murder." *Sun* (NY), September 17, 1912.
73. "Co-ed and hat pin rout a burglar." *East Oregonian* (Pendleton, OR), October 23, 1912.
74. "Big robber jabbed with a hatpin by woman agent." *Evening World* (NY), November 30, 1912.
75. "Girl with a hatpin captures ex-convict robbing a letter box." *Evening World* (NY), April 4, 1913.
76. "Hatpin halts burglars." *New York Tribune*, July 28, 1913.
77. "Rules for women in holdup." *San Francisco Call*, September 19, 1913.
78. "Hatpin stab proves fatal." *Sun* (NY), January 15, 1914.
79. "Justified slaying is verdict in case of Milwaukee girl." *Bisbee Daily Review*, January 21, 1914.
80. "Heroine's hatpin routs a burglar choking a woman." *Evening World* (NY), July 14, 1914.
81. "To jab him if he flirts." *Tulsa Daily World*, December 16, 1916.
82. "Woman stabs negro thug on street with hat pin." *Washington Herald*, December 18, 1916.
83. "All in a day's work." *Washington Times*, July 27, 1919.
84. "Boy bandit in U.S. Navy garb robs 15." *Washington Times*, October 24, 1919.
85. "Her hatpin routs footpad." *Washington Times*, March 18, 1921.
86. "Hold-up man is routed by woman with hatpin." *Washington Times*, March 23, 1922.
87. "Girls of Boston start warfare against flirts." *Washington Times*, December 31, 1922.

Chapter 5

1. "Two brokers who failed." *San Francisco Call*, May 9, 1896.
2. "The hatpin in politics." *Indianapolis Journal*, October 6, 1900.
3. "Messenger boy strikers foiled." *Evening Times* (Washington), September 1, 1902.
4. "Girl uses her fist." *St. Paul Globe*, August 30, 1902.
5. "Negro girls cause terror in park." *New York Tribune*, April 28, 1903.
6. "Girl pickets use hat pins." *St. Paul Globe*, August 25, 1904.
7. "Hatpins for insulter." *New York Tribune*, March 26, 1905.
8. "Armed with hatpins girls defy hugger." *St. Louis Republic*, December 17, 1905.
9. "Women join general fight in subway car." *Evening World* (NY), March 5, 1906.
10. "Hatpins and hair and awful riot." *Washington Times*, July 25, 1906.
11. "Hatpins on his left, hatpins on his right, so Mulligan runs away." *Washington Times*, August 21, 1907.
12. "Armed with hatpins, women hustle man into station house." *Washington Times*, October 14, 1907.
13. "Chauffeur threatened by hatpin brigade." *Seattle Star*, September 17, 1908.
14. "Hatpins and red pepper for hugger." *Marion Daily Mirror* (Ohio), February 23, 1909.
15. "Women use hatpins when in big crowds." *San Francisco Call*, October 24, 1909.
16. "Women rioters in New York soak meat with oil." *Bisbee Daily Review*, April 8, 1910.
17. "London suffragettes raise Cain—220 jailed." *Day Book* (Chicago), November 22, 1911.
18. "Women form hatpin squad for defense." *Seattle Star*, January 11, 1913.
19. "Garment work and police fight today." *Bryan Daily Eagle and Pilot* (TX), January 18, 1913.
20. "Hatpin as protection." *Times Dispatch* (VA), January 27, 1913.
21. "Women battle to hear evangelist." *Washington Times*, February 1, 1913.
22. "Police make raid on suffragettes." *Daily Capital Journal* (Salem, OR), April 30, 1913.
23. "Girl workers menace pickets with hat pins." *Albuquerque Evening Herald*, June 5, 1913.
24. "Poisoned hatpin and gas pipe are weapons of women in struggle." *Seattle Star*, July 18, 1913.
25. "Holloway prison again holds Pankhurst woman." *Albuquerque Evening Herald*, July 21, 1913.
26. "Hatpins drawn in riot." *New York Tribune*, August 8, 1913.
27. "Hatpins flash in wild fight." *Tacoma Times*, June 16, 1917.

Chapter 6

1. "Killed him with her hat pin." *Sun* (NY), August 6, 1890.
2. "Pinned through the nose." *Los Angeles Herald*, August 1, 1891.
3. "Broke off in him." *Comet* (Johnson City, TN), February 15, 1894.
4. "Not exactly news." *Belmont Chronicle* (St. Clairsville, Ohio), February 22, 1894.
5. "Died of a pin prick." *Abbeville Press and Banner* (SC), July 31, 1895.
6. "Point of hat pin." *St. Paul Globe*, March 13, 1899.
7. "Hatpin in his flesh." *Indianapolis Journal*, January 8, 1900.
8. "News of the stage." *New York Tribune*, March 4, 1903.
9. "Hatpin scratch fatal." *Evening Statesman* (Walla Walla, WA), February 25, 1907.
10. "The hatpin danger." *Evening Star* (Washington), February 17, 1907.
11. "Conductor jabbed on nose by hatpin." *Los Angeles Herald*, December 28, 1908.
12. "The riotous hatpin." *New York Tribune*, September 10, 1909.
13. "Hatpin stuck in his eye." *New York Tribune*, January 13, 1911.
14. "Aged sea captain killed by hatpin." *Washington Herald*, February 16, 1911.
15. "Hat pin pierces passenger's eye." *Rock Island Argus* (Illinois), June 13, 1911.
16. "Hatpin in actor's eye." *New York Tribune*, August 3, 1911.
17. "Woman's hatpin spears a man." *East Oregonian* (Pendleton, OR), October 18, 1911.
18. "Priest stabbed with hatpin." *Mathews Journal* (Mathews, VA), November 2, 1911.
19. "Hatpin destroys eye." *Crittenden Record-Press* (Marion, KY), March 28, 1912.
20. "His eye put out by big hatpin." *Daily Capital Journal* (Salem, OR), May 6, 1912.
21. "Jabbed in eye by woman's hatpin." *Seattle Star*, May 6, 1912.
22. "Hatpin pierced his nose." *New York Tribune*, December 22, 1912.
23. "Hatpin pierces Caruso." *San Francisco Call*, January 6, 1913.

Chapter 7

1. "Hat pins." *Evening Statesman* (Walla Walla, WA), July 25, 1909.

2. "Berlin police officer wars on hat pins." *Deseret Evening News* (Salt Lake), November 24, 1910.
3. "Berlin bars long hatpins." *Washington Herald*, March 28, 1911.
4. "Make fight on army rules." *El Paso Herald*, June 3, 1911.
5. "Long hatpins barred in German railroad cars." *Salt Lake Tribune*, July 2, 1911.
6. "Heavy fines for long hatpins." *Tacoma Times*, August 10, 1911.
7. No title. *Washington Times*, August 17, 1911.
8. "Ladies must wear hatpin protectors." *Evening Herald* (Klamath Falls, OR), July 20, 1912.
9. "Paring German headgear." *Sun* (NY), April 8, 1913.
10. "Bar unprotected hatpins." *Sun* (NY), October 26, 1913.
11. "Germany crusades against long hatpins." *Washington Herald*, November 9, 1913.
12. "Women's hatpins." *Caucasian* (Shreveport, LA), August 17, 1909.
13. "Josh Wise says." *Spokane Press*, November 16, 1910.
14. "Hatpin agitation extends to Paris." *San Francisco Call*, December 10, 1912.
15. "Hatpin guard rule enforced." *Sun* (NY), January 11, 1914.
16. "Paris women invincible." *East Oregonian* (Pendleton, OR), April 6, 1914.
17. "Bar long hatpins." *Seattle Star*, May 19, 1917.
18. "Hatpin pricks; girl is jailed." *Seattle Star*, February 10, 1911; "Hatpin causes arrest." *Watchman and Southron* (Sumter, SC), February 25, 1911.
19. "War is waged on hatpins." *San Francisco Call*, May 23, 1913.
20. "Hatpins seized." *Washington Herald*, February 15, 1911.
21. "Women forbidden to wear long hatpins." *Salt Lake Tribune*, June 4, 1911.
22. "Clergy in arms against big hats." *Washington Herald*, September 3, 1911.
23. "Penalty for hatpins if they wickedly protrude." *Evening Herald* (Klamath Falls, OR), December 23, 1911.
24. "Swiss make hatpins unlawful." *New York Tribune*, January 21, 1912.
25. "Hatpin deadly weapon." *Washington Times*, October 28, 1913; "Penalty for bare hatpins." *Sun* (NY), December 8, 1913.
26. "Prefer jail to paying fines." *Salt Lake Tribune*, October 31, 1912.
27. Sophie Irene Loeb. "The everyday rights of everyday persons." *Evening World* (NY), November 15, 1912.
28. "Saving eyes in Stockholm." *Sun* (NY), February 9, 1913.
29. "Europe fights long hatpins." *New York Tribune*, May 11, 1913.

Chapter 8

1. "The hatpin." *Rock Island Argus* (Illinois), December 9, 1895.
2. "Dangerous weapons." *St. Paul Globe*, April 2, 1897.
3. "Must the long hatpin go." *Sun* (NY), August 23, 1897.
4. "Voice of the press." *Record-Union* (Sacramento), September 23, 1897.
5. "Women's hatpins." *Virginia Gazette* (Williamsburg, VA), September 25, 1897.
6. "The deadly hatpin." *Roanoke Times* (VA), October 9, 1897.
7. "Hatpins and evolution." *Kansas City Journal* (MO), March 8, 1898.
8. "Law against hat pins." *Evening World* (NY), February 20, 1900.
9. No title. *Worthington Advance* (MN), March 2, 1900.
10. No title. *El Paso Herald*, March 8, 1900.
11. "For the better half." *El Paso Herald*, March 10, 1900.
12. "A crisis for the hatpin." *Omaha Daily Bee*, March 11, 1900.
13. "The deadly hat pin." *Spokane Press*, June 20, 1903.
14. "A weapon of defense." *St. Paul Globe*, September 11, 1903.
15. "The lethal hatpin." *Indianapolis Journal*, September 27, 1903.
16. "The homicidal hatpin." *San Francisco Call*, January 15, 1904.
17. "The modern girl's weapons." *St Paul Globe*, September 4, 1904.
18. "Woman's weapon of defense." *Omaha Daily Bee*, November 27, 1904.
19. "A moot parliament." *New York Tribune*, January 14, 1905.
20. "The deadly hatpin." *Salt Lake Tribune*, March 23, 1906.
21. "The offending hatpin." *Truth* (Salt Lake), October 27, 1906.
22. "The insider." *San Francisco Call*, April 11, 1907.
23. "Fair inventor may save lives of men." *San Francisco Call*, April 16, 1907.
24. "A point in woman's favor." *Omaha Daily Bee*, May 27, 1907.
25. No title. *New York Tribune*, January 10, 1908.
26. "The hatpin as a weapon." *Washington Herald*, March 8, 1908.
27. "Appropriations and hatpins." *Evening Statesman* (Walla Walla, WA), January 21, 1909.
28. "Lawmaker wants ban put on hat pins." *Tacoma Times*, January 21, 1909.

29. "Hat pins." *East Oregonian* (Pendleton, OR), January 26, 1909.
30. "Hat pins must not be over ten inches." *Daily Capital Journal* (Salem, OR), January 27, 1909.
31. "Law to protect from deadly hatpin." *Washington Times*, January 28, 1909.
32. "Oregon Legislature has passed a law limiting hatpins to 10 inches long." *Evening World* (NY), February 1, 1909.
33. No title. *Brownsville Herald* (TX), February 4, 1909.
34. No title. *San Mateo Item* (Florida), March 6, 1909.
35. "Blow that killed the hatpin bill." *Evening Herald* (Klamath Falls, OR), February 8, 1909.
36. "Hat pins in Oregon." *Washington Herald*, October 15, 1909.
37. "Some freak legislation." *Times Dispatch* (Richmond, VA), October 19, 1909.
38. "The deadly hatpin." *Valentine Democrat* (Nebraska), February 11, 1909.
39. "War on hatpin." *Spokane Press*, February 22, 1909.
40. Cynthia Grey. "France has set fashion America should follow." *Tacoma Times*, September 18, 1909.
41. Alton E. Gasso. "Hat pins are really menacing." *Muskogee Cimeter* (OK), February 4, 1910.
42. "Hatpins of the ladies." *Ogden Standard*, February 12, 1910.
43. "War on hatpins." *New York Tribune*, February 12, 1910.
44. "Citizen wounded by hat harpoon." *San Francisco Call*, February 22, 1910.
45. "Will ignore the hat pin." *Daily Capital Journal* (Salem, OR), February 22, 1910.
46. "Not a sign of relief yet in sight." *Washington Times*, February 27, 1910.
47. "Would banish long hatpins." *Ogden Standard*, March 1, 1910.
48. "The hatpin up." *New York Tribune*, March 1, 1910.
49. "The hat pin and the hat. They are institutions." *Washington Herald*, March 2, 1910.
50. "Crusade waged against hatpins." *Washington Times*, March 5, 1910.
51. "Long hat pins are abolished." *Ogden Standard*, March 8, 1910.
52. "To arms, ye women of Chicago. Hatpins barred by ordinance." *Seattle Star*, March 8, 1910.
53. "Ban placed upon the deadly snickersnee." *Evening Statesman* (Walla Walla, WA), March 8, 1910.
54. "The long hat pin." *Evening Statesman* (Walla Walla, WA), March 8, 1910.
55. "Long hat pins public nuisance." *Deseret Evening News* (Salt Lake), March 8, 1910; "To put a ban on deadly hatpin." *East Oregonian* (Pendleton, OR), March 8, 1910.
56. "A joke with a sharp point." *New York Tribune*, March 11, 1910.
57. "Ordinance limiting length of hat pins." *Deseret Evening News* (Salt Lake), March 12, 1910.
58. "Suggestions follow passing of hat pin." *Ogden Standard*, March 14, 1910.
59. "Shame! Cry women." *New York Tribune*, March 15, 1910.
60. "Long hatpins against law." *Ogden Standard*, March 22, 1910.
61. "The hatpin law in Chicago." *Daily Capital Journal* (Salem, OR), March 22, 1910.
62. "Earnest words to the hat brigade." *Spokane Press*, March 22, 1910.
63. "Chicago council bars long hatpins." *San Francisco Call*, March 22, 1910.
64. "Short hatpins after April 1." *New York Tribune*, March 23, 1910.
65. "Won't hurt Louisville." *Kentucky Irish American* (Louisville), March 26, 1910.
66. "Long hat pins." *Caucasian* (Shreveport, LA), March 27, 1910.
67. "Hatpin woman's undoing." *Marion Daily Mirror* (Ohio), April 2, 1910.
68. "Hatpin leads to arrest." *Manning Times* (SC), April 13, 1910.
69. "A fine present for your mother-in-law." *Daily Capital Journal* (Salem, OR), May 19, 1910.
70. No title. *Jasper Weekly Courier* (Indiana), May 20, 1910.
71. "The dangerous hatpin." *Dakota County Herald* (Dakota City, Nebraska), June 24, 1910.
72. "Beauty squad of police to make hat pin arrests." *Evening World* (NY), June 6, 1912.
73. "Light hats for high brows; Chicago's war on hatpins." *Hawaiian Star* (Honolulu), June 17, 1912.
74. "Society beauty squad to wage war on long hatpin." *East Oregonian* (Pendleton, OR), June 18, 1912.
75. "Chicago's beauty squad in the antihatpin war." *Hawaiian Star* (Honolulu), June 25, 1912.
76. "Chicago mayor puts ban on hat ticklers." *San Francisco Call*, December 3, 1913.
77. "Should enact a law against women wearing long hat pins." *Salt Lake Herald-Republican*, March 3, 1910.
78. "Armed hats." *Los Angeles Herald*, March 10, 1910.
79. "Hat pin crusade grows." *Paducah Evening Sun* (KY), March 10, 1910.
80. "Hatpin crusade begun." *Washington Herald*, April 25, 1910; "Garrulous girls may be suppressed." *Washington Times*, October 26, 1910.

81. "Yes! There should be a reform in hatpins." *Spokane Press*, March 14, 1910.
82. "Two eyes jabbed out by hatpins in crowd." *Washington Herald*, March 16, 1910.
83. "Hatpins must be abolished." *Washington Herald*, March 17, 1910.
84. "Current comment." *Seattle Republican*, March 18, 1910.
85. "Length of hatpins is none of men's business." *Salt Lake Herald-Republican*, March 20, 1910.
86. "Hatpin ordinance allowed to die." *Washington Times*, March 21, 1910.
87. "Long hatpins find defender." *Deseret Evening News* (Salt Lake), March 22, 1910.
88. No title. *Virginia Citizen* (Irvington, VA), April 29, 1910.
89. "The talk of the day." *New York Tribune*, March 22, 1910.
90. "Is hat pin man's menace? Police chief's opinion." *Salt Lake Herald-Republican*, March 27, 1910.
91. "War declared on hatpins." *Times Dispatch* (Richmond, VA), March 28, 1910.
92. "Gets two hatpin wounds." *Sun* (NY), April 2, 1910.
93. "Seattle makes war on hat pins." *Daily Capital Journal* (Salem, OR), April 4, 1910.
94. "How long should hat pins be?" *Seattle Star*, April 5, 1910.
95. "Driveling rot, says pretty steno, about hatpin rule." *Seattle Star*, April 7, 1910.
96. "Seattle to drive out long hatpins—one man blinded." *Tacoma Times*, May 8, 1912.
97. "Women boost for hatpin law." *Seattle Star*, May 27, 1913.
98. "Recommend new ban upon hatpin." *Seattle Star*, May 28, 1913.
99. "Ladies, watch your hatpins!" *Seattle Star*, June 3, 1913.
100. "Congress may legislate against long hat pins." *Los Angeles Herald*, April 5, 1910.
101. "Hatpins may be barred in the District next." *Washington Times*, April 6, 1910.
102. "Representative Coudrey and hat pins." *Washington Times*, April 8, 1910.
103. "Commissioners worried by the hatpin problem." *Washington Times*, April 9, 1910.
104. "Decides District needs no hat protection." *Washington Times*, April 19, 1910.
105. "The bystander." *Hawaiian Gazette* (Honolulu), April 12, 1910.
106. "Boss of the establishment." *Omaha Daily Bee*, May 9, 1910.
107. R. Ellis Wales. "If San Francisco police should pinch wearers of deadly hatpins." *San Francisco Call*, May 15, 1910.
108. "Hats on and why." *San Francisco Call*, June 5, 1910.
109. Barbara Boyd. "Heart and home talks." *Washington Herald*, June 17, 1910.
110. "Legislatures and milliners." *Washington Herald*, July 4, 1910.
111. "Hat pin is dangerous." *Evening Standard* (Ogden), August 17, 1910.
112. "Stick them with hat pins! Says Galloway." *Los Angeles Herald*, September 22, 1910.
113. "Pittsburg to shorten hatpins to nine inches." *Spokane Press*, September 24, 1910.
114. "She's only woman in M.U. law school." *University Missourian* (Columbia, MO), October 7, 1910.
115. "Long hatpins O.K, says judge." *Morning Standard* (Ogden), November 20, 1910.
116. "Long hatpins a peril." *New York Tribune*, December 2, 1910.
117. "Deadly hat pin is on the move." *Tulsa Daily World*, December 31, 1910.
118. No title. *Hawaiian Star* (Honolulu), January 11, 1911.
119. Cy Clemmons. "Many acute dangers of hatpins." *Dakota County Herald* (Dakota City, Nebraska), December 9, 1910.
120. Cynthia Grey. "Cynthia Grey's after supper talks." *Spokane Press*, December 10, 1910.
121. "Kansas City women must muzzle hat pins." *Salt Lake Tribune*, December 28, 1910.
122. "The dangerous hatpin." *St. Landry Clarion* (Opelousas, LA), January 11, 1911.
123. "Kansas City may get a hatpin ordinance." *Tulsa Daily World*, January 10, 1911.
124. "Bar hatpin." *Seattle Star*, March 19, 1911; "Kansas City bars pointed hatpins." *Washington Herald*, March 29, 1911.
125. "Deadly hat pin is on the move." *Tulsa Daily World*, December 31, 1910.
126. "Hatpin bill in South Dakota." *Omaha Daily Bee*, January 9, 1911.
127. "Hatpin bill is referred to Military Affairs Committee." *Omaha Daily Bee*, January 15, 1911; "Hatpin bill beaten by Dakota's solons." *Omaha Daily Bee*, January 19, 1911.
128. "Law-mill grind." *Dakota Farmer's Leader* (Canton, SD), January 20, 1911.
129. "Alderman Keep Volkmann." *Sun* (NY), January 11, 1911.
130. "Long 'uns must go." *Watchman and Southron* (Sumter, SC), January 21, 1911.
131. "Perils of long hatpins told by the clubwomen in pleas to aldermen." *Evening World* (NY), January 26, 1911.
132. "Daggers in the lady's hats." *Sun* (NY), January 27, 1911.
133. "The lady and the hat pin." *Evening World* (NY), January 28, 1911.
134. "Long hatpin o.k., aldermen won't make 'em shorter." *Evening World* (NY), January 31, 1911.
135. "Her hatpin is let alone." *Sun* (NY), February 1, 1911.

136. "Long hatpins must go." *New York Tribune*, February 8, 1911.
137. "Hatpin doomed to oblivion." *Weekly Journal-Miner* (Prescott, AZ), February 15, 1911.
138. "Aldermen still fear to cut hatpins short." *Evening World* (NY), October 3, 1911.
139. "War on big hat pins." *New York Tribune*, February 1, 1911.
140. "Would withdraw hatpin bill." *New York Tribune*, February 2, 1911.
141. "Bay State urges hatpin scabbard." *San Francisco Call*, January 29, 1913.
142. "Hatpins in Massachusetts." *Washington Herald*, February 22, 1913.
143. "Foss will sign bill barring long hatpins." *Washington Times*, March 9, 1913; "Hatpins with buttons." *San Francisco Call*, March 11, 1913.
144. "Removes hat pin menace." *New York Tribune*, March 11, 1913.
145. "The question in Boston." *Evening World* (NY), April 9, 1913.
146. "Society." *Goodwin's Weekly* (Salt Lake), June 7, 1913.
147. "New hatpin bill from Hatfield." *Omaha Daily Bee*, February 4, 1911.
148. "Kennedy has deadly hatpins as exhibits." *San Francisco Call*, February 9, 1911.
149. "File all your hatpins ladies then read this." *San Francisco Call*, February 18, 1911.
150. "Fun poked at hat pin bill but it passes." *San Francisco Call*, March 4, 1911.
151. "Montclair suffragettes rush to shorten hatpins." *Evening World* (NY), February 10, 1911.
152. No title. *Hawaiian Star* (Honolulu), March 21, 1911.
153. "Hatpin jabs legislator." *New York Tribune*, March 24, 1911.
154. "Long hatpin fined." *Washington Herald*, April 4, 1911.
155. "Guard hatpins, ladies, if you travel in Jersey." *Evening World* (NY), April 3, 1913.
156. "New hatpin law arouses the ire of Jersey women." *Evening World* (NY), April 5, 1913.
157. "Dangerous weapons." *New York Tribune*, April 17, 1911.
158. "A splendid idea." *Seattle Star*, June 26, 1911.
159. "The hatpin no joke." *Omaha Daily Bee*, August 4, 1911.
160. "The dangerous weapon." *Evening Standard* (Ogden), August 7, 1911.
161. "The murderous hatpin." *Coconino Sun* (Flagstaff, AZ), September 1, 1911.
162. "Pete just scratches along." *Washington Times*, September 9, 1911.
163. "Hatpins and women." *Colfax Chronicle* (LA), September 30, 1911.
164. No title. *Spanish American* (Roy, New Mexico), October 7, 1911.
165. "Hatless women adopt resolution against hat pins." *Evening World* (NY), November 17, 1911.
166. "Queen Mary and the hatpin." *Washington Herald*, November 17, 1911.
167. No title. *Goodwin's Weekly* (Salt Lake), November 18, 1911.
168. "Renew war on long hatpins." *Albuquerque Evening Herald*, March 2, 1912.
169. "A public servant who has been doing things." *Tulsa Daily World*, March 2, 1912.
170. "The deadly hat pin." *Washington Times*, March 14, 1912.
171. "War on long hatpins." *New York Tribune*, March 22, 1912.
172. "Women fight long hatpin." *New York Tribune*, March 28, 1912.
173. "Adieu to the long hatpin." *Seattle Star*, May 15, 1912.
174. "Hat pin measure." *Caucasian* (Shreveport, LA), December 31, 1912.
175. "To enforce hatpin law." *New York Tribune*, March 21, 1913.
176. "Eleven arrested." *Caucasian* (Shreveport, LA), April 3, 1913.
177. "The long hat pin will have to go." *St. Landry Clarion* (Opelousas, LA), June 1, 1912.
178. "Hatpin woman's weapon; it's like her tongue." *Evening World* (NY), July 6, 1912.
179. "Hatpins and pinheads." *Era-Leader* (Franklin, LA), July 16, 1914.
180. "Woman to wear on hatpins." *New York Tribune*, April 14, 1912.
181. "Thoughtful women." *University Missourian* (Columbia, MO), May 1, 1912.
182. "The long hatpin menace to society." *Daily Ardmoreite* (Ardmore, OK), May 14, 1912.
183. "Ban on hat pin." *San Francisco Call*, June 9, 1912.
184. "Against long hatpins." *Daily Capital Journal* (Salem, OR), June 12, 1912.
185. "Milady's hat pins restricted." *San Francisco Call*, June 26, 1912.
186. "Knell of hat pin sounded." *San Francisco Call*, July 3, 1912.
187. "Hat pins unsanitary supervisors are told. *East Oregonian* (Pendleton, OR), June 18, 1912.
188. "Everybody's doing it." *Kennewick Courier* (WA), July 19, 1912.
189. "Supervisors get stuck on hatpin." *San Francisco Call*, August 21, 1912.
190. "Short hatpins the rule, ladies." *San Francisco Call*, September 5, 1912.
191. "Long hatpins under the ban." *San Francisco Call*, July 7, 1912.
192. "Hatpins will be regulated." *San Francisco Call*, August 31, 1912.

193. "Mayor on hat pins." *New York Tribune*, September 27, 1912.
194. "Smoking law to curb hat pins." *San Francisco Call*, November 10, 1912.
195. "Hat pins and cigars barred." *Evening Herald* (Klamath Falls, OR), November 14, 1912.
196. "To regulate hatpins." *Daily Capital Journal* (Salem, OR), November 20, 1912.
197. "Hat feathers to be banished." *Evening Standard* (Ogden), December 4, 1912.
198. "Oh girls! $500 fine for long hat pins." *Seattle Star*, December 4, 1912.
199. "Los Angeles frowns on civic dance hall." *San Francisco Call*, December 11, 1912.
200. "Judge says hat pin is deadly weapon." *Seattle Star*, November 21, 1912.
201. "Safe and sane hatpins." *Washington Times*, January 26, 1913.
202. "No pistols for women." *San Francisco Call*, January 29, 1913.
203. "Puts muzzle on hatpins." *Times Dispatch* (Richmond, VA), March 9, 1913.
204. "When hat pin guards become the rage." *Rock Island Argus* (Illinois), March 15, 1913.
205. "Law forbids free lunch." *Sun* (NY), March 21, 1913.
206. Frances Shaffer. "Protecting world against hatpin." *Washington Herald*, April 21, 1913.
207. "Hat pins." *St. Landry Clarion* (Opelousas, LA), May 24, 1913.
208. Marguerite Mooers Marshall. "Use hatpins or fists on mashers, says Mrs. Brophy, who did it." *Evening World* (NY), August 9, 1913.
209. "Tulsa's special ordinance." *Daily Ardmoreite* (Ardmore, OK), October 14, 1913.
210. "Her thoughtfulness." *Ottumwa Courier* (Iowa), October 21, 1913.
211. Sophie Irene Loeb. "The long hatpin: an arraignment." *Evening World* (NY), March 26, 1914.
212. "Long hat-pins in women's hats." *Ogden Standard*, April 2, 1914.
213. Frederick Lewis Allen. *Only Yesterday: An Informal History of the 1920s*. New York: Harper & Row, 1931, pp. 94–96.

Bibliography

Newspaper Articles with Titles

"Accused of trying to stab him with hatpin." *Paducah Evening Sun* (KY), July 19, 1909.
"Actress in fight stabs with hatpin." *Los Angeles Herald*, April 22, 1909.
"Adieu to the long hatpin." *Seattle Star*, May 15, 1912.
"Advantages and disadvantages of the new hat." *Bisbee Daily Review*, May 2, 1908.
"Against long hatpins." *Daily Capital Journal* (Salem, OR), June 12, 1912.
"Aged sea captain killed by hatpin." *Washington Herald*, February 16, 1911.
"Aiming at theater hats." *Evening Star* (Washington), January 20, 1897.
"Alderman keep Volkmann." *Sun* (NY), January 11, 1911.
"Aldermen still fear to cut hatpins short." *Evening World* (NY), October 3, 1911.
"All in a day's work." *Washington Times*, July 27, 1919.
Allen, Frederick Lewis. *Only Yesterday: An Informal History of the 1920s*. New York: Harper & Row, 1931.
"Another bad case of hatpin." *San Francisco Call*, July 19, 1897.
"Another triumph for the big hat pin." *Salt Lake Tribune*, June 15, 1906.
"Answers to correspondents." *San Francisco Call*, February 5, 1901.
"Anti-hat ordinances galore." *Kansas City Journal* (MO), January 23, 1897.
"Appropriations and hatpins." *Evening Statesman* (Walla Walla, WA), January 21, 1909.
"Armed hats." *Los Angeles Herald*, March 10, 1910.
"Armed with hatpins girls defy hugger." *St. Louis Republic*, December 17, 1905.
"Armed with hatpins, women hustle man into station house." *Washington Times*, October 14, 1907.
"Arrival of the hatpin." *Daily Ardmoreite* (Ardmore, OK), September 18, 1902.
"Attacked by female bandits." *Times* (Washington), October 5, 1899.
"Attacks lawyers with hatpins." *Mathews Journal* (VA), August 1, 1912.
"Attacks rubber company man." *New York Tribune*, October 24, 1904.
"Ban on hat pin." *San Francisco Call*, June 9, 1912.
"Ban placed upon the deadly snickersnee." *Evening Statesman* (Walla Walla, WA), March 8, 1910.
"Bar hatpin." *Seattle Star*, March 29, 1911.
"Bar long hatpins." *Seattle Star*, May 19, 1917.
"Bar unprotected hatpins." *Sun* (NY), October 26, 1913.
"Bay state urges hatpin scabbard." *San Francisco Call*, January 29, 1913.
"Beauty squad of police to make hat pin arrests." *Evening World* (NY), June 6, 1912.
"Becky Fream arrested." *Sun* (NY), July 24, 1895.
"Berlin bars long hatpins." *Washington Herald*, March 28, 1911.
"Berlin police officer wars on hat pins." *Deseret Evening News* (Salt Lake), November 24, 1910.

"Beware of the hatpin." *Salt Lake Herald*, May 23, 1902.
"Big robber jabbed with a hatpin by woman agent." *Evening World* (NY), November 30, 1912.
"Bigger closets needed." *Sun* (NY), October 4, 1908.
"Blow that killed the hatpin bill." *Evening Herald* (Klamath Falls, OR), February 8, 1909.
"Bold attempt at assault." *Marion Daily Mirror* (Ohio), May 4, 1911.
Bordoni, Irene. "Irene Bordoni describes her favorite hat." *Ogden Standard*, September 27, 1917.
"Boss of the establishment." *Omaha Daily Bee*, May 9, 1910.
Bottomley, Julia. "The Panama hat." *Baxter Springs News* (Baxter Springs, Kansas), July 20, 1911.
"Boy bandit in U.S. Navy garb robs 15." *Washington Times*, October 24, 1919.
Boyd, Barbara. "Heart and home talks." *Washington Herald*, June 17, 1910.
"Brave Barbara Stack." *Rock Island Argus* (Illinois), February 5, 1898.
"Brings a robber to grief with a hatpin." *St. Paul Globe*, September 8, 1903.
"Broke off in him." *Comet* (Johnson City, TN), February 15, 1894.
"Button protects police officer." *Salt Lake Tribune*, April 13, 1913.
"The bystander." *Hawaiian Gazette* (Honolulu), April 12, 1910.
"Car sinks hatpin into her skull." *San Francisco Call*, May 2, 1908.
"Catches masher with hatpin." *Alexander Gazette* (VA), August 23, 1910.
"Cermack to the rescue with bill limiting specifications for hats." *Rock Island Argus* (Illinois), April 24, 1909.
"Charge model with crime." *Evening Statesman* (Walla Walla, WA), January 1, 1907.
"Chauffeur threatened by hatpin brigade." *Seattle Star*, September 17, 1908.
"Chicago council bars long hatpins." *San Francisco Call*, March 22, 1910.
"Chicago mayor puts ban on hat ticklers." *San Francisco Call*, December 3, 1913.
"Chicago's beauty squad in the anti-hatpin war." *Hawaiian Star* (Honolulu), June 25, 1912.
"Citizen wounded by hat harpoon." *San Francisco Call*, February 22, 1910.
Clemmons, Cy. "Many acute dangers of hatpins." *Dakota County Herald* (Dakota City, Nebraska), December 9, 1910.
"Clergy in arms against big hats." *Washington Herald*, September 3, 1911.
"Co-ed and hat pin rout a burglar." *East Oregonian* (Pendleton, OR), October 23, 1912.
"Commissioners worried by the hatpin problem." *Washington Times*, April 9, 1910.
"Complains of short hatpins." *Rich Hill Tribune* (Rich Hill, MO), December 12, 1907.
"Conductor jabbed on nose by hatpin." *Los Angeles Herald*, December 28, 1908.
"Congress may legislate against long hat pins." *Los Angeles Herald*, April 5, 1910.
"A crisis for the hatpin." *Omaha Daily Bee*, March 11, 1900.
"Crowd tries to rescue prisoners." *New York Tribune*, August 6, 1903.
"Crowd's enthusiasm causes president to mount railing." *St. Louis Republic*, May 1, 1903.
"Crusade waged against hatpins." *Washington Times*, March 5, 1910.
"Current comment." *Seattle Republican*, March 18, 1910.
"Daggers in the lady's hats." *Sun* (NY), January 27, 1911.
"The dangerous hatpin." *Dakota County Herald* (Dakota City, Nebraska), June 24, 1910.
"The dangerous hatpin." *St. Landry Clarion* (Opelousas, LA), January 14, 1911.
"Dangerous hatpins will go." *University Missourian* (Columbia, MO), March 18, 1912.
"The dangerous weapon." *Evening Standard* (Ogden), August 7, 1911.
"Dangerous weapons." *New York Tribune*, April 17, 1911.
"Dangerous weapons." *St. Paul Globe*, April 2, 1897.
"A dangerous woman." *Barton County Democrat* (Great Bend, Kansas), March 11, 1904.
"Deadly hat pin is on the move." *Tulsa Daily World*, December 31, 1910.
"The deadly hat pin." *Scranton Tribune* (PA), January 14, 1898.
"The deadly hat pin." *Spokane Press*, June 20, 1903.
"The deadly hat pin." *Washington Times*, March 14, 1912.
"The deadly hatpin." *Roanoke Times* (VA), October 9, 1897.
"The deadly hatpin." *Valentine Democrat* (Nebraska), February 11, 1909.

"Deadly hatpin again." *San Francisco Call*, October 17, 1904.
"Defend honor with hatpin." *Spokane Press*, October 14, 1907.
"Delegate Kinney would bar high hats from theaters." *St. Louis Republic*, January 15, 1902.
"Detective stabbed by woman." *New York Tribune*, September 1, 1900.
"Died of a pin prick." *Abbeville Press and Banner* (SC), July 31, 1895.
"Driveling rot, says pretty steno, about hatpin rule." *Seattle Star*, April 7, 1910.
"Drummer jabbed with hatpins." *Deseret Evening News* (Salt Lake), October 9, 1901.
"Earnest words to the hat brigade." *Spokane Press*, March 22, 1910.
"Eleven arrested." *Caucasian* (Shreveport, LA), April 3, 1913.
"Europe fights long hatpins." *New York Tribune*, May 11, 1913.
"Eva Tanguay is arrested." *New York Tribune*, March 2, 1910.
"Everybody's doing it." *Kennewick Courier* (WA), July 19, 1912.
"Express rates on high hats to be subject of dignified inquiry." *Los Angeles Herald*, January 28, 1910.
"Fads in hat pins." *Evening Star* (Washington), November 1, 1895.
"Fair inventor may save lives of men." *San Francisco Call*, April 16, 1907.
"Fair miss sits on a burglar." *San Francisco Call*, March 18, 1901.
"Fancy hat pins." *Evening Star* (Washington), May 27, 1906.
"Fancy hat pins are now all the rage." *Minneapolis Journal*, November 4, 1906.
"Fashionable hat pins." *Washington Times*, December 30, 1906.
"Fight with hatpins." *Evening Standard* (Ogden), August 14, 1911.
"File all your hatpins ladies then read this." *San Francisco Call*, February 18, 1911.
"A fine present for your mother-in-law." *Daily Capital Journal* (Salem, OR), May 19, 1910.
"Fined for using hatpin on trolley conductor." *Washington Times*, January 11, 1911.
"Fined $10 for her bit of fun at the Gotham." *Evening World* (NY), January 26, 1907.
"For and about women." *Omaha Daily Bee*, September 13, 1903.
"For the better half." *El Paso Herald*, March 10, 1900.
"Foss will sign bill barring long hatpins." *Washington Times*, March 9, 1913.
"Fought like a tigress." *Minneapolis Journal*, April 20, 1905.
"Freak hat legislation may cost him his job." *Tacoma Times*, May 11, 1909.
"Fun pokes at hat pin bill, but it passes." *San Francisco Call*, March 4, 1911.
"Garment work and police fight today." *Bryan Daily Eagle and Pilot* (TX), January 18, 1913.
"Garrulous girls may be suppressed." *Washington Times*, October 26, 1910.
Gasso, Alton E. "Hat pins are really menacing." *Muskogee Cimeter* (OK), February 4, 1910.
"Germany crusades against long hatpins." *Washington Herald*, November 9, 1913.
"Gets two hatpin wounds." *Sun* (NY), April 2, 1910.
"Girl attacks cop with wicked hatpin." *Evening World* (NY), March 7, 1905.
"Girl, hatpin and club rout bold burglar." *El Paso Herald*, July 11, 1910.
"Girl in unwritten law case, wields hatpin in courtroom." *Los Angeles Herald*, December 1, 1910.
"Girl pickets use hat pins." *St. Paul Globe*, August 25, 1904.
"Girl puts ruffian to flight with hat pin." *Minneapolis Journal*, November 14, 1904.
"Girl uses hatpin with telling effect." *Washington Times*, January 23, 1906.
"Girl uses her fist." *St. Paul Globe*, August 30, 1902.
"Girl with a hatpin captures ex-convict robbing a letter box." *Evening World* (NY), April 4, 1913.
"Girl with hatpin, battles 5 thugs." *Minneapolis Journal*, December 16, 1906.
"Girl workers menace pickets with hat pins." *Albuquerque Evening Herald*, June 5, 1913.
"Girls capture highwayman." *New York Tribune*, April 3, 1910.
"Girls chase assailants." *Los Angeles Herald*, September 28, 1907.
"Girl's hatpin routs masher." *St. Louis Republic*, May 31, 1903.
"Girls of Boston start warfare against flirts." *Washington Times*, December 31, 1922.
"Girls use hatpins to check linemen." *Washington Times*, November 24, 1910.

"Great variety of hatpins demanded by fashion causes comment." *Washington Times*, February 12, 1909.
Grey, Cynthia. "Cynthia Grey's after supper talks." *Spokane Press*, December 10, 1910.
Grey, Cynthia. "France has set fashion America should follow." *Tacoma Times*, September 18, 1909.
"Guard hatpins, ladies, if you travel in Jersey." *Evening World* (NY), April 3, 1913.
"Hat feathers to be banished." *Evening Standard* (Ogden), December 4, 1912.
"Hat pin a legal weapon for women to employ." *St. Louis Republic*, September 16, 1902.
"The hat pin and the hat. They are institutions." *Washington Herald*, March 2, 1910.
"Hat pin and yell save her." *Omaha Daily Bee*, November 6, 1904.
"Hat-pin battle aired in court." *Deseret Evening News* (Salt Lake), July 15, 1908.
"Hat pin crusade grows." *Paducah Evening Sun* (KY), March 10, 1910.
"The hat-pin danger." *Evening Star* (Washington), February 17, 1907.
"Hat pin for weapon." *St. Louis Republic*, August 22, 1900.
"Hat pin is dangerous." *Evening Standard* (Ogden), August 17, 1910.
"Hat pin killed Mrs. MacDonald." *Daily Capital Journal* (Salem, OR), July 2, 1910.
"Hat pin measure." *Caucasian* (Shreveport, LA), December 31, 1912.
"Hat pin pierces passenger's eye." *Rock Island Argus* (Illinois), June 13, 1911.
"Hat pin thrust makes 'em howl." *Washington Times*, March 2, 1909.
"Hat pin, woman's weapon." *Minneapolis Journal*, May 18, 1906.
"Hat pins." *East Oregonian* (Pendleton, OR), January 26, 1909.
"Hat pins." *Evening Statesman* (Walla Walla, WA), July 25, 1909.
"Hat pins." *St. Landry Clarion* (Opelousas, LA), May 24, 1913.
"Hat pins." *Tulsa Daily World*, December 21, 1911.
"Hat pins a favorite weapon." *Sun* (NY), December 5, 1896.
"Hat pins and cigars barred." *Evening Herald* (Klamath Falls, OR), November 14, 1912.
"Hat pins in Oregon." *Washington Herald*, October 15, 1909.
"Hat pins must not be over ten inches." *Daily Capital Journal* (Salem, OR), January 27, 1909.
"Hat pins unsanitary supervisors are told." *East Oregonian* (Pendleton, OR), June 18, 1912.
"Hatless women adopt resolution against hat pins." *Evening World* (NY), November 17, 1911.
"The hatpin." *Red Cloud Chief* (Red Cloud, Nebraska), October 25, 1895.
"The hatpin." *Rock Island Argus* (Illinois), December 9, 1895.
"Hatpin." *Seattle Star*, January 31, 1901.
"Hatpin agitation extends to Paris." *San Francisco Call*, December 10, 1912.
"The hatpin as a weapon." *Washington Herald*, March 8, 1908.
"Hatpin as protection." *Times Dispatch* (VA), January 27, 1913.
"A hatpin baffled workmen." *New York Tribune*, July 2, 1910.
"Hatpin bill beaten by Dakota's solons." *Omaha Daily Bee*, January 19, 1911.
"Hatpin bill in South Dakota." *Omaha Daily Bee*, January 9, 1911.
"Hatpin bill is referred to military affairs committee." *Omaha Daily Bee*, January 15, 1911.
"Hatpin caused death." *Evening Standard* (Ogden), September 16, 1912.
"Hatpin causes arrest." *Watchman and Southron* (Sumter, SC), February 25, 1911.
"The hatpin craze." *Carlsbad Current* (NM), February 19, 1909.
"Hatpin crusade begun." *Washington Herald*, April 25, 1910.
"Hatpin Curtis is sentenced." *Seattle Star*, April 5, 1901.
"Hatpin deadly weapon." *Washington Times*, October 28, 1913.
"Hatpin destroys eye." *Crittenden Record-Press* (Marion, KY), March 28, 1912.
"Hatpin doomed to oblivion." *Weekly Journal-Miner* (Prescott, AZ), February 15, 1911.
"Hatpin enters woman's scalp." *San Francisco Call*, December 8, 1901.
"Hatpin fight in car." *New York Tribune*, May 31, 1903.
"Hatpin foils bandit." *Minneapolis Journal*, August 15, 1905.
"Hatpin foils men." *Washington Herald*, August 31, 1907.
"Hatpin for defense." *Bennington Evening Banner* (VT), April 5, 1911.
"Hatpin for her weapon." *Valentine Democrat* (Nebraska), July 3, 1902.

"Hatpin guard rule enforced." *Sun* (NY), January 11, 1914.
"Hatpin halts burglars." *New York Tribune*, July 28, 1913.
"Hatpin in actor's eye." *New York Tribune*, August 3, 1911.
"Hatpin in her head." *Evening Times* (Washington), September 10, 1896.
"Hatpin in his flesh." *Indianapolis Journal*, January 8, 1900.
"Hatpin in policeman." *Evening World* (NY), January 26, 1900.
"The hatpin in politics." *Indianapolis Journal*, October 6, 1900.
"Hatpin jabs legislator." *New York Tribune*, March 24, 1911.
"The hatpin law in Chicago." *Daily Capital Journal* (Salem, OR), March 22, 1910.
"Hatpin leads to arrest." *Manning Times* (SC), April 13, 1910.
"Hatpin leads to divorce." *Bemidji Daily Pioneer* (MN), March 23, 1910.
"Hatpin menace to go." *Sun* (NY), November 17, 1912.
"Hatpin Minnie busy." *Evening World* (NY), September 26, 1906.
"Hatpin nearly ends life of detective." *San Francisco Call*, May 15, 1910.
"The hatpin no joke." *Omaha Daily Bee*, August 4, 1911.
"Hatpin ordinance allowed to die." *Washington Times*, March 21, 1910.
"Hatpin pierced his nose." *New York Tribune*, December 22, 1912.
"Hatpin pierces Caruso." *San Francisco Call*, January 6, 1913.
"Hatpin pricks; girl is jailed." *Seattle Star*, February 10, 1911.
"Hatpin routs mere man." *New York Tribune*, August 27, 1912.
"Hatpin saves her honor." *Norfolk Weekly News-Journal* (VA), November 13, 1903.
"Hatpin scratch fatal." *Evening Statesman* (Walla Walla, WA), February 25, 1907.
"Hatpin stab proves fatal." *Sun* (NY), January 15, 1914.
"Hatpin stuck in his eye." *New York Tribune*, January 13, 1911.
"Hatpin to the rescue." *Daily Ardmoreite* (Ardmore, OK), January 12, 1911.
"The hatpin up." *New York Tribune*, March 1, 1910.
"The hatpin used with deadly effect." *Arizona Republican* (Phoenix), June 15, 1910.
"Hatpin woman's undoing." *Marion Daily Mirror* (Ohio), April 2, 1910.
"Hatpin woman's weapon; it's like her tongue." *Evening World* (NY), July 6, 1912.
"Hatpin wound is fatal." *Rock Island Argus* (Illinois), December 17, 1906.
"Hatpins and evolution." *Kansas City Journal* (MO), March 8, 1898.
"Hatpins and hair and awful riot." *Washington Times*, July 25, 1906.
"Hatpins and pinheads." *Era-Leader* (Franklin, LA), July 16, 1914.
"Hatpins and red pepper for hugger." *Marion Daily Mirror* (Ohio), February 23, 1909.
"Hatpins and women." *Colfax Chronicle* (LA), September 30, 1911.
"Hatpins as weapons." *St. Louis Republic*, June 19, 1900.
"Hatpins drawn in riot." *New York Tribune*, August 8, 1913.
"Hatpins flash in wild fight." *Tacoma Times*, June 16, 1917.
"Hatpins for insulter." *New York Tribune*, March 26, 1905.
"Hatpins help girl rout an assailant." *Salt Lake Tribune*, April 23, 1911.
"Hatpins in Massachusetts." *Washington Herald*, February 22, 1913.
"Hatpins may be barred in the district next." *Washington Times*, April 6, 1910.
"Hatpins must be abolished." *Washington Herald*, March 17, 1910.
"The hatpin's new renown." *San Francisco Call*, January 11, 1898.
"Hatpins of the ladies." *Ogden Standard*, February 12, 1910.
"Hatpins on his left, hatpins on his right, so Mulligan runs away." *Washington Times*, August 21, 1907.
"Hatpins saved girls their money." *St. Louis Republic*, December 30, 1905.
"Hatpins seized." *Washington Herald*, February 15, 1911.
"Hatpins weapons of women robbers." *Evening World* (NY), July 31, 1903.
"Hatpins will be regulated." *San Francisco Call*, August 31, 1912.
"Hatpins with buttons." *San Francisco Call*, March 11, 1913.
"Hats are out of order in woman's clubs." *San Francisco Call*, November 28, 1910.
"Hats off in church." *Kansas City Journal* (MO), July 4, 1897.

"Hats on and why." *San Francisco Call*, June 5, 1910.
"Hats on or off in church." *Washington Herald*, July 25, 1910.
"Heavy fines for long hatpins." *Tacoma Times*, August 10, 1911.
"Her hatpin is let alone." *Sun* (NY), February 1, 1911.
"Her hatpin routs footpad." *Washington Times*, March 18, 1921.
"Her thoughtfulness." *Ottumwa Courier* (Iowa), October 21, 1913.
"Heroine's hatpin routs a burglar choking a woman." *Evening World* (NY), July 14, 1914.
"The high hat ordinance." *Kansas City Journal* (MO), January 23, 1897.
"High hats at theaters." *Record-Union* (Sacramento), March 17, 1897.
"High hats in theaters." *Marietta Daily Leader* (Ohio), March 25, 1896.
"His eye put out by big hatpin." *Daily Capital Journal* (Salem, OR), May 6, 1912.
"Hold-up man is routed by woman with hatpin." *Washington Times*, March 23, 1922.
"Holds the hatpins." *Daily News* (Newport News, VA), May 15, 1909.
"Holloway prison again holds Pankhurst woman." *Albuquerque Evening Herald*, July 21, 1913.
"The homicidal hatpin." *San Francisco Call*, January 15, 1904.
"How about the hatpin as a teacher for mashers?" *Marion Daily Mirror* (Ohio), August 16, 1910.
"How long should hat pins be?" *Seattle Star*, April 5, 1910.
"The insider." *San Francisco Call*, April 11, 1907.
"Is hat pin man's menace? Police chief's opinions." *Salt Lake Herald-Republican*, March 27, 1910.
"Is stabbed by negress." *Ogden Standard*, July 7, 1909.
"Jabbed a cop with her hatpin." *Sun* (NY), December 4, 1896.
"Jabbed in eye by woman's hatpin." *Seattle Star*, May 6, 1912.
"Jabbed with a hatpin." *Sun* (NY), September 21, 1897.
"Jealous woman attacks her rival with hatpin." *Rock Island Argus* (Illinois), June 1, 1904.
"Jeered her harem skirt." *New York Tribune*, February 27, 1911.
"Jennie used her hat pin." *Daily Capital Journal* (Salem, OR), September 1, 1909.
"A joke with a sharp point." *New York Tribune*, March 11, 1910.
"Josh Wise says." *Spokane Press*, November 16, 1910.
"Judge says hat pin is deadly weapon." *Seattle Star*, November 21, 1912.
"Judge says women have right to wield hatpins." *Washington Times*, September 8, 1903.
"Justified slaying is verdict in case of Milwaukee girl." *Bisbee Daily Review*, January 21, 1914.
"Justifies use of hatpin." *Florida Star* (Titusville, FL), October 10, 1902.
"Kansas City bars pointed hatpins." *Washington Herald*, March 29, 1911.
"Kansas City may get a hatpin ordinance." *Tulsa Daily World*, January 10, 1911.
"Kansas City women must muzzle hat pins." *Salt Lake Tribune*, December 28, 1910.
"Keith O'Brien." *Salt Lake Tribune*, July 18, 1911.
"Kennedy has deadly hatpins as exhibits." *San Francisco Call*, February 9, 1911.
"Killed by her hat pin." *Critic* (Washington), December 26, 1890.
"Killed by her hat pin." *Los Angeles Herald*, December 26, 1890.
"Killed by her hat pin." *Wichita Eagle*, November 18, 1887.
"Killed by her hatpin." *Abbeville Press and Banner* (SC), March 6, 1895.
"Killed him with her hat pin." *Sun* (NY), August 10, 1890.
"Kills woman with hatpin." *Times Dispatch* (Richmond, VA), June 30, 1903.
"Kissers routed by sharp hatpins." *St. Louis Republic*, April 28, 1901.
"Knell of hat pin sounded." *San Francisco Call*, July 3, 1912.
Knickerbocker, Cholly. "The mode of the moment in hats." *Washington Times*, November 24, 1907.
"Ladies must wear hatpin protectors." *Evening Herald* (Klamath Falls, OR), July 20, 1912.
"Ladies, watch your hatpins." *Seattle Star*, June 3, 1913.
"The lady and the hat pin." *Evening World* (NY), January 28, 1911.
"Large theater hats must go." *Los Angeles Herald*, January 31, 1895.
"Law against hat pins." *Evening World* (NY), February 20, 1900.

"The law against hats." *Rock Island Argus* (Illinois), April 26, 1909.
"Law forbids free lunch." *Sun* (NY), March 21, 1913.
"Law to protect from deadly hatpin." *Washington Times*, January 28, 1909.
"Law-mill grind." *Dakota Farmer's Leader* (Canton, SD), January 20, 1911.
"Lawmaker wants ban put on hat pins." *Tacoma Times*, January 21, 1909.
"Legislator wars on freak hat." *Albuquerque Citizen*, May 10, 1909.
"Legislatures and milliners." *Washington Herald*, July 4, 1910.
"Length of hatpins is none of men's business." *Salt Lake Herald-Republican*, March 20, 1910.
"The lethal hatpin." *Indianapolis Journal*, September 27, 1903.
"Light hats for high brows; Chicago's war on hatpins." *Hawaiian Star* (Honolulu), June 17, 1912.
"Live topics about town." *Sun* (NY), October 25, 1895.
Loeb, Sophie Irene. "The everyday rights of everyday persons." *Evening World* (NY), November 15, 1912.
Loeb, Sophie Irene. "The long hatpin: an arraignment." *Evening World* (NY), March 26, 1914.
"London suffragettes raise cain—220 jailed." *Day Book* (Chicago), November 22, 1911.
"The long hat pin." *Evening Statesman* (Walla Walla, WA), March 8, 1910.
"The long hat pin will have to go." *St. Landry Clarion* (Opelousas, LA), June 1, 1912.
"Long hat pins." *Caucasian* (Shreveport, LA), March 27, 1910.
"Long hat pins are abolished." *Ogden Standard*, March 8, 1910.
"Long hat pins public nuisance." *Deseret Evening News* (Salt Lake), March 8, 1910.
"Long hat-pins in women's hats." *Ogden Standard*, April 2, 1914.
"Long hatpin fined." *Washington Herald*, April 4, 1911.
"The long hatpin menace to society." *Daily Ardmoreite* (Ardmore, OK), May 14, 1912.
"Long hatpin o.k., aldermen won't make 'em shorter." *Evening World* (NY), January 31, 1911.
"Long hatpins a peril." *New York Tribune*, December 2, 1910.
"Long hatpins against law." *Ogden Standard*, March 22, 1910.
"Long hatpins are imported as needles." *Deseret Evening News* (Salt Lake), July 26, 1910.
"Long hatpins barred in German railroad cars." *Salt Lake Tribune*, July 2, 1911.
"Long hatpins find defender." *Deseret Evening News* (Salt Lake), March 22, 1910.
"Long hatpins must go." *New York Tribune*, February 8, 1911.
"Long hatpins o.k., says judge." *Morning Standard* (Ogden), November 20, 1910.
"Long hatpins under the ban." *San Francisco Call*, July 7, 1912.
"Long 'uns must go." *Watchman and Southron* (Sumter, SC), January 21, 1911.
"Los Angeles frowns on civic dance hall." *San Francisco Call*, December 11, 1912.
"Low life murder." *Watchman and Southron* (Sumter, SC), December 19, 1906.
"Maid attacks Mary Pickford with a hatpin." *Seattle Star*, August 2, 1917.
"Maidens fight over a young man's hand." *San Francisco Call*, July 23, 1898.
"Make fight on army rules." *El Paso Herald*, June 3, 1911.
"Man routed by hatpin held in city hall." *Los Angeles Herald*, January 16, 1910.
"The man-eater sent up again." *Sun* (NY), January 18, 1897.
"Many more Merry Widows and Broadway must be widened." *Los Angeles Herald*, March 22, 1908.
"Many women held as shoplifters; all deny guilt." *New York Tribune*, December 15, 1919.
Marshall, Frances. "Fashion's latest word in smart creations." *Washington Herald*, November 22, 1914.
Marshall, Marguerite Mooers. "Use hatpins or fist on mashers, says Mrs. Brophy, who did it." *Evening World* (NY), August 9, 1913.
"Mayor on hat pins." *New York Tribune*, September 27, 1912.
"Messenger boy strikers foiled." *Evening Times* (Washington), September 1, 1902.
"Milady's hat pins restricted." *San Francisco Call*, June 26, 1912.
"The modern girl's weapons." *St. Paul Globe*, September 4, 1904.

"Montclair suffragettes rush to shorten hatpins." *Evening World* (NY), February 10, 1911.
"A moot parliament." *New York Tribune*, January 14, 1905.
"More attacks cause lynch spirit to rise." *Albuquerque Citizen*, August 6, 1907.
"More hatpins than ever." *Minneapolis Journal*, August 11, 1905.
"Mortally hurt by a hat pin." *Sun* (NY), November 12, 1887.
"The murderous hatpin." *Coconino Sun* (Flagstaff, AZ), September 1, 1911.
"Must the long hatpin go." *Sun* (NY), August 23, 1897.
"Mysterious fire gets skyscraper." *San Francisco Call*, May 6, 1910.
"Negro girls cause terror in park." *New York Tribune*, April 28, 1903.
"New hatpin bill from Hatfield." *Omaha Daily Bee*, February 4, 1911.
"New hatpin law arouses the ire of Jersey women." *Evening World* (NY), April 5, 1913.
"New hatpins as weapons are deadly." *Seattle Star*, November 29, 1909.
"New use for hat pins." *Perrysburg Journal* (Ohio), May 15, 1897.
"No hats in theaters." *Baxter Springs News* (Baxter Springs, Kansas), February 13, 1897.
"No pistols for women." *San Francisco Call*, January 29, 1913.
"Not a sign of relief yet in sight." *Washington Times*, February 27, 1910.
"Not exactly news." *Belmont Chronicle* (St. Clairsville, Ohio), February 22, 1894.
"Not milliners." *Wheeling Daily Intelligencer* (W. VA), January 27, 1897.
"Notes of the stage." *New York Tribune*, March 4, 1903.
"Of hats and plays." *St. Paul Globe*, December 2, 1903.
"The offending hatpin." *Truth* (Salt Lake), October 27, 1906.
"Officer insulted her." *Deseret Evening News* (Salt Lake), June 30, 1908.
"Oh, girls! $500 fine for long hat pins." *Seattle Star*, December 4, 1912.
"Ordinance limiting length of hat pins." *Deseret Evening News* (Salt Lake), March 12, 1910.
"Oregon legislature has passed a law limiting hatpins to 10 inches long." *Evening World* (NY), February 1, 1909.
"Overstepping the bounds." *San Francisco Call*, February 3, 1899.
"Paring German headgear." *Sun* (NY), April 8, 1913.
"Paris women invincible." *East Oregonian* (Pendleton, OR), April 6, 1914.
"Patrolman is stabbed with long hat pin." *Seattle Star*, November 5, 1909.
Patterson, Ethel Lloyd. "Women's fall hats so small shoe horns needed, not hatpins." *Evening World* (NY), August 2, 1911.
"Penalty for bare hatpins." *Sun* (NY), December 8, 1913.
"Penalty for hatpins if they wickedly protrude." *Evening Herald*, December 23, 1911.
"Perils of long hatpins told by the clubwomen in pleas to aldermen." *Evening World* (NY), January 26, 1911.
"Pete just scratches along." *Washington Times*, September 9, 1911.
"Pinless hat offers solution of long hatpin controversy." *Salt Lake Herald-Republican*, April 3, 1910.
"Pinned through the nose." *Los Angeles Herald*, August 1, 1891.
"Pittsburg to shorten hatpins to nine inches." *Spokane Press*, September 24, 1910.
"A point in woman's favor." *Omaha Daily Bee*, May 27, 1907.
"Point of hat pin." *St. Paul Globe*, March 13, 1899.
"Poisoned hatpin and gas pipe are weapons of women in struggle." *Seattle Star*, July 18, 1913.
"Police fear hatpins more than revolvers." *Spokane Press*, October 26, 1906.
"Police make raid on suffragettes." *Daily Capital Journal* (Salem, OR), April 30, 1913.
"Police matron's work." *New York Tribune*, July 11, 1909.
"Policeman took off her hat." *Sun* (NY), October 3, 1909.
"Prefer jail to paying fines." *Salt Lake Tribune*, October 31, 1912.
"Pricked by a hat-pin." *St. Paul Globe*, October 21, 1891.
"Priest stabbed with hatpin." *Mathews Journal* (Mathews, VA), November 2, 1911.
"A public servant who has been doing things." *Tulsa Daily World*, March 2, 1912.
"Punctures assailant." *Democratic Banner* (Mt. Vernon, Ohio), November 4, 1910.
"Put to flight with a hatpin." *St. Paul Globe*, November 11, 1902.

"Puts muzzle on hatpins." *Times Dispatch* (Richmond, VA), March 9, 1913.
"Queen Mary and the hatpin." *Washington Herald*, November 17, 1911.
"The question in Boston." *Evening World* (NY), April 9, 1913.
"Real reason for the anti-big hat bill." *Morning Examiner* (Ogden), April 25, 1909.
"Rebellion against tyranny of big lid." *San Francisco Call*, January 30, 1910.
"Recommend new ban upon hatpin." *Seattle Star*, May 28, 1913.
"Recovering from the hatpin wound." *Sun* (NY), October 15, 1897.
"Red pepper and a hatpin." *San Francisco Call*, February 2, 1899.
"Regulating size of women's hats." *Washington Herald*, July 25, 1910.
"Removes hat pin menace." *New York Tribune*, March 11, 1913.
"Renew war on long hatpins." *Albuquerque Evening Herald*, March 2, 1912.
"Representative Coudrey and hat pins." *Washington Times*, April 8, 1910.
"Rhinestone hatpins." *Wenatchee Daily World* (WA), February 4, 1910.
"Riot in church led by negroes." *St. Louis Republic*, July 31, 1903.
"The riotous hatpin." *New York Tribune*, September 10, 1909.
"Robbers routed by a woman." *Salt Lake Herald*, January 10, 1898.
"Routed men with hatpins." *Evening Times* (Washington), May 2, 1900.
"Rules for women in holdup." *San Francisco Call*, September 19, 1913.
"Safe and sane hatpins." *Washington Times*, January 26, 1913.
"A salesgirl goes crazy." *New York Tribune*, September 21, 1897.
"Sallie Slick and her surprising Aunt Amelia." *Times* (Richmond, VA), July 13, 1902.
"Saving eyes in Stockholm." *Sun* (NY), February 9, 1913.
"Says woman robbed and then beat him." *Evening World* (NY), May 1, 1906.
Schenck, S. C. "Theater millinery." *North Platte Semi-Weekly Tribune* (Nebraska), February 19, 1897.
"Scratched by her hatpin." *New York Tribune*, September 19, 1910.
"Seattle makes war on hat pins." *Daily Capital Journal* (Salem, OR), April 4, 1910.
"Seattle to drive out long hatpins—one man blinded." *Tacoma Times*, May 8, 1912.
Shaffer, Frances. "Protecting world against hatpin." *Washington Herald*, April 21, 1913.
"Shame! Cry women." *New York Tribune*, March 15, 1910.
"She broke up the meeting." *Sun* (NY), April 21, 1894.
"She jabs policeman with her hat pin." *St. Paul Globe*, November 5, 1904.
"She used a hat pin." *Scranton Tribune* (PA), September 23, 1898.
"She used a hatpin to restore peace." *Evening World* (NY), March 21, 1903.
"She's only woman in M.U. law school." *University Missourian* (Columbia, MO), October 7, 1910.
"Short hatpins after April 1." *New York Tribune*, March 23, 1910.
"Short hatpins the rule, ladies." *San Francisco Call*, September 5, 1912.
"Should enact a law against women wearing long hat pins." *Salt Lake Herald-Republican*, March 3, 1910.
"Size of women's hats." *Washington Herald*, February 12, 1910.
"Size of women's hats." *Washington Herald*, April 11, 1910.
"Smoking law to curb hat pins." *San Francisco Call*, November 10, 1912.
"Society." *Goodwin's Weekly* (Salt Lake), June 7, 1913.
"Society beauty squad to wage war on long hatpin." *East Oregonian* (Pendleton, OR), June 18, 1912.
"Some freak legislation." *Times Dispatch* (Richmond, VA), October 19, 1909.
"The souvenir pin craze." *Lafayette Advertiser* (LA), October 28, 1893.
"A splendid idea." *Seattle Star*, June 26, 1911.
"Stabbed cop with hat pin." *Evening World* (NY), March 31, 1904.
"Stabbed him with a hat pin." *Guthrie Daily Leader* (OK), December 11, 1895.
"Stabbed him with a hat pin." *Times Dispatch* (Richmond, VA), March 22, 1903.
"Stabbed with a hat pin." *St. Paul Globe*, October 12, 1897.
"Stabbed with a hat pin." *St. Paul Globe*, March 8, 1900.

"Stabbed with a hat pin." *Springfield Daily Republic* (Ohio), May 8, 1888.
"Stabbed with a hatpin." *Alexandria Gazette* (VA), March 30, 1904.
"Stabbed with a hatpin." *Daily Journal* (Salem, OR), August 22, 1903.
"Stabbed with a hatpin." *Evening Times* (Washington), March 7, 1898.
"Stabbed with a hatpin by a jealous woman." *San Francisco Call*, March 25, 1900.
"Stabs a masher with her hatpin." *Washington Times*, October 18, 1909.
"Stabs hugger with hatpin." *Los Angeles Herald*, January 26, 1906.
"Stage hand is punctured." *New York Tribune*, March 4, 1910.
"Stick them with hat pins! Says Galloway." *Los Angeles Herald*, September 22, 1910.
"Stuck hatpin into a masher." *Evening World* (NY), May 27, 1903.
"Suggestions follow passing of hat pin." *Ogden Standard*, March 14, 1910.
"Supervisors get stuck on hatpin." *San Francisco Call*, August 21, 1912.
"Surprise, wrath and profanity." *Sun* (NY), February 15, 1897.
"Suspected of murder with hat pin." *Deseret Evening News* (Salt Lake), December 29, 1906.
"Swiss make hatpins unlawful." *New York Tribune*, January 21, 1912.
"Tailored chapeaux of velour and felt will do away with hatpins." *Washington Times*, September 25, 1914.
"Take the pin from his lung." *Omaha Daily Bee*, October 16, 1897.
"The talk of the day." *New York Tribune*, March 22, 1910.
"That hat pin stabbing." *Sun* (NY), October 22, 1895.
"The theater hat." *Austin Weekly Statesman* (TX), December 24, 1891.
"The theater hat." *Evening Star* (Washington), October 27, 1894.
"The theater hat." *St. Paul Globe*, December 28, 1892.
"The theater hat." *St. Paul Globe*, February 16, 1895.
"The theater hat in Ohio." *Evening Star* (Washington), March 26, 1896.
"Theater hat ordinance." *Evening Times* (Washington), February 26, 1897.
"They used a hatpin." *Evening World* (NY), August 11, 1891.
"Things heard and seen." *Evening Star* (Washington), June 16, 1906.
"Thoughtful women." *University Missourian* (Columbia, MO), May 1, 1912.
"Threatened to use hatpin on stepfather." *Salt Lake Tribune*, July 29, 1907.
"Throttle is open." *Rock Island Argus* (Illinois), May 8, 1909.
"To arms, ye women of Chicago. Hatpins barred by ordinance." *Seattle Star*, March 8, 1910.
"To enforce hatpin law." *New York Tribune*, March 21, 1913.
"To jab him if he flirts." *Tulsa Daily World*, December 16, 1916.
"To put ban on deadly hatpin." *East Oregonian* (Pendleton, OR), March 8, 1910.
"To regulate hatpins." *Daily Capital Journal* (Salem, OR), November 20, 1912.
"To stop the goo-goo habit." *Indianapolis Journal*, April 26, 1903.
"Tried to stab a policeman." *Evening World* (NY), January 7, 1893.
"Tried to stab a policeman." *Evening World* (NY), December 30, 1893.
"Tries to stab man with her hatpin in court house hall." *Evening World* (NY), January 17, 1913.
"Tulsa's special ordinance." *Daily Ardmoreite* (Ardmore, OK), October 14, 1913.
"Two brokers who failed." *San Francisco Call*, May 9, 1896.
"Two eyes jabbed out by hatpins in crowd." *Washington Herald*, March 16, 1910.
"Used a hat pin." *Kansas City Journal* (MO), June 23, 1895.
"Used a hat pin." *San Francisco Call*, March 30, 1897.
"Used a hat pin in justification." *Times Dispatch* (VA), July 4, 1906.
"Used hatpin on assailant." *Salt Lake Herald*, January 12, 1904.
"Used hatpin on negro assailant." *St. Louis Republic*, July 11, 1904.
"Used her hatpin." *Minneapolis Journal*, September 8, 1902.
"Uses hatpin on holdup." *Salt Lake Herald-Republican*, February 14, 1910.
"Uses her hatpin to capture negro." *St. Louis Republic*, February 17, 1901.
"Vicious woman stabs officer with hatpin." *Seattle Star*, March 25, 1901.

"Voice of the press." *Record-Union* (Sacramento), September 23, 1897.
Wales, R. Ellis. "If San Francisco police should pinch wearers of deadly hatpins." *San Francisco Call*, May 15, 1910.
"War declared on hatpins." *Times Dispatch* (Richmond, VA), March 28, 1910.
"War is waged on hatpins." *San Francisco Call*, May 23, 1913.
"War on a boat." *Evening Times* (Washington), June 19, 1896.
"War on big hat pins." *New York Tribune*, February 1, 1911.
"War on hatpin." *Spokane Press*, February 22, 1909.
"War on hatpins." *New York Tribune*, February 12, 1910.
"War on long hatpins." *New York Tribune*, March 22, 1912.
"A weapon of defense." *St. Paul Globe*, September 11, 1903.
"Wex Jones news of tomorrow." *El Paso Herald*, October 6, 1910.
"When hat pin guards become the rage." *Rock Island Argus* (Illinois), March 15, 1913.
"Will ignore the hat pin." *Daily Capital Journal* (Salem, OR), February 22, 1910.
"With hat pin girl fought hiwayman." *Washington Times*, October 23, 1905.
"With her hat pin." *Daily Public Ledger* (Maysville, KY), December 9, 1898.
"Woman drives off robbers with hatpin." *Minneapolis Journal*, February 3, 1905.
"Woman hat-pinned burglar." *Evening Star* (Washington), June 1, 1906.
"Woman in crowded car stabbed with hatpin." *San Francisco Call*, July 11, 1906.
"Woman made a scene in court." *Evening World* (NY), July 23, 1901.
"Woman routs robber with her hatpin." *Los Angeles Herald*, January 7, 1907.
"Woman stabs a prison matron." *Evening World* (NY), January 5, 1893.
"Woman stabs negro thug on street with hatpin." *Washington Herald*, December 18, 1916.
"Woman to war on hatpins." *New York Tribune*, April 14, 1912.
"Woman used hatpin." *Gainesville Daily Sun* (FL), March 9, 1906.
"Woman uses hat pin on officer." *Omaha Daily Bee*, August 22, 1909.
"Woman uses hatpin in effective way." *Salt Lake Tribune*, June 4, 1911.
"Woman wields hat pin." *Salt Lake Herald-Republican*, August 8, 1910.
"Woman with hat pin routs two highwaymen." *San Francisco Call*, August 27, 1909.
"Woman's handy weapon against thieves." *New York Tribune*, February 7, 1904.
"Woman's hatpin spears a man." *East Oregonian* (Pendleton, OR), October 18, 1911.
"Woman's hatpin stops murder." *Sun* (NY), September 17, 1912.
"A woman's weapon." *Los Angeles Herald*, July 19, 1897.
"Woman's weapon of defense." *Omaha Daily Bee*, November 27, 1904.
"Women battle to hear evangelist." *Washington Times*, February 1, 1913.
"Women boost from hatpin law." *Seattle Star*, May 27, 1913.
"Women fight long hatpin." *New York Tribune*, March 28, 1912.
"Women fight with hatpins." *New York Tribune*, February 24, 1912.
"Women forbidden to wear long hatpins." *Salt Lake Tribune*, June 4, 1911.
"Women form hatpin squad for defense." *Seattle Star*, January 11, 1913.
"Women join general fight in subway car." *Evening World* (NY), March 5, 1906.
"Women prisoners mutiny." *New York Tribune*, December 28, 1900.
"Women rioters in New York soak meat with oil." *Bisbee Daily Review*, April 8, 1910.
"Women use hat pins to check train rush." *Seattle Star*, August 4, 1909.
"Women use hatpins when in big crowds." *San Francisco Call*, October 24, 1909.
"Women's hatpins." *Caucasian* (Shreveport, LA), August 17, 1909.
"Women's hatpins." *Virginia Gazette* (Williamsburg, VA), September 25, 1897.
"Won't hurt Louisville." *Kentucky Irish American* (Louisville, KY), March 26, 1910.
"Would banish long hatpins." *Ogden Standard*, March 1, 1910.
"Would withdraw hatpin bill." *New York Tribune*, February 2, 1911.
"Wounds thug with hatpin." *San Francisco Call*, July 25, 1905.
"Written at random." *Paducah Sun* (KY), January 22, 1898.
"Yes! There should be a reform in hatpins." *Spokane Press*, March 14, 1910.
"Young woman uses hatpin on an offensive masher." *St. Louis Republic*, April 20, 1903.

Newspapers with Untitled Articles

Brownsville Herald (TX), February 4, 1909.
El Paso Herald, March 8, 1900.
Goodwin's Weekly (Salt Lake), November 18, 1911.
Hawaiian Star (Honolulu), January 11, 1911.
Hawaiian Star (Honolulu), March 21, 1911.
Intermountain Catholic (Salt Lake), May 15, 1909.
Jasper Weekly Courier (Indiana), May 20, 1910.
New York Tribune, December 26, 1890.
New York Tribune, January 10, 1908.
Omaha Daily Bee, October 3, 1910.
Princeton Union (MN), October 14, 1897.
St. Louis Republic, May 2, 1903.
San Francisco Call, July 26, 1898.
San Francisco Call, May 22, 1901.
San Mateo Item (FL), March 6, 1909.
Spanish American (Roy, NM), October 7, 1911.
Sun (NY), September 22, 1897.
Virginia Citizen (Irvington, VA), April 29, 1910.
Washington Times, August 17, 1911.
Worthington Advance (MN), March 2, 1900.

Index

Aaronson, Anna 98
abolition called for 121
accidental uses 102–108
accidents 46–48, 117, 121
advertising 5, 37
agitation against, peak 116
Alameda, CA 31
Almendinger, Charles 94
Alter, J.C.C. 140–141
alteration 36
American Suffragettes 171
Anderson, E.J. 106–107, 147
Anderson, Ella 122
Andrews, Mayme 79
Annapolis, MD 30
anti-hat sentiment 11
arrests 15, 170; Chicago 137; mass arrests 72; of men 12
assaults 53
Atchison, Kansas 11
Atkinson, Edgar L. 95
attacks: foiled 74–94; humorous, on bills 10; spontaneous 98–99
Avery, Rachel Foster 156

Baden, Switzerland 113
Badger California Club 174
bail 52
Bailey, Richard 146
Bands, Harry 55
Bannick, Claude G. 56
Barlow, Samuel H. 145
Barnum, Thilo F. 53
Bauer, Hugo 153
Bauler, Herman J. 131–133
Bavarian Minister of Communications 115
beauty squad 139–140
Beaver, Nellie 47–48
Becker, Della 87–88
begging 50
Benach, Mrs. Morris 85
Benham, Julia 96
Berlin, Germany 109

Berlin Elevated Railways Company 110
Blake, Lillie Devereux 124
Blaker, Leoti 79–80
blood poisoning 57, 92–93, 103
Boardman, Captain 84–85
Bonita 68
Bonneau, Janette 96
Bordoni, Irene 35
Boston 161–163
Bottomley, Julia 43
Bowen, Jessie 59–60
Bowers, Martin 62
Boyd, Barbara 150–151
Brennan, John 86–87
Brennan, Sarah 90
Brockington, Mary 76–77
Brockington, Virginia 76–77
Brooks, John 63–64
Brophy, Viola 177
Brown, Abe 88
Brown, Belle 52
Brown, Darius 155–156
Brown, Jennie 49
Brown, Maggie 65
Brown, May 56
Brown, Nellie 69–70
Brussels, Belgium 142
Bryan, Carrie 171
Buchanan, W.C. 87
Budapest, Hungary 113
Bullocks, Carrie 83–84
Burnett, George 91
Burrell, Reverend 132
Busco, Florence 53
Byrnes, James 86–87

California Legislature 163–164
California State Board of Health 174
Canancamp, Alfred 107–108
Cannon, Lottie 88
Cantell, Frances 55–56
Carlyle, Anastasia 123
Carsensen, C.C. 57

205

cartoons, editorial 38, 116, 126, 127, 137, 138, 142, 143, 155, 159, 165, 177
Caruso, Enrico 108
Caswell, George 90
Chapman, Gladys 96–97
Chappell, Mrs. James 89–90
Cherry, Kate 65
Chicago City Council 11, 131–137
Chicago, ordinance 132–138
Chicago Police Department 139–140
Chicago streets 140
Chickering, Mrs. Clifford C. 139
chivalry 73
churches 31; and hats 13–14
Cincinnati 172
cinemas 88–89, 93
citizens, rescued 79, 81, 91, 93
Clancy, James 89
Clark, Annie 96
Clark, May 175
Clas, Laura 48; lawsuits 48
class elements 9, 13, 62, 118, 139–140
Clay, Mary 90
clergymen 34
closet space 20
clothing 90
collection crazes 36
Collins, Maude 137
columnists 18
Connecticut 176–177
conscription 101
Conway, Irene 88
Cook County, Illinois 8
Cook County League of Women's Clubs 168
corks 45, 168, 171
cost 40
costumes, women's 180
Coudrey, Harry 147–149
court case 153
co-workers 61–62
Croft, Lizzie 62
Crow, Herbert 61
crusades against: Germany 112
crusades 42–43, 117, 128–130, 169; against big hats 12
Cue, Ora 45
Cullinane, Timothy 52
Curtis, Annie 52
custom production 44

Dahnken, Minnie 147
damages awarded 114
Davenport, Lizzie 51
Davis, Ed 106
Davis, May E. 132
deaths 57, 64–65, 66–67, 92–93, 101, 103, 104, 105; self-inflicted 46–48
debtors 51–52
demise 180
demonization 117–118, 122–123
Denney, J.N. 146

Dent, George 80
department stores 60–61
Derby, George T. 85
Dickson, E.L. 88–89
Dietz, Sadie 49
discrimination against women 11
divorces 69
Donohue, Edward 60
Dowling, Frank 160
Downes, Henrietta 96
Drescher, Alderman 157–160
Driscoll, Florence 49–50
drug addicts 66–67
Dugan, Robert E. 105
Dumble, Laura 193
Dupont, Alphonse 170–171

Easton, Mrs. D.E.F. 34
Ebell Club 34–35
Eckhardt, Nellie 81
Edison Electric Lighting Company 69
editorials against 173
editorials 14, 25, 166–168; against 104–105, 118, 122, 133–134, 142–143, 154, 159–160, 162, 169, 173; ambivalent 118, 120–121, 124–125; on hats 6–7, 8; praising 74, 78, 89, 93; satirical 162–163; urging legislation 131; weaponization 50, 59, 60, 61, 62, 64
Eickhoff, Mrs. Henry 34
electricity poles 69
Elwood, Robert 63
England, Andrew 105–106
Englemenn, Richard 113
Enright, Mrs. George 91
Epstein, Gretchen 113
Equi, Marie D. 101
Era Club 169
Europe 115
evangelist meetings 100
Evans, Lillian 63
express companies 27

falls 46–47
Farrar, Geraldine 108
fashion 31, 34, 35, 114, 124, 151; as attack cause 90; changes 180; necessity 37
fasteners: alternate 45; need for 5; return to old 121
fathers 86
fear 123–124, 143
Federation of Women's Clubs NYS 168
Feighor, Ruth 106
female clothing, regulation 128
feminism 5
fines 52, 70, 89, 135, 155, 162, 175, 176; for big hats 15
Finley, Michael 50
Finnegan, Lizzie 84
fire, in bib hat 31
First Baptist Church, Indianapolis 13–14
Fitzgerald, Margaret E. 130

Index

foreign countries 109–115
Fosdick, Representative (OH) 10
Foss, Governor (MA) 162
Foster, Benjamin 59
Fox, Rose 64
Franklin, Bud 76
Franklin, Ethel 57
Frederick, Josephine 89
freedom of movement 5
freight rates, for hats 27

Gardner, Emma 76
garment strike 100
Gasso, Alton E. 129
Gates, Mary 86
Gaynor, Henry 99
Gaynor, William 174
Geneva, Switzerland 113–114
Germany 109–111
Gilson, Emma 76
Gilson, Rose 76
Glaus, Oscar 91
Grady, Mary 58
Graham, Mrs. Andrew J. 139
Grandy, Beatrice 85
Grant, Louisa 96
Grant, Mrs. Eugene J. 168
Greeley, Edward Addison 122
Green Gladys 88
Green, Edward L. 81
Green, Simon 49
Greville, Violet 18
Grey, Cynthia 129, 154
Griffith, W.H. 86
Gross, Felix 85
group use 95–101
guards, for points 42, 45, 110, 112, 115, 123, 140, 155, 164, 168
Gunderland, J. 53–54
guns 55; permits barred to women 176

hair: false 6; styles 6
Hall, Hattie 68
Hamburg, Germany 110–111
Hammell, Irene 53
Handy, Fanny 52
Hanna, Senator 12
Hanover, Germany 109
Hansen, Clara 81–82
Harlan, James S. 27–28
Harnett, Lizzie 60–61
Harrington, Mary 84
Harris, Bridget 50
Harrison, Mayor 139–141
Haskell, Olive 52
hats: adornment on 12, 21, 141, 175; big hats 18, 34–35; etiquette 31–32; manufacturers 22; novel uses for big hats 20; reasons for big hats 32–33; removal 6, 8, 17; size of 5–34; small 34–35; wearing of 5
Hauser, Rose 93

Haverelkoss, Sadie 92
Hawaii 164
hearings, New York 158–160
Heath, Georgia 71
Hermann, M.S. 152
Hermes, Catherine 92–93
Herold, Raener 92
Hess, Clarence 68–69
Hetlich, William 68
Hickman, Velma 106
Hillis, James D. 142
Hilton, G.G. 76
Hilton, George C. 20–21, 23–25, 26–27
Hilton, Mrs. George C. 23–24, 26
Hinckley, Francis 133
Hogan, Walter 56
holders for 40–41
Honolulu ordinance 149
hotel detectives 67
Hotel Gotham (New York) 67
Hubble, Annie 84
Hurse, Bertha 51
hyperbole 123–124, 140, 141, 156
hyping 38–44
hysteria 122–123

Illinois House of Representatives 20–21
importing 41
Indianapolis 11, 12, 13–14, 141–142
Industrial Workers of the World (IWW) 101
injuries 106, 142, 147, 151; eye 105, 106
Interstate Commerce Commission 27

Jackson, C.A. 155–156
jealousy 59, 61, 63, 64–65, 69–70
Jenks, Mary 47
jewelers 38, 44
jewels, added 36
Johnson, Forest 57
Johnson, Hilda 69
Johnson, Laura Brown 51–52
Johnson, Sadie 70
Jones, A.F. 161
Jones, Alexander J. 8
Jones, John 98–99
Jones, Maggie 59
Jones, Mrs. Morgan 175
Jones, Nellie 52
Jones, Paul 103
Jordan, Mrs. Arthur 14
Joyce, Kate 53

Kalichman, Ida 94
Kansas 12, 128
Kansas City, MO 154–156; City Council 11
Kaufman, Marian 139
Keeler, Eva L. 97
Kelly, Minnie 54
Kennedy, Maggie 86
Kent, William 176
Kierce, Maggie 59–60

208   INDEX

Kiernan, Philomena 153
Kinney, Thomas 15
Kinston, Ethel Violet 152–153
Kirkpatrick, James P. 165
Kirshman, Elizabeth 84
Klimm, Frank J. 172–174
Knickerbocker, Cholly 18
Krotchstil, Hannah 90

labor disputes 95–98, 100, 101
Lander, Rose 57
Lang, Ellen 118
Lang, Mary 71
Lang, Nellie 50
Larkin, Emma 87
Lawler, Mollie 50
laws, unwritten 62, 69–70
lawsuits 69, 105
Le Blanc, Marguerite 88
Leclerc, John B. 164
legal ruling, self-defense 77
legislating reform, women's clothes 119–120
legislation: 8, 10, 11, 12, 30, 144, 145–146, 147–149, 153–154, 166–168; California 163–164; call for 120–121; Connecticut 176–177; Louisiana 171; Massachusetts 161–163; Michigan 168–169; Nebraska 163; New Jersey 164–166; New York 118–120; Oregon 125–126; penalties 8, 12, 15; results 166–168, 179–180; South Dakota 157
legislators attacked 25
Lehar, Franz 20
length 36, 39–40, 116–117, 123, 127–128, 130, 131–137, 140–141, 146–147, 148
Lenhart, Florence 90–91
Leonard, Emma 65
Lerner, Fannie 101
Levine sisters 69
Levy, Philip 104
Levy, Samuel 57
Lial, Joseph 63
licensing 121
Lichtenstein, Edna 170
lock-ups 49
Loeb, Sophie Irene 114–115, 178–179
Logan, Daniel 149
London (UK) 99–100, 101, 114
Lord, George 168–169
Los Angeles 174–175
Los Angeles Herald 18–20
Los Angeles police 152
Louisiana 170–171
Louisville, KY 137; City Council 12
Lundquist 83
Luthardt, William 140
Lynch, Bertha 75
Lynch, Matron 49
Lynn, MA 146
Lyon, France 112

MacDonald, Mrs. Peter 48
Mack, Daniel 106

magistrate, favoring legislation 152
males, fear of 136, 138, 140–141
marital disputes 58–59
marketing 5
Marquardt, Hattie 77
Marshall, Eustice 70
Marshall, Eva 63
Martinon, Mrs. John 34
mashers 73–94, 97
Mason, Julia 106
Matz, Adam 68
May, Agnes L. 88
McArdle, Mary 91–92
McArthur, F.B. 65
McCarmont, Jennie 83
McCord, Kitty 58–59
McCord, Tom 58–59
McCullough, Mrs. James 158
McGovern, Mary 50, 118
McMahon, C.H. 145
medical press 121
medical profession 179
Meller, Rudolph 97
merchandising 36–45
Merry Widow hat 19–20
messenger girls 95–96
Metcalf, Clara 90
Michaud, Tony 112
Michigan 168–169
Miller, Harriet 130
Miller, Howard T. 104
Milliners' Jobbers' Association 27
Milwaukee 176
Minnesota 16–17
Misell, Margaret 67–68
Mishow, Ella 76
Missouri House of Delegates 11
mockery 119–120, 132–136; of legislation 125–126
Moore, Emma 59
moral suasion 10, 15
Moran, Edward J. 146
Morris, C.W. 56–57
Morton's Opera House 14
Moss, Lulu 84
Moulton, Alice 53
Mulligan, John 98
Mulroney, Mary 51
Murphy, Kate 86–87
Murphy, Margaret 87
Murphy, May 61–62
Myers, Edward 106
Myers, Emily 80

Navansky, John 96
Nebraska 163
needles 41
Neil, Catherine 66–67
Neil, Joseph M. 66–67
Nelson, Anna 77
Neumann, Anna Raetta 54

Neuse, William 81
New Jersey 164–166
New Orleans 15, 169–170
New Orleans police 170
New York City Council ordinance 157–161
New York Police Department 85
New York State Assembly 118–120
New York Telephone Company 69
Newton, William 161–162
Noble, C.E. 107
non-removal of hats, reasons 13
Norris, Jean 72
Nougier, F. 60
numbers of hatpins used 37, 40, 116–117

O'Brien, Loretta 63–64
Ohio 9–10
Olembeck, Bessie 64
Omaha City Council ordinance 144
ordinances 11, 13, 15, 132–138, 149; Indianapolis 141–142; Kansas City 154–156; Los Angeles 175; Milwaukee 176; New Orleans 169–170; New York City 157–161; Omaha 144; Philadelphia 153–154; Pittsburgh 152; San Francisco 172–174; Seattle 146–147; Tulsa 178
Oregon Legislature 125–126
outdoor crowds 95

Paducah, KY 14
Panama hat 43
Pankhurst, Emmeline 101
parades 31, 99
Paris, France 111–113
Parry, Mrs. D.M. 13–14
Parsons, Edward 52
Pate, Minnie 90
Patterson, Ethel Lloyd 43
Pavlole, Michael 92
Pelsgrove, Carrie 47
Pendergast, Christina 54
pepper, red 99
Perkins, Nellie M. 97
Philadelphia 153
Phillips, N. Taylor 118–120
Phillips, S.H. 103
picketing 96
Pickett, Helen 83
Pickford, Mary 71
Pierce, Ralph 56
Pilong, Frank 65
Pittsburgh ordinance 152
police: fear of hatpins 54–55, 85; instructions 54–55; reluctance to enforce ordinances 139–140; urge use of hatpins 84–85, 92; as victims 49–57
Pollard, James 58
polygamy 38
Ponderford, Ethel 146–147
Portsmouth, UK 115
Posten, Joseph 77–79
press coverage 129

prison sentences 50, 54, 60
prisoners, transporting 55
property disputes 70–71
protests, male 12
protrusion, of points 124, 140, 147, 153, 157–160, 169–170, 173, 176
psychology 151
public safety 121, 148, 169
Putnam, Albert 133–134

Queen Mary 168

racism 55–56
railroads 48, 68, 106, 112–113
Rayner, Lulu 80
reformers 123
Reich, Beulah 93
retailers 22
Revelle, Thomas 146
rhinestones 41
Rhode Island 164
Rhodes, Ann 122
Richardson, Albert 93
Riley, C.C. 55
Riley, Mary 52
rioters 65, 98, 99–100, 101
Ripkine, Katherine 71
robberies 53, 56, 63, 65; foiled 74–94
Robinson, Ada 75
Rodgers, A.L. 47
Rottanzi, Supervisor 13
Rubens George C. Councilman 141–142
rural residents 11
Russ, Robert R. 123
Russell, H. Everett 161
Ryan, Mary 53

Saarbrucken, Germany 110
St. Louis 12
St. Louis House of Delegates 15
Sallie Slick (comic) 77, 78
Salt Lake City police 145
San Francisco 15
San Francisco Board of Health 172–174
San Francisco Board of Supervisors 13, 130–131
Sanford, Dan 105
satire 42, 149–150; of big hats 19–20
Saunders, Birdie 59
Saville, Mrs. Louis 70–71
Sayman, Nettie 83
scabs (labor) 98
Schenck, S.C. 12
Schmucker, Councilman 153–154
Scott, Laura 65
Scotton, Edna 88
searches of women, for 54–55
Seattle City Council 146–147
Sebastian, Charles 176
Second Amendment cited 119
self-defense 74–94, 152–153, 177; court case 85; instructionst 82

selfishness 10, 173
Seller, Bertha 65–66
sentences 137–138
sexual harassers 73–94
Shaffer, Frances 177
Shaffer, Mabel 76
Shamberger, Madeline 91
shaming 19–20
Sherwood, Lottie 49
shoplifting 72
Simmons College (Boston) 100
Simpson, Josephine 71
Slater, John F. 137
Smith, Effie 64–65
Smith, Gertrude 63
Smith, James 66
Smith, Jennie 56
Smoot, Reed 38
society women 139–140
South Dakota 156–157
Spokane, WA 54–55
Springfield, IL 20–21
Stahl, William 92
Star (Washington) 10
status 5
Steer, Emma 55
Stephen Merritt's Mission (NYC) 58
Stephens, Zurella 90
Stevens, Solomon 70–71
Stevenson, Edgar 117–118
Stewart, Mrs. Oliver W. 25
Stockholm, Sweden 115
Stockton, C.W. 28
Stoddart, Samuel 63
Stoner, Cora 49
Street, Pansy 67–68
streetcars 55, 64, 66, 68, 70, 83, 84, 98–99, 109, 115
strikes by employees 100–101
students 100
Suedmeyer, Rose 76
suffrage movement 144
suffragettes 25, 99–100
Sunday, W.A. (Billy) 100
Swafford, G.B. 75–76
Sweeney, Daniel 92–93
Sydney, Australia 114–115
Sylvester, Richard 144–145
Sylvia, Aggie 50–51
symbolic use 38

Taggart, Mayor 11
Tanguay, Eva 68–69
tariffs 41
Taylor, Marcia 89
theater managers 8, 12
theaters 6–8, 11, 30–31; accidental pinning to seats 104–105
Thill, Mrs. Charles F. 88
Thomas, E.H. 148–149
Thompson, Georgiana 76
Thornton, Agnes 91
Tindall, William 148
Todd, Mayor 12
Tracy, Dolly 77–79
transit, public 73–74, 79–80, 97–98, 103–107, 105
Trautman, Mrs. Ralph 160
Trotter, Maud 65
Tulsa 178

United States Constitution 11
United States House of Congress 147–148
United States Senate 38
unsanitary 172, 178
uses for haptins 41–42; bad 46–72; good 73–93; novel 73–74
utility companies, attacked 69

vagrancy 57
Veigler, Bessie 93
Vienna, Austria 113
views, obstructed 6, 8, 15, 99

Waggener, Mayor 11
Wagner, Mary Swain 171
Walker, S.D. 87
Walsh, James 79
Ward, Emma 62
Ward, John 155
Ward, Mae 67
Wardell, Max 147
Washington 120
Washington, Booker T. 65
Washington, D.C. 10, 147–149
Washington, D.C., Police Department 84–85
Washington, D.C., police, in favor 144–145
Waters, Frances 49
weaponization 37, 56, 116, 122, 124–125, 144, 161; bad uses 46–72; compared to other weapons 75, 116, 123–124; concealment 121–122; deadly 117, 119, 175; good uses 73–94; natural choice 118
Webber, Mabel 56
Weingartner, Franz 87
Welch, Anna 94
Wellborn, Charles 175
Wells, Alice Stebbins 92
West Virginia Legislature 12
west vs. east 73–74
Western Union messengers 95–96
Whalen, W.D. 83
Wilder, Adelaide 86
Willense, Cornelius 53
Williams, Joel 101–102
Williams, Sadie 74–75
Willisten, Mrs. William 83
Wilson, Rosa 80
Winston, Bertha 64–65
Wisconsin 128
Wittig, Walter 30
Woman's Circle, Indianapolis 13–14

Woman's League of Chicago 171
women: against big hats 34–35; against hatpins 130, 140, 147, 154, 158–160, 167–168, 171–172; and Chicago efforts 132–139;
women's attire 133
Women's Democratic Club (NYC) 129–130
women's rights 153
World's Fair (St. Louis) 64
Wynn, Emma 47

Young, Cora 101–102
Young, Florence 86
Young, Margaret A. 57
Young Ladies Protective Association of Educational Hill (PA) 99

Zemp, Harvey 69–70
Zurich, Switzerland 114
Zwerling, Ethel 69

www.ingramcontent.com/pod-product-compliance
Ingram Content Group UK Ltd.
Pitfield, Milton Keynes, MK11 3LW, UK
UKHW042001140426
5217IPUK00015B/918